Lesson files . . . and so much more

The *Adobe Premiere Pro CS3 Classroom in a Book* DVD includes the lesson files that you'll need to complete the exercises in this book, as well as other content to help you learn more about Adobe Premiere Pro CS3 and use it with greater efficiency and ease. The diagram below represents the contents of the DVD, which should help you locate the files you need.

Lessons

Each lesson has its own folder inside the Lessons folder. You will need to copy all these lesson folders to your hard drive before you can begin the book.

Lynda.com Movies

QuickTime tutorial movies by Lynda.com (www.lynda.com)

Adobe Press

Find information about other Adobe Press titles, covering the full spectrum of Adobe products, in the Adobe Press folder.

Adobe Certified

Information about how to become an Adobe Certified Expert or instructor is in the Adobe Certified folder.

Adobe Design Center

Find a wealth of information on Digital Video and DVD production in the AdobeDesignCenter.pdf file.

Contents

Getting Started

1 Touring Adobe Premiere Pro CS3

2 Shooting and Capturing Great Video Assets

9 **Adding Video Effects**

10 **Putting Clips in Motion**

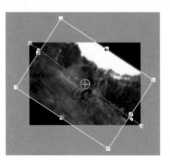

11 **Changing Time**

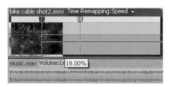

12   Acquiring and Editing Audio

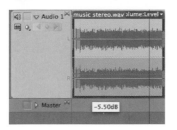

13   Sweetening Your Sound and Mixing Audio

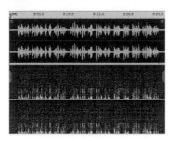

14   Compositing Techniques

15 **Color, Nested Sequences, and Shortcuts**

16 **Project Management**

17 **Using Photoshop and After Effects to Enhance Your Video Projects**

18 **Exporting Frames, Clips, and Sequences**

19 **Authoring DVDs with Adobe Premiere Pro CS3 and Encore CS3**

Getting Started

Adobe® Premiere® Pro CS3, the essential editing tool for video enthusiasts and professionals, enhances your creative power and freedom. Adobe Premiere Pro is the most scalable, efficient, and precise video editing tool available. Whether you're working with DV, HD, HDV, or any other format, the superior performance of Adobe Premiere Pro lets you work faster and more creatively. The complete set of powerful and exclusive tools lets you overcome any editorial, production, and workflow challenge to deliver the high-quality work you demand.

About Classroom in a Book

Adobe Premiere Pro CS3 Classroom in a Book® is part of the official training series for Adobe graphics and publishing software. The lessons are designed so that you can learn at your own pace. If you're new to Adobe Premiere Pro, you'll learn the fundamental concepts and features you'll need to use the program. Classroom in a Book also teaches many advanced features, including tips and techniques for using the latest version of this software.

The lessons in this edition include opportunities to use new features, such as improved slow motion with time remapping, improved editing efficiency, direct-to-disk recording, and the ability to publish Adobe Encore® CS3 projects to DVD, Blu-ray Disc, or Flash. All these features are further enhanced through the inclusion of a redesigned interface with new conveniences. Adobe Premiere Pro CS3 is now available for Windows and Mac OS.

Prerequisites

Before beginning to use *Adobe Premiere Pro CS3 Classroom in a Book*, make sure that your system is set up correctly and that you've installed the required software and hardware. You should have a working knowledge of your computer and operating system. You should know how to use the mouse and standard menus and commands, and also how to open, save, and close files. If you need to review these techniques, see the printed or online documentation included with your Macintosh or Microsoft® Windows® system.

Installing Adobe Premiere Pro CS3

You must purchase the Adobe Premiere Pro CS3 software separately. For system requirements and complete instructions on installing the software, see the document Adobe Premiere Pro ReadMe.html on the application DVD.

Install Adobe Premiere Pro from the Adobe Premiere Pro CS3 application DVD onto your hard disk; you cannot run the program from the DVD. Follow the onscreen instructions.

Make sure that your serial number is accessible before installing the application; you can find the serial number on the registration card or on the back of the DVD case.

Optimizing performance

Editing videos is memory- and processor-intensive work for a desktop computer. A fast processor and a lot of memory will make your editing experience much faster and more efficient. 1GB of memory is the minimum, and 2GB is recommended for editing HDV or HD media. Adobe Premiere Pro CS3 takes advantage of multicore processors on Windows and Macintosh systems, and will run on Macintosh computers with multicore Intel processors.

A dedicated 7200-RPM or faster hard drive is recommended for SD or HDV media. A RAID 0 striped disk array or SCSI disk subsystem is recommended for HD. Performance will be significantly affected if you attempt to store media files and program files on the same hard drive.

Copying the lesson files

The lessons in *Adobe Premiere Pro CS3 Classroom in a Book* use specific source files, such as image files created in Adobe Photoshop® CS3 and Adobe Illustrator® CS3, audio files, and videos. To complete the lessons in this book, you must copy all the files from the *Adobe Premiere Pro CS3 Classroom in a Book* DVD (inside the back cover of this book) to your hard drive. You will need about 3.5GB of storage space in addition to at least 10GB you'll need to operate Adobe Premiere Pro CS3.

While each lesson stands alone, some lessons use files from other lessons, so you'll need to keep the entire collection of lesson assets on your hard drive as you work through the book. Here's how to copy those assets from the DVD to your hard drive.

1   Open the *Adobe Premiere Pro CS3 Classroom in a Book* DVD in My Computer or Windows Explorer (Windows) or in the Finder (Mac OS).

2   Right-click (Windows) or Control-click (Mac OS) the folder called Lessons, and choose Copy.

3   Navigate to the location you set to store your Adobe Premiere Pro CS3 projects. The default location is My Documents\Adobe\Premiere Pro\3.0 (Windows) or Documents/Adobe/Premiere Pro/3.0 (Mac OS).

4   Right-click (Windows) or Control-click (Mac OS) the 3.0 folder, and choose Paste. Repeat steps 3 and 4 for the Movies folder.

That will load all the lesson assets and movies to your local folder. It'll take a couple of minutes to finish this, depending on the speed of your DVD drive.

How to use these lessons

Each lesson in this book provides step-by-step instructions for creating one or more specific elements of a real-world project. The lessons stand alone, but most of them build on previous lessons in terms of concepts and skills. So the best way to learn from this book is to proceed through the lessons in sequential order.

The organization of the lessons is workflow-oriented rather than feature-oriented. The lessons follow the typical sequential steps video editors use to complete a project, starting with laying down a cuts-only video and proceeding through the process, all the way to applying special effects. This real-world approach differs from the reference manual approach you'll find in the *Adobe Premiere Pro CS3 User Guide*.

Note: *Many aspects of Adobe Premiere Pro CS3 can be controlled by multiple techniques, such as menu commands, context menus, and keyboard shortcuts. Sometimes more than one of the methods is described in any given procedure so that you can learn different ways of working, even when the task is one you've done before.*

Additional resources

Adobe Premiere Pro CS3 Classroom in a Book is not meant to replace documentation that comes with the program. This book explains only the commands and options actually used in the lessons, so there's much more to learn about Adobe Premiere Pro. Classroom in a Book aims to give you confidence and skills so that you can start creating your own projects. For more comprehensive information about program features, see:

• The *Adobe Premiere Pro CS3 User Guide,* which is included with the Adobe Premiere Pro CS3 software and contains descriptions of all features.

• Adobe Premiere Pro Help, an online version of the user guide, which you can view by starting Adobe Premiere Pro and then choosing Help > Adobe Premiere Pro Help.

• The Adobe website (*www.adobe.com*), which you can explore by choosing Help > Online Support if you have a connection to the World Wide Web.

• Adobe Design Center (*http://www.adobe.com/designcenter*), where you can find a wealth of tips, tutorials, plug-ins, actions, and other design inspiration and instructional content.

Adobe certification

The Adobe training and certification programs are designed to help Adobe customers improve and promote their product-proficiency skills. There are three levels of certification:

* Adobe Certified Expert (ACE)

* Adobe Certified Instructor (ACI)

* Adobe Authorized Training Center (AATC)

The Adobe Certified Expert (ACE) program is a way for expert users to upgrade their credentials. You can use Adobe certification as a catalyst for getting a raise, finding a job, or promoting your expertise.

If you are an ACE-level instructor, the Adobe Certified Instructor program takes your skills to the next level and gives you access to a wide range of Adobe resources.

Adobe Authorized Training Centers offer instructor-led courses and training on Adobe products, employing only Adobe Certified Instructors. A directory of AATCs is available at *http://partners.adobe.com.*

For information on the Adobe Certified programs, visit *www.adobe.com/support/ certification/main.html.*

workflow

workspace

Timeline

It's time to roll up your sleeves and dive into Adobe Premiere Pro CS3. But before you make your first edit or apply your first transition, you will see a brief overview of video editing and how Adobe Premiere Pro fits into the video production workflow, and get an introduction to its improved workspace. Even those who are old hands at editing videos on a desktop computer will find the new workspace features in Adobe Premiere Pro CS3 worthy of exploration.

1 Touring Adobe Premiere Pro CS3

Topics covered in this lesson:

- What's new in Adobe Premiere Pro CS3

- Nonlinear editing in Adobe Premiere Pro CS3

- Standard digital video workflow

- Incorporating Adobe® Creative Suite® 3 Production Premium into the workflow

- Touring the Adobe Premiere Pro workspace

- Customizing the workspace

Getting started

We've come a long way from clunky old videotape machines and expensive production equipment to professional-level editing on a desktop computer. To get started, we will first look at some of the exciting new features included with Adobe Premiere Pro CS3. We'll review the basic workflow most video editors follow, and see how Adobe Premiere Pro fits within the different versions of Adobe Creative Suite. Finally, you'll be introduced to custom workspaces in Adobe Premiere Pro CS3.

New Features in Adobe Premiere Pro CS3

- **Adobe® OnLocation™ CS3**—Eliminates the capture process by recording SD and HD video directly from your camera to a laptop or workstation. Instantly review any shot. Log clips during your shoot. Avoid problems and improve quality on location with the virtual reference monitor, comprehensive waveform monitor, Vectorscope, and audio spectrum analyzer. (Adobe OnLocation is

Windows-only software, and therefore requires Boot Camp if you want to run it on Mac OS.) For more information, see Lesson 3.

•   **Adobe® Encore® CS3**—Create DVDs and take advantage of Blu-ray Disc technology. Work with the same Encore authoring interface and features used to create standard-definition DVDs. Author once, deliver twice: Automatically convert HD Blu-ray Disc projects into standard-definition DVDs. Encore now allows the project to be exported as interactive Flash content for easy web viewing of your DVD project. For more information, see Lesson 19.

•   **High quality slow motion with time remapping**—Create dramatic slow- and fast-motion effects without exporting clips to another application. With precise keyframe control, real-time feedback, and advanced frame-blending quality, you can easily increase or decrease speed, and even make a clip run backwards before resuming normal forward motion. For details, see Lesson 10.

•   **Smart File Search**—Find files faster with search tools that instantly update their results list as you type. Sort and organize assets into multiple project panels, each with its own graphical or text view setting. You'll see this in action later in this lesson.

•   **Improved editing efficiency**—Work faster with powerful and flexible editing tools. No more waiting for audio to render when working with nested sequences. Replace any clip in the timeline with a new clip while preserving the replaced clip's attributes, filters, and settings. For details, see Lesson 15.

•   **Output for mobile devices**—Make your video viewable on the latest delivery platforms. Encode video for cell phones, portable media players, and other mobile devices. For more information, see Lesson 18.

•   **Flash Video export with markers converted to cue points**—Encode video and audio for Flash projects and web playback with direct Flash Video (FLV) export. Adobe Premiere Pro timeline markers become Flash cue points that trigger interactivity and navigation. For details, see Lesson 18.

Nonlinear editing in Adobe Premiere Pro CS3

Adobe Premiere Pro is a nonlinear editor (NLE). Unlike older videotape editing systems, where you generally need to lay down edits consecutively and contiguously, Adobe Premiere Pro lets you place, replace, trim, and move clips anywhere you want in your final edited video.

On videotape systems, if you decide to insert a sound bite in the middle of a story already edited on tape, you need to insert that sound bite over your existing edits and re-edit everything after it. Or you can make a dub (copy) of the story segment after the new edit point and re-record that part after adding the sound bite (causing generation quality loss in the process).

Adobe Premiere Pro lets you do things non-sequentially. With Adobe Premiere Pro (and other NLEs), you can make changes by simply dragging clips or segments around within your final video. You can edit video segments separately and tie them together later. You can even edit the closing sequence first.

NLEs have another huge benefit over videotape-editing systems: immediate access to your video clips. No longer do you need to endlessly fast-forward or rewind through tons of tape to find that one elusive-but-essential shot. With Adobe Premiere Pro, it's a mouse click away.

Presenting the standard digital video workflow

There is a basic workflow for creating videos with NLEs such as Adobe Premiere Pro. After a while, it'll become second nature. Generally, that workflow follows these steps:

1 Shoot the video.

2 Capture (transfer) the video to your hard drive. Or, use Adobe OnLocation to record video directly to your workstation hard drive (bypassing the capture step).

3 Build your edited video by selecting, trimming, and adding clips to a timeline.

4 Place transitions between clips, apply video effects to clips, and composite (layer) clips.

5 Create text, credits, or basic graphics, and apply them to your project.

6 Add audio—be it narration, music, or sound effects.

Note: Audio can also be the first thing you lay down when editing a video.

7 Mix multiple audio tracks and use transitions and special effects on your audio clips.

8 Export your finished project to videotape, a file on your desktop computer, streaming video for Internet playback, or to a DVD.

Adobe Premiere Pro supports each of these steps with industry-leading tools. Since this book is geared to the beginning and intermediate video editor, becoming proficient with these standard workflow tools is the primary goal of the upcoming lessons.

Enhancing the workflow with high-level features

Adobe Premiere Pro goes well beyond providing a full-featured toolset for standard digital video editing. It is loaded with extra features that can enhance the video production process and improve the quality of your finished product.

You are not likely to incorporate many of these features in your first few video projects. But as you ramp up your skills and expectations, you will begin to tap these high-productivity features. The following topics will be covered in this book:

- **Advanced audio editing**—Adobe Premiere Pro provides audio effects and editing unequaled by any other nonlinear editor, or by most audio software. Create and place 5.1 surround-sound audio channels, make sample-level edits, apply multiple audio effects to any audio clip or track, and use the included state-of-the-art plug-ins and other Virtual Studio Technology (VST) plug-ins.

- **Color correction**—Correct and enhance the look of your footage with advanced color-correction filters.

- **Keyframe controls**—Adobe Premiere Pro CS3 gives you the precise control you need to fine-tune your visual and motion effects without requiring you to export to a compositing application.

- **Broad hardware support**—Choose from a wide range of capture cards and other hardware to best fit your needs and budget. Adobe Premiere Pro CS3 support extends from low-cost computers for digital video (DV) and compressed high-definition video (HDV) format editing, up to high-performance workstations capturing high-definition (HD) video. When it's time to upgrade your hardware to work with HD and film, you don't need to leave the familiar Adobe Premiere Pro interface—unlike with some proprietary systems that provide different interfaces for different formats.

- **Clip Notes**—Speed your client review-and-approval process by embedding Adobe Premiere Pro projects in PDF documents. Your client watches the video with Adobe Reader® software, enters comments into the feedback form in the PDF file, and then e-mails the comments to you.

- **GPU-accelerated video effects**—Use the graphics processing unit (GPU) on modern graphics cards to create real-time page curls, page rolls, spheres with video mapped on them, and other image-distortion effects that typically require expensive hardware or long render times.

- **High-definition video support**—Work with every high-definition format, including HDV, HDCAM, DVCPRO HD, D5-HD, and 4K film scans. Adobe Premiere Pro CS3 supports these formats at any resolution (720p, 1080i, 1080p) and frame rate (24fps, 23.98fps, 30fps, 60fps, and so on).

- **Multicam editing**—You can easily and quickly edit any production shot with multiple cameras. Adobe Premiere Pro displays all the camera tracks in a split-view monitor, and you set the edits by clicking in the appropriate screen or by making single keystrokes.

- **Project Manager**—Manage your media through a single dialog box. View, delete, move, search for, and reorganize clips and bins. Consolidate your projects by moving just the media actually used in a project, and copying that media to a single location. Then reclaim drive space by deleting unused media.

Incorporating Adobe Creative Suite 3 Production Premium into the workflow

Even with all of the exciting extra features in Adobe Premiere Pro, there are some digital video production tasks that it cannot do. For example:

- High-end 3D motion effects

- Detailed text animations

- Layered graphics

- Vector artwork

- Music creation

- Advanced audio mixing, editing, and effects processing

To incorporate one or more of these features into a production, you can turn to Adobe Creative Suite 3 Production Premium software. It has all the tools you need to produce some absolutely amazing videos, including:

- Adobe Premiere Pro CS3

- Adobe After Effects® CS3 Professional

- Adobe Photoshop® CS3 Extended

- Adobe Soundbooth™ CS3

- Adobe Encore® CS3
- Adobe Illustrator® CS3
- Adobe Flash® CS3 Professional
- Adobe Dynamic Link
- Adobe Bridge CS3
- Adobe OnLocation™ CS3 (Windows only)
- Adobe Ultra® CS3 (Windows only)

Here's a brief description of Adobe Premiere Pro software's ten Creative Suite 3 Production Premium teammates:

• **Adobe After Effects CS3 Professional**—The tool of choice for motion graphics and visual effects artists.

• **Adobe Photoshop CS3**—The industry standard image-editing and graphic-creation product.

• **Adobe Soundbooth CS3**—Easy yet powerful audio editing, audio cleanup, audio sweetening, and music creation.

• **Adobe Encore CS3**—A high-quality DVD-authoring product designed to work closely with Adobe Premiere Pro, After Effects, and Photoshop CS3. Now publishes to standard DVD, Blu-ray Disc, and interactive SWF files. Encore CS3 is now included with Adobe Premiere Pro CS3.

• **Adobe Illustrator CS3**—Professional vector graphics creation software for print, video production, and the web.

• **Adobe Dynamic Link**—A cross-product connection that allows you to work in real time with native After Effects files in Adobe Premiere Pro and Encore CS3 without rendering first.

• **Adobe Bridge**—A visual file browser that provides centralized access to your Creative Suite project files, applications, and settings.

• **Adobe Flash CS3 Professional**—The industry standard for creating rich, interactive web content.

• **Adobe OnLocation CS3 (Windows only)**—Powerful direct-to-disk recording and monitoring software to help you produce superior-quality results from your video camera. Adobe OnLocation CS3 is now included with Adobe Premiere Pro CS3.

- **Adobe Ultra CS3 (Windows only)**—An easy-to-use keyer that allows composites of bluescreen and virtual sets, including shadows, reflections, and advanced tracking shots.

Adobe Creative Suite 3 Production Premium workflow

Your Adobe Premiere Pro/Adobe Creative Suite Production Studio Premium workflow will vary depending on your production needs. Here are a few mini-workflow scenarios:

- Use Adobe OnLocation to record video direct to disk.

- Use Photoshop CS3 to touch up still images from a digital camera, a scanner, or an Adobe Premiere Pro video clip. Then export them to Adobe Premiere Pro.

- Create layered graphics in Photoshop CS3 and then open them in Adobe Premiere Pro. You can opt to have each layer appear on a separate track in a timeline, allowing you to apply effects and motion to selected layers.

- Build custom music tracks using Adobe Soundbooth CS3, and then export them to Adobe Premiere Pro.

- Use Adobe Soundbooth to do professional-quality audio editing and sweetening on an existing Adobe Premiere Pro video or a separate audio file.

- Using Dynamic Link, open Adobe Premiere Pro video sequences in After Effects CS3. Apply complex motion and animation, and then send those updated motion sequences back to Adobe Premiere Pro. You can play After Effects compositions in Adobe Premiere Pro CS3 without first waiting to render them.

- Use After Effects CS3 to create and animate text in ways far beyond the capabilities of Adobe Premiere Pro. Export those compositions to Adobe Premiere Pro.

- Import video projects created in Adobe Premiere Pro into Encore CS3 to use in DVD projects. You can use those videos as the foundation of a project or as motion menus.

Most of this book will focus on a "standard" workflow involving only Adobe Premiere Pro. However, several lessons will demonstrate how you can incorporate Adobe Creative Suite 3 Production Premium components within your workflow for even more spectacular results.

Touring the Adobe Premiere Pro workspace

You'll dive into nonlinear editing in the next lesson. At this point, we'll take a brief tour of the video editing workspace. In this lesson, you will use an Adobe Premiere Pro project from this book's companion DVD.

1 Make sure you've copied all the lesson folders and contents from the DVD to your hard drive. The default directory is: My Documents\Adobe\Premiere Pro\3.0\Lessons in Windows or Documents/Adobe/Premiere Pro/3.0/Lessons in Mac OS.

Note: It's best to copy all the lesson assets from the DVD to your hard drive and leave them there until you complete this book; some lessons refer back to assets from previous lessons.

2 Start Adobe Premiere Pro.

3 Click Open Project.

4 In the Open Project window, navigate to the Lesson 01 folder in the Lessons folder, and then double-click the Lesson 1.prproj project file to open the first lesson in the Adobe Premiere Pro workspace.

Note: You may be prompted with a dialog box asking where a particular file is. This will happen when the original files were saved on a hard drive other than the one you're using. You'll need to tell Adobe Premiere Pro where the file is: In this case, navigate to the Lesson 1 folder and select the file that the dialog box is prompting you for.

The workspace layout

If you've never seen a nonlinear editor, this workspace might overwhelm you. Not to worry. A lot of careful consideration went into its design and layout. The principal elements are identified in the next figure.

The Adobe Premiere Pro workspace might seem daunting to first-time NLE users, but you'll soon see the logic behind its layout.

Each workspace item appears in its own panel. You can dock multiple panels in a single frame. Some items with common industry terms stand alone, such as Timeline,

Audio Mixer, and Program Monitor. All the new (and some old) names are listed in the following workspace descriptions.

- **Timeline panel**—This is where you'll do most of your actual editing. You create sequences (Adobe's term for edited video segments or entire projects) in the Timeline panel. One strength of sequences is that you can nest them—place sequences in other sequences. In this way, you can break up a production into manageable chunks.

More tracks than you can use

You can layer—or composite—video clips, images, graphics, and titles in an unlimited number of tracks. Video clips in higher-numbered tracks cover whatever is directly below them on the timeline. Therefore, you need to give clips in higher-numbered tracks some kind of transparency or reduce their size if you want to let clips in lower tracks show through. Compositing will be covered in several upcoming lessons.

- **Monitors**—You use the Source Monitor (on the left) to view and trim raw clips (your original footage). To place a clip in the Source Monitor, double-click bike cable shot1.mov in the Project panel. The Program Monitor (on the right) is for viewing your project-in-progress.

Single or dual monitor view

Some editors prefer working with only one monitor screen. The lessons throughout this book reflect a two-monitor workflow. You can change to a single monitor view if you choose. Click the Close button in the Source tab to close that monitor. In the main menu, choose Window > Source Monitor to open it again.

- **Project panel**—This is where you place links to your project's assets: video clips, audio files, graphics, still images, and sequences. You use bins—or folders—to organize your assets.

- **Effects panel**—Click the Effects tab (by default docked with the History and Info tabs) to open the Effects panel (below). Effects are organized by Presets, Audio Effects, Audio Transitions, Video Effects, and Video Transitions. If you open the various effects bins you'll note that they include numerous audio effects to spice up your sound; two audio crossfade transitions; video scene transitions, such as dissolves and wipes; and many video effects to alter the appearance of your clips.

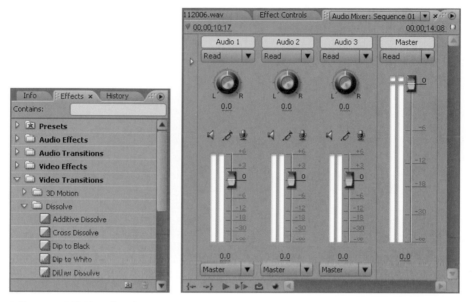

Effects panel (left) and Audio Mixer (right)

- **Audio Mixer**—Click the Audio Mixer tab to the right of the Effect Controls tab (above). This interface looks a lot like audio production studio hardware with its volume sliders and panning knobs—one set of controls for each audio track in the Timeline, plus a Master track.

- **Tools panel**—Each icon in this panel (below) represents a tool that performs a specific function, typically a type of edit. Older versions of Adobe Premiere Pro had many more tools, but now the Selection tool (⬚) is context-sensitive. It changes appearance to indicate the function that matches the circumstances.

- **Effect Controls panel**—Click the Effect Controls tab (below), and then click any clip in the Timeline to display that clip's effect parameters in the Effect Controls panel. This will give you a small taste of many lessons to come. Two video effects are always present for every video, still, or graphic: Motion and Opacity. Each effect parameter (in the case of Motion: Position, Scale Height and Width, Rotation, and Anchor Point) is adjustable over time using keyframes. The Effect Controls panel is an immensely powerful tool that gives you incredible creative latitude. It comes up in many of this book's lessons.

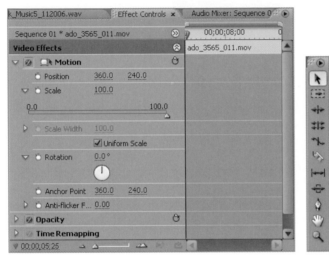

Effect Controls panel (left) and Tools panel (right)

- **Info panel**—Click the Info tab to the left of the Effects tab. This panel presents a data snapshot of any asset you've selected in the Project panel or any clip or transition selected in a sequence.

- **History panel**—Click the History tab to the right of the Effects tab. This panel tracks every step you take in your video production and lets you back up if you don't like your latest efforts. When you back up to a previous condition, all steps that came after that point are also undone. You cannot extract a single misstep buried within the current list.

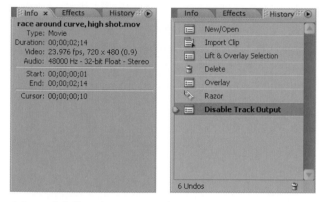

Info panel (left) and History panel (right)

Customizing the workspace

You can customize the workspace to create a layout that works best for you.

- As you change the size of one frame, other frames change size to compensate.
- All panels within frames are accessible via tabs.
- All panels are dockable—you can drag a panel from one frame to another.
- You can drag a panel out of a frame to become a separate floating panel.

You can save your workspace as a custom workspace; you can save as many custom workspaces as you like.

In this lesson you'll try out all of those functions and save a customized workspace. Before changing the interface layout, you'll adjust its brightness.

1   Choose Edit > Preferences > User Interface (Windows) or Premiere Pro > Preferences > User Interface (Mac OS).

```
General...
Audio...
Audio Hardware...
Audio Output Mapping...
Auto Save...
Capture...
Device Control...
Label Colors...
Label Defaults...
Media...
Scratch Disks...
Titler...
Trim...
User Interface...
```

2   Drag the Brightness slider to the left or right to suit your needs. When done, click OK.

```
User Interface
  User Interface Brightness

  Darker        Default Brightness        Lighter
```

💡 **Cave-like editing bays**

As you approach the darkest setting, the text switches to white on gray. This is to accommodate those editors who work in editing bays in darkened rooms.

3   Click the Effects tab, and then position your pointer on the vertical divider between the Effects panel and the Timeline panel. Then, drag left and right to change the sizes of those frames.

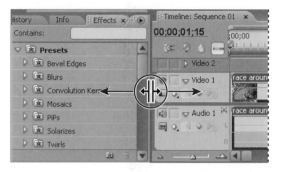

4   Place the pointer on the horizontal divider between the Effect Controls panel and the Timeline panel. Drag up and down to change the sizes of these frames.

5   Click the drag handle in the upper left corner of the History tab, and drag it to the top of the interface, next to the Project tab, to dock the History panel in that frame.

Note: *As you move a panel around, Adobe Premiere Pro displays a drop zone. If the panel is a rectangle, it will go into the selected frame. If it's a trapezoid, it'll go into its own frame.*

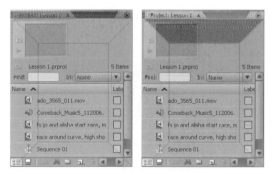

Rectangular drop zone (left) and trapezoidal drop zone (right)

💡 **Dealing with a crowded frame**

When the History panel is added to the frame with the Project panel, you may not be able to see all the tabs. In this case, a slider appears above the tabs. Slide it left or right to reveal all the tabs. You can also open a hidden (or any other) panel directly from a menu by choosing Window and then clicking a panel name.

6   Drag the Effect Controls drag handle to a point near the bottom of the Project panel to place it in its own frame.

As shown in the following figure on the left, the drop zone is a trapezoid that covers the lower portion of the Project panel. Release the mouse button, and your workspace should look something like the following figure on the right.

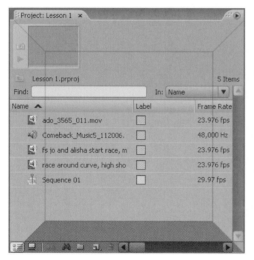
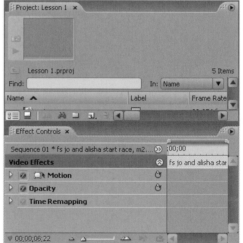

7 Click the Program Monitor's drag handle and hold down the Ctrl (Windows) or Command (Mac OS) key while dragging it out of its frame. Its drop zone image is much more distinct, indicating you are about to create a floating panel.

8 Drop the Program Monitor anywhere, creating a floating panel. Expand it by dragging from the corner.

9 As you gain editing acumen, you might want to create and save a customized workspace. To do that, choose Window > Workspace > New Workspace. Type a workspace name, and click OK.

10 If you want to return the workspace to its default layout, choose Window > Workspace > Reset Current Workspace.

Review

▶ **Review questions**

1   Why is Adobe Premiere Pro considered a nonlinear editor?

2   Describe the basic video editing workflow.

3   What purpose does the Project panel serve?

4   Can you save a customized workspace?

5   What is the purpose of the Source Monitor? What is the purpose of the Program Monitor?

6   How and why do you create a floating panel?

▶ **Review answers**

1   Adobe Premiere Pro lets you place video, audio, and graphics anywhere on a sequence (timeline), rearrange media clips within a sequence, add transitions, apply effects, and do any number of other video editing steps in just about any order that suits you.

2   Shoot your video; transfer it to your computer; create a sequence of video, audio, and still-image clips on the timeline; apply effects and transitions; add text and graphics; edit your audio; and export the finished product.

3   You store and organize links to your media assets in the Project panel.

4   Yes. Any customized workspace can be saved by using the Window > Workspace > New Workspace feature.

5   You use the monitor panels to view your project and your original clips. When working with two monitors—Source and Program—you can view and trim your raw footage in the Source Monitor and use the Program Monitor to view the timeline sequence as you build it.

6   Frequently you need much more real estate when working in a panel. The Effect Controls panel, for example, can display enough parameters to fill a full screen. To expand your view of a panel by creating a floating panel, hold down Ctrl (Windows) or Command (Mac OS) while dragging the panel's drag handle.

cutaways

capture

00;00;00

scene detection

1/3 1/3 1/3

It's time to do some work with your own videos. You've heard of garbage in, garbage out? That truism also applies to video editing. So, your first task is to shoot some great-looking video. Then use Adobe Premiere Pro CS3 to capture that video—transfer it from your camcorder or VCR to your hard drive. Adobe Premiere Pro offers several ways to do that. Each is easy and fast.

2 | Shooting and Capturing Great Video Assets

Topics covered in this lesson:

- Twenty tips for shooting great video
- Capturing an entire videotape
- Using batch capture and scene detection
- Tackling manual analog video capture

Getting started

The purpose of this book is to help you use Adobe Premiere Pro to make professional-looking videos. To do that, you need to start with high-quality raw material. This lesson gives you 20 tips for shooting great video, and four methods to transfer or capture your video to your workstation.

Twenty tips for shooting great video

With your camcorder of choice in hand, it's time to venture off and shoot videos. If you're new to videography, following these tips will help you create better videos. If you're an old hand, think of this list of shooting axioms as a way to snap out of your routine and juice things up a bit:

- Get a closing shot.
- Get an establishing shot.
- Shoot plenty of video.
- Adhere to the "rule of thirds."
- Keep your shots steady.
- Follow the action.
- Use trucking shots.
- Find unusual angles.
- Lean forward or backward.
- Get wide shots.
- Get tight shots.
- Shoot matched action.
- Get sequences.
- Avoid fast pans and snap zooms.
- Shoot cutaways.
- Don't break the "plane."
- Use lights.
- Grab good "bites."
- Get plenty of natural sound.
- Plan your shoot.

Get a closing shot

Your closing images are what stick in people's minds. You should be constantly on the lookout for that one shot or sequence that best wraps up your story.

Get an establishing shot

An establishing shot sets a scene in one image. Although super-wide shots work well (aerials in particular), consider other points of view: from the cockpit of a race car, a close-up of a scalpel with light glinting off its surface, or paddles dipping frantically in roaring white water. Each grabs the viewer's attention and helps tell your story.

The establishing shot sets the scene: an isolated mountain range. The second tells the story: a race is about to start.

Shoot plenty of video

Videotape is cheap and expendable. Shoot a whole lot more raw footage than you'll put in your final production. Five times as much is not unusual. Giving yourself that latitude might help you grab shots you would have missed otherwise.

Adhere to the rule of thirds

It's called the "rule of thirds" but it's more like the rule of four intersecting lines. When composing your shot, think of your viewfinder as being crisscrossed by two horizontal and two vertical lines. The center of interest should fall along those lines or near one of the four intersections, not the center of the image.

Consider all those family photos where the subject's eyes are smack dab in the center of the photo. Those are *not* examples of good composition.

Another way to follow the rule of thirds is to look around the viewfinder as you shoot, not just stare at its center. Check the edges to see whether you're filling the frame with interesting images. Avoid large areas of blank space.

The rule of thirds: Putting your image's most important elements along the lines or at their intersections will make it more pleasing to the eye.

Keep your shots steady

You want to give viewers the sense that they're looking through a window or, better yet, are there on location. A shaky camera shatters that illusion.

When possible, use a tripod. The best "sticks" have fluid heads that enable you to make smooth pans or tilts.

If it's impractical to use a tripod try to find some way to stabilize the shot: Lean against a wall, put your elbows on a table, or place the camcorder on a solid object.

Follow the action

This might seem obvious, but keep your viewfinder on the ball (or sprinter, speeding police car, surfer, conveyor belt, and so on). Your viewers' eyes will want to follow the action, so give them what they want.

One nifty trick is to use directed movement as a pan motivator. That is, follow a leaf's progress as it floats down a stream and then continue your camera motion past the leaf—panning—and widen out to show something unexpected: a waterfall, a huge industrial complex, or a fisherman.

Use trucking shots

Trucking or dolly shots move with the action. For example, hold the camera at arm's length right behind a toddler as he motors around the house, put the camera in a grocery cart as it winds through the aisles, or shoot out the window of a speeding train.

Find unusual angles

Getting your camcorder off your shoulder, away from eye level, leads to more interesting and enjoyable shots. Ground-level shots are great for gamboling lambs or cavorting puppies. Shoot up from a low angle and down from a high angle. Shoot through objects or people while keeping the focus on your subject.

Lean forward or backward

The zoom lens can be a crutch. A better way to move in close or away from a subject is simply to lean in or out. For example, start by leaning way in with a tight shot of someone's hands as he works on a wood carving; then, while still recording, lean way back (perhaps widening your zoom lens as well) to reveal that he is working in a sweatshop full of folks hunched over their handiwork.

Get wide and tight shots

Our eyes work like medium-angle lenses. So we tend to shoot video that way. Instead, grab wide shots and tight shots of your subjects. If practical, get close to your subject to get the tight shot rather than use the zoom lens. Not only does it look better, but the proximity leads to clearer audio.

Using a wide and a tight shot can create greater interest.

Shoot matched action

Consider a shot from behind a pitcher as he throws a fastball. He releases it, and then it smacks into the catcher's glove. Instead of a single shot, grab two shots: a medium shot from behind the pitcher showing the pitch and the ball's flight toward the catcher, and a tight shot of the catcher's glove. Same concept for an artist: Get a wide shot of her applying a paint stroke to a canvas, and then move in for a close shot of the same action. You'll edit them together to match the action.

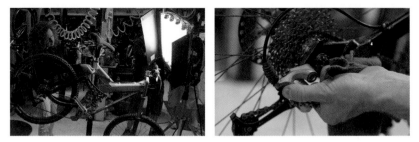

Matched action keeps the story flowing smoothly while helping to illustrate a point.

Get sequences

Shooting repetitive action in a sequence is another way to tell a story, build interest, or create suspense. A bowler wipes his hands on a rosin bag, dries them over a blower, wipes the ball with a towel, picks the ball up, fixes his gaze on the pins, steps forward, swings the ball back, releases it, slides to the foul line, watches the ball's trajectory, and then reacts to the shot. Instead of simply capturing all this in one long shot, piecing these actions together in a sequence of edits is much more compelling. You can easily combine wide and tight shots, trucking moves, and matched action to turn repetitive material into attention-grabbing sequences.

Avoid fast pans and snap zooms

These moves fall into MTV and amateur video territory. Few circumstances call for such stomach-churning camerawork. In general, it's best to minimize all pans and zooms. As with a shaky camera, they remind viewers that they're watching TV.

If you do zoom or pan, do it for a purpose: to reveal something, to follow someone's gaze from his or her eyes to the subject of interest, or to continue the flow of action (as in the floating leaf example earlier). A slow zoom in, with only a minimal change to the focal length, can add drama to a sound bite. Again, do it sparingly.

Keep on rolling along

Don't let this no-fast-moves admonition force you to stop rolling while you zoom or pan. If you see something that warrants a quick close-up shot or you need to suddenly pan to grab some possibly fleeting footage, keep rolling. You can always edit around that sudden movement later.

If you stop recording to make the pan or zoom or adjust the focus, you might lose some or all of whatever it was you were trying so desperately to shoot. You will also miss any accompanying natural sound.

Shoot cutaways

Avoid jump cuts by shooting cutaways. A jump cut is an edit that creates a disconnect in the viewer's mind. A cutaway—literally a shot that cuts away from the current shot—fixes jump cuts.

Cutaways are common in interviews where you might want to edit together two 10-second sound bites from the same person. Doing so would mean the interviewee would look like he suddenly moved. To avoid that jump cut—that sudden disconcerting shift—you make a cutaway of the interview. That could be a wide shot, a hand shot, or a reverse-angle shot of the interviewer over the interviewee's shoulder. You then edit in the cutaway over the juncture of the two sound bites to cover the jump cut.

The same holds true for a soccer game. It can be disconcerting to simply cut from one wide shot of players on the field to another. If you shoot some crowd reactions or the scoreboard, you can use those cutaways to cover up what would have been jump cuts.

A cutaway of the racer's face as she prepares with her mechanic.

Don't break the plane

This avoids another viewer disconnect. If you're shooting in one direction, you don't want your next shot to be looking back at your previous camera location. For instance, if you're shooting an interview with the camera peering over the left shoulder of the interviewer, you want to shoot your reverse cutaways behind the interviewee and over his right shoulder. That keeps the camera on the same side of the plane—an imaginary vertical flat surface running through the interviewer and interviewee.

To shoot over your interviewee's left shoulder would break that plane, meaning the viewer would think the camera that took the previous shot should somehow be in view.

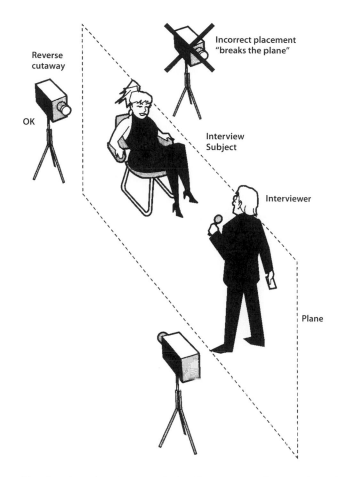

The plane is an imaginary vertical wall running, in this case, through the reporter and interviewee. Breaking the plane—particularly when shooting a reverse cutaway—leads to camera shots that cause viewer disconnects.

In general, you want to keep all your camera positions on one side of that plane, even when shooting large-scale events like football games. Otherwise, viewers may lose track of the direction of play.

There are exceptions. Consider videotaping a rock group performance. Camera crew members typically scramble all over the stage, grabbing shots from multiple angles, and frequently appear on camera themselves.

💡 Switch sides

If you conduct formal, sit-down interviews with more than one person for the same piece, consider shooting each subject from a different side of the interviewer. Shoot one subject with the camera positioned over the left shoulder of the reporter, and for the next interview position the camera over the right shoulder of the reporter. That avoids a subtle jump cut that happens when you edit two bites from two individuals who are both facing the same way.

Use lights

Lights add brilliance, dazzle, and depth to otherwise bland and flat scenes. Consider using an onboard camcorder fill light and, if you have the time, money, patience, or personnel, a full lighting kit with a few colored gels. In a pinch, do whatever you can to increase available light. Open curtains, turn on all the lights, or bring a couple of desk lamps into the room. One caveat: Low-light situations can be dramatic, and flipping on a few desk lamps can destroy that mood in a moment.

Image courtesy of Lowel-Light Mfg.

Grab good "bites"

Your narrator presents the facts. The people in your story present the emotions, feelings, and opinions. Don't rely on interview sound bites to tell the who, what, where, when, and how. Let those bites explain the why.

In a corporate backgrounder, have the narrator say what a product does and let the employees or customers say how enthusiastic they are about that product.

Your narrator should be the one to say, "It was opening night and this was her first solo." Let the singer, who is recalling this dramatic moment, say, "My throat was tight and my stomach was tied in knots."

In general, even though your interviews might take forever, use only short sound bites in your final production. Use those bites as punctuation marks, not paragraphs.

💡 Exceptions for idiosyncratic characters

None of these admonitions are carved in stone. Some characters you'll videotape are so compelling, quirky, or humorous that your best bet is to let them be the primary narrator. Then you'll want to consider what scenes you can use to illustrate their commentary. You don't want to fill your entire video with a "talking head."

Get plenty of natural sound

Think beyond images. Sound is tremendously important. Listen for sounds you can use in your project. Even if the video quality is mediocre, grab that audio. Your camcorder's onboard microphone is not much more than a fallback. Consider using additional microphones: shotgun mics to narrow the focus of your sound and avoid extraneous noise, lavalieres tucked out of sight for interviews, and wireless mics when your camera can't be close enough to get just what you need.

Plan your shoot

When you consider a video project, plan what you need to shoot to tell the story. Videotaping your kid's soccer championship match, a corporate backgrounder, or a medical procedure each require planning to ensure success. Know what you want your final video project to say and think of what you need to videotape to tell that story.

Even the best-laid plans and most carefully scripted projects might need some adjusting once you start recording in the field. No matter how you envision the finished project, be willing to make changes as the situation warrants.

Capturing video

Before you can edit your own video, you need to transfer it to your computer's hard drive. In NLE parlance, you need to *capture* it. Capture is a somewhat-misleading term used throughout the NLE world. All that Adobe Premiere Pro does during DV capture is to place the video data in a movie file "wrapper" without changing the original DV data.

The capture process in the analog world takes several steps: transfer, conversion, compression, and wrapping. Your camcorder transfers the video and audio as analog data to a video capture card. That card's built-in hardware converts the waveform signal to a digital form, compresses it using a codec (compression/decompression) process, and then wraps it in the AVI file format.

Three DV capturing scenarios

Adobe Premiere Pro offers tools to take some of the manual labor out of the capturing process. There are three basic approaches:

- Capture your entire videotape as one long clip.

- Log each clip's In and Out points for automated batch capturing.

- Use the scene detection feature in Adobe Premiere Pro to automatically create separate clips whenever you pressed the pause/record button on your camcorder.

To do this lesson, you need a DV camcorder. Most DV camcorders have a FireWire (IEEE 1394) cable that you hook up to your computer's FireWire connector. If your computer does not have a FireWire connector, it is recommended that you buy a FireWire/USB combination card.

You can work with HDV or with a professional-level camcorder with a Serial Digital Interface (SDI) connector and a specialized video capture card.

Adobe Premiere Pro handles HDV and SDI capture with the same kind of software device controls used with a standard DV camcorder. SDI requires an extra setup procedure. Refer to Adobe Premiere Pro Help for more on that.

If you have an analog camcorder, you need a video capture card that supports S-video or composite video connectors. The only option with most analog camcorders is to manually start and stop recording. Most analog capture cards do not work with remote device control or have timecode readout, so you can't log tapes, do batch capture, or use the scene-detection feature.

Capturing an entire tape

1   Connect the camcorder to your computer.

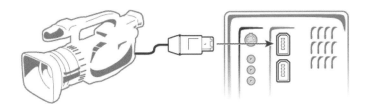

2   Turn on your camcorder and set it to the playback mode: VTR or VCR. Do not set it to the Camera mode.

💡 Use AC, not a battery

When capturing video, use your camcorder's AC adapter, not its battery. Here's why: When using a battery, camcorders can go into sleep mode, and the battery will often run out before you're done.

__Note:__ Windows might note that you've powered up your camcorder by displaying a Digital Video Device connection message. Mac OS may start a default associated application, such as iPhoto.

3   In Windows, if the Digital Video Device message did pop up, click Take No Action, select the Always Perform The Selected Action option, and click OK. (The next time you fire up your camcorder, you should not see this connection query.) In Mac OS, if iPhoto or another application starts up, see Help for that application for information about which application to open when a camera is connected.

💡 **Project settings for SDI or HDV**

This project assumes you are recording from a DV camcorder: standard 4:3 format or widescreen anamorphic 16:9 screen ratio. If you are working with SDI or HDV, you need to start Adobe Premiere Pro, click New Project, and select the preset project settings that match your camcorder.

4   Start Adobe Premiere Pro, click Open Project, navigate to the Lesson 02 folder, and double-click Lesson 2.prproj.

5   Choose File > Capture to open the Capture panel.

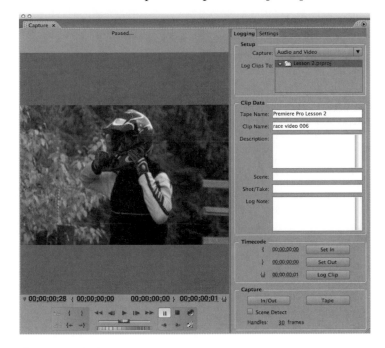

Capture panel with video capture in progress

6   Look above the Capture panel preview pane to make sure your camcorder is connected properly.

Note: If a message says No Device Control or Capture Device Offline, you'll need to do some troubleshooting. The most obvious fix is to make sure the camcorder is turned on and the cables are connected. For more troubleshooting tips, refer to Adobe Premiere Pro Help.

7   Insert a tape into your camcorder. You will be prompted to give the tape a name.

8   Type a name for your tape in the text box. Be sure not to give two tapes the same name; Adobe Premiere Pro remembers clip in/out data based on tape names.

9 Use the VCR-style device controls in the Capture panel to play, fast-forward, rewind, pause, and stop your tape. If you have never used a computer to control a camcorder, this will seem pretty cool.

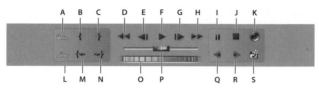

Capture panel playback controls: ***A.*** *Next Scene* ***B.*** *Set In Point* ***C.*** *Set Out Point* ***D.*** *Rewind* ***E.*** *Step Back*
F. *Play* ***G.*** *Step Forward* ***H.*** *Fast Forward* ***I.*** *Pause* ***J.*** *Stop* ***K.*** *Record* ***L.*** *Previous Scene* ***M.*** *Go To In Point*
N. *Go To Out Point* ***O.*** *Jog* ***P.*** *Shuttle* ***Q.*** *Slow Reverse* ***R.*** *Slow Play* ***S.*** *Scene Detect*

10 Try some of the other VCR-style buttons:

• Shuttle (the slider toward the bottom) enables you to move slowly or zip quickly—depending on how far you move the slider off center—forward or backward through your tape.

• Single-frame Jog control (below the Shuttle)

• Step Forward and Step Back, one frame at a time

• Slow Reverse and Slow Play

Note: *To help you identify these buttons, move the pointer over them to see tool tips.*

11 Rewind the tape to its beginning or to wherever you want to start recording.

12 In the Setup area of the Logging tab, note that Audio and Video is the default setting. If you want to capture only audio or only video, change that setting.

13 Click the Tape button in the Capture area of the Logging tab or the Record button in the Capture panel to start recording.

You'll see (and hear) the video in the Capture panel and on your camcorder.
Since there is a slight delay during capture, you'll hear what sounds like an echo. Feel free to turn down the speaker on either your camcorder or your computer.

14 Click the red Record button or the black Stop button when you want to stop recording. The Save Captured Clip dialog box appears.

15 Give your clip a name (add descriptive information if you want), and click OK.

Adobe Premiere Pro stores all clips you capture during this lesson in the Lesson 02 folder on your hard drive. You can change the default location by choosing Edit > Preferences > Scratch Disks (Windows) or Premiere Pro > Preferences > Scratch Disks (Mac OS).

Using batch capture and scene detection

When you perform a batch capture, you log the In and Out points of a number of clips and then have Adobe Premiere Pro automatically transfer them to your computer.

Use the logging process to critically view your raw footage. You want to look for "keeper" video, the best interview sound bites, and any natural sound that will enhance your production.

The purpose of using a batch capture is threefold: to better manage your media assets, to speed up the video capture process, and to save hard disk space (one hour of DV consumes 13GB).

Use a clip naming convention

Think through how you're going to name your clips. You might end up with dozens of clips, and if you don't give them descriptive names, it'll slow down editing.

You might use a naming convention for sound bites such as "Bite-1," "Bite-2," and so forth. Adding a brief descriptive comment, such as "Bite-1 Laugh," will help.

Here are the steps to follow:

1 In the Capture panel, click the Logging tab.

2 Change the Handles setting (at the bottom of the Logging tab) to 30 Frames.

This adds one second to the start and finish of each captured clip, which will give you enough head and tail frames to add transitions without covering up important elements of the clip.

💡 **Using the mouse drag method to change numeric values**

When changing the Handles value, you can click the current number and type a new figure, or simply position your pointer over the Handles number and drag left or right to lower or raise the value. This method of changing a numeric value works throughout Adobe Premiere Pro.

3 In the Clip Data area of the Logging tab, give your tape a unique name.

4 Log your tape by rewinding and then playing it.

When you see the start of a segment you want to transfer to your computer, stop the tape, rewind to that spot, and click the Set In button in the Timecode area of the Logging tab.

5 When you get to the end of that segment (you can use Fast Forward or simply Play to get there), click Set Out. The in/out times and the clip length will be displayed.

> 💡 **Three other ways to set In and Out points**
>
> *There are other means to set In points and Out points for selected clips: Click the brackets ({ or }) on the play controls, use the keyboard shortcuts—I for In and O for Out—or you can change the in/out time directly in the Timecode area by dragging left or right over the timecode.*

6 Click Log Clip to open the Log Clip dialog box.

7 Change the clip name, if needed, add appropriate notes if you want, and then click OK. That adds this clip's name with its in/out times and tape name info to the Project panel (with the word "Offline" next to it). You'll go there later to do the actual capture.

8 Log clips for the rest of your tape using the same method.

Each time you click Log Clip, Adobe Premiere Pro automatically adds a number to the end of your previous clip's name. You can accept or override this automated naming feature.

9   When you've finished logging your clips, close the Capture panel.

All your logged clips will be in the Project panel, with the Offline icon next to each.

10   Add the Media Type column by choosing Edit Columns from the Project panel menu. Select the Media Type column, and then click OK. Notice the Media Type column displays "Offline" for the logged clips. You can use this column to sort all offline clips together.

11   In the Project panel, select all the clips that you want to capture (see the following tip for three methods to do that).

Project: Lesson 2 ✕						
6 Items Selected						
Lesson 2.prproj						7 Items
Find:					In: Name	
Name ▼	Media Type	Media Start	Media End	Media Duration	Video In Point	Video Out Point
Sequence 01	Sequence				00;00;00;00	23;00;00;01
race video 001.mov	Offline	00;00;00;2	00;00;12;16	00;00;11;19	00;00;01;28	00;00;11;16
race video 002.mov	Offline	00;00;19;1	00;00;30;12	00;00;11;02	00;00;20;11	00;00;29;12
race video 003.mov	Offline	00;00;37;0	00;00;48;06	00;00;11;05	00;00;38;02	00;00;47;06
race video 004.mov	Offline	00;00;49;2	00;01;11;19	00;00;21;19	00;00;50;29	00;01;10;19
race video 005.mov	Offline	00;01;18;0	00;01;42;11	00;00;24;12	00;01;19;00	00;01;41;11
race video 006.mov	Offline	00;01;48;1	00;02;52;18	00;01;04;09	00;01;49;10	00;02;51;18

💡 **Three ways to select more than one item**

There are usually three ways to select more than one file in a window. If the filenames are contiguous, click the top one and Shift-click the last one in the group, or click off to one side and above the top clip and drag down to the last one to marquee-select a group (the marquee-select method—creating the gray rectangle—was used in the previous figure). If the filenames are scattered about, click one first, and then Ctrl-click (Windows) or Command-click (Mac OS) each additional one in turn.

12 Choose File > Batch Capture.

That opens a very simple Batch Capture dialog box that allows you to override the camcorder settings or add more handle frames.

Batch Capture

☐ Capture with handles: 0 frames
☐ Override Capture Settings

Capture Settings

Capture Format
QuickTime

OK
Cancel
Edit...

13 Leave the Batch Capture options unselected, and click OK.

The Capture panel opens, as does another little dialog box telling you to insert the proper tape (in this case, it's probably still in the camcorder).

14 Insert the tape, and click OK.

Adobe Premiere Pro now takes control of your camcorder, cues up the tape to the first clip, and transfers that clip and all other clips to your hard drive.

15 When the process is complete, take a look at your Project panel to see the results. Offline files have become movies.

Using scene detection

Instead of manually logging In and Out points, you might want to use the Scene Detect feature. Scene Detect analyzes your tape's Time/Date stamp, looking for breaks such as those caused when you press the camcorder's pause button while recording.

When Scene Detect is on and you perform a capture, Adobe Premiere Pro automatically captures a separate file at each scene break it detects. Scene Detect works whether you are capturing an entire tape or just a section between specific In and Out points.

To turn on Scene Detect, do either of the following:

- Click the Scene Detect button (below the Record button in the Capture panel).

- Select the Scene Detect option in the Capture area of the Logging tab.

Then you can either set In and Out points and click Record, or cue your tape to wherever you want to start capturing and click Record. In the latter case, click Stop when done.

Your clips will show up in the Project panel. No need to batch-capture them—Adobe Premiere Pro captures each clip on the fly. Adobe Premiere Pro will then name the first captured clip by putting a 01 after the name you put in the Clip Name box, and then increment the number in each new clip name by one.

Note: Automatic scene detection isn't available for HDV or HD assets.

Tackling manual analog movie capture

If you need to transfer analog video—consumer-level VHS, SVHS, Hi-8, or professional-grade video such as Beta-SP—you need a video capture card with analog inputs. Most analog capture cards have consumer-quality composite connectors as well as S-video and sometimes top-of-the-line component connections.

Check your card's documentation for setup and compatibility issues.

With analog video, you have only one capture option—to do it manually:

1   Open the Capture panel (File > Capture).

2   Use the controls on the camcorder to move the videotape to a point several seconds before the frame you want to begin capturing.

3   Press the Play button on the camcorder, and then click the red Record button in the Capture panel.

4   When your clip has been captured, click the Stop button in the Capture panel and on the camcorder. Your clip will show up in the Project panel.

Review

▶ **Review questions**

1   Why is getting the closing shot so important?

2   If you're shooting a formal sit-down interview and the camera is positioned over the left shoulder of the interviewer, where should you place the camera for reverse cutaways?

3   What does Scene Detect do when selected?

4   When you open the Capture panel, you don't see an image in the video monitor and you can't control your DV camcorder. What could be going on?

5   During the capture process, how do you add extra frames to ensure you have enough footage for transitions?

6   Is the actual media captured to your hard disk during a batch capture?

▶ **Review answers**

1   Your closing shot is what viewers take away from your video. You want to do what you can to make it memorable.

2   Place the camera behind the interview subject and shoot over his right shoulder.

3   Enabling Scene Detect causes clips to be automatically logged at each point where the camcorder was stopped or paused.

4   This could be one of several things: Your camcorder is not turned on (or if you're using a battery, it might be in sleep mode); you have it in Camera mode instead of VCR/VTR; or you haven't inserted your tape.

5   You would put a number of frames in the Handles option in the Capture area of the Logging tab.

6   No. Only information about the clip is captured, such as tape name and In and Out points. The clip will be displayed as "Offline" in the Project panel.

analyze

monitor

direct to disk

If you are shooting studio work, or have a notebook computer that you can locate with your camera, then you have a perfect environment for Adobe OnLocation. Adobe OnLocation allows you to bypass the time-consuming step of capturing video and also provides tools for ensuring your camera and lighting are set up perfectly, before ever recording a frame of video.

3 Adobe OnLocation

Topics covered in this lesson:

- Setting up Adobe OnLocation

- Calibrating your camera with SureShot

- Recording live video

- Analyzing video with Adobe OnLocation

- Analyzing audio with Adobe OnLocation scopes

Getting started

Adobe OnLocation enables you to record video from your camcorder direct to disk, bypassing the slow process of recording to tape and then capturing. Because editors are often up against tight deadlines, this capability can be a huge boost in productivity. Adobe OnLocation can save time and improve the quality of your shots by providing professional monitoring tools and scopes while you shoot.

Setting up Adobe OnLocation

Adobe OnLocation communicates with camcorders and other OHCI-compliant devices using the IEEE 1394 standard. Connect your camera to your desktop or notebook computer, as described in Lesson 2, via FireWire cable. However, instead of capturing video to Adobe Premiere Pro, you will be recording live video direct to your computer. This requires your computer to be "on location" with your camcorder.

1   Connect the camcorder to your computer.

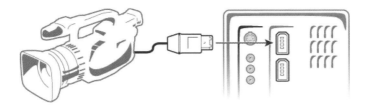

2   Turn on your camcorder and set it to the camera mode.

3   If the Digital Video Device dialog box appears, click Take No Action, select the Always Perform The Selected Action option, and click OK.

4   Start Adobe OnLocation. The first time Adobe OnLocation opens, you will see a long scrolling window with many components. These software components behave like the hardware components they resemble. We will declutter the Adobe OnLocation desktop so we can focus on a few core components for recording video direct to disk.

Note: Adobe OnLocation is optimized for higher-resolution screens. If you run in 1024x768 resolution, it maximizes screen real estate by doing away with the standard bars at the top and bottom of the screen. All the menu choices are in a context menu; you can right-click (Windows) or Control-click (Mac OS) to select a different device or to quit the application.

5   Close all the individual components on the Adobe OnLocation desktop (click the power button in each component). Notice that each component is designed to resemble its hardware counterpart, so the power button will look different in each component. There are three examples in the illustration below. Powering the component off will remove it from the desktop.

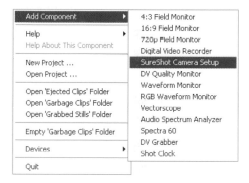

6   Add the SureShot camera setup component to the desktop by choosing Component > SureShot Camera Setup.

7   Add the 4:3 field monitor component to the desktop by choosing Component > 4:3 Field Monitor.

8   If you have more than one 1394 device, or audio devices, you may need to tell Adobe OnLocation which device you want it to use. Choose the correct 1394 device from the Devices menu.

Calibrating your camera with SureShot

You can dramatically improve your videos by fine-tuning your camera setup before recording a single frame of video. The SureShot component in Adobe OnLocation is an excellent tool to help you calibrate you camera's focus, exposure, and white balance. For this fine-tuning of your camera setup, it will be helpful to set your camcorder to manual focus, manual exposure, and manual white balance so you have complete control over these attributes.

Frame

1   Point your camera at your subject and place the focus chart (which is included in the box with Adobe OnLocation) next to the subject.

2   Zoom in with your camera lens so the focus chart takes up most of the frame.

3   Use the slider in the SureShot component to crop the frame to include just the focus chart. Notice the cropped portion of the frame is yellow.

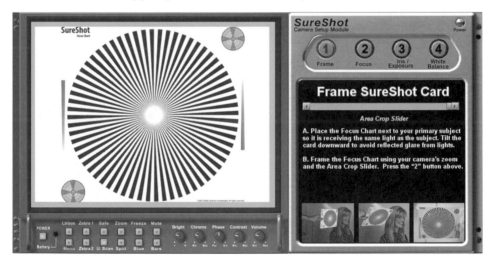

Focus

1   Click the Focus button in the SureShot component.

2   Adjust the focus on your camcorder until the Focus indicator in the SureShot component grows as large as possible. You will also notice the focus fine-tuning in the monitor window.

Iris/Exposure

1   Click the Iris/Exposure button in the SureShot component.

2   Flip the focus chart over so the exposure side of the card is visible. Keep the card in the same position as in the focus step.

3   Adjust the exposure on your camera so that the light meter in the SureShot component has the green box illuminated, and the white line as far to the right as possible without illuminating the red box. Achieving this exposure gives you the maximum range of darks to whites without overexposing the video.

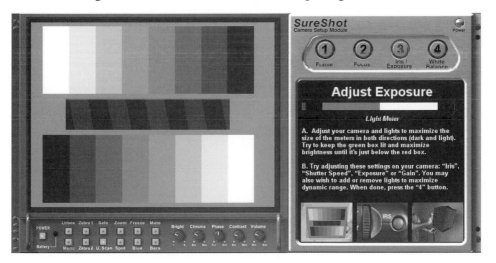

💡 **About Exposure**

Exposure is determined by multiple things:

Lighting: The ambient or created lighting of your shot. You may need to adjust the physical lighting of your scene to achieve the best exposure.

Iris or aperture: Adjust the aperture of your camera to let more or less light into the camera. The wider your iris, the shallower your depth of field.

Shutter speed: Adjust the shutter speed to allow light into the camera for shorter or longer periods of time. Shutter speeds of 1/60 second are typical for shoots not involving very fast action.

Gain: The amount your camera electronically enhances the amount of light.

White Balance

White-balancing your shot is important to help ensure that the camera records the correct colors. When properly white-balanced, the recorded images will accurately reflect the real colors in the scene.

1 Place the included white-balance card in the same position as the exposure card.

2 Click the White Balance button in the SureShot component.

3 Adjust the white balance on your camera until the white-balance meter in the SureShot component is maximized to the right. When properly set, the white card in the field monitor component will appear white rather than gray or a different hue.

ᗪ **White-balance controls on camcorders**

Manual: Some camcorders allow you to manually dial any color temperature. This is the most flexible method.

Presets: Some camcorders have white-balance presets such as Indoors, Outdoors, and so on. Scroll through them to see which one best matches your scene.

Custom presets: Some camcorders can "learn" custom white-balance settings by pointing the camera at a white card and pressing a button on the camcorder to "learn" the color temperature.

Review the documentation for your camcorder to learn how to set the white balance properly on your camera.

That's it. By following these steps your camera will record an optimally exposed and focused video. Close the Sure Shot component when you are finished.

Recording live video

Recording live video from your camera to your computer can save you hours of time in capturing and logging tapes. Recording direct to your computer's hard drive happens in real time, and the clips recorded are available immediately for editing, simply by importing them into Adobe Premiere Pro. Now that your camera is set up and calibrated, you'll record some video direct to your hard drive.

1   Start a new Adobe OnLocation project by choosing File > New Project. Choose a folder on your hard drive where you want to store your project, and give the project a name. Note that your recorded video clips will be stored in this location as well.

2   Close (power off) all components on the Adobe OnLocation desktop. You will add only the components helpful for recording video.

3   Add the Digital Video Recorder (Component > Digital Video Recorder).

4   Add the Field Monitor by choosing Component > 4:3 Field Monitor.

5   If your camera is on and is the selected device in the Devices menu, you should see the live video displayed in the field monitor.

💡 **Aspect Ratio**

This project assumes you're using an SD camera at 4:3 aspect ratio. If you're shooting in 16:9 aspect ratio or shooting HDV, choose the appropriate field monitor for that format.

You can change the aspect ratio in the field monitor by using the following keyboard shortcuts:

F8 = 4:3

Control F8 = 16:9

6   Click the red Record button at the top of the Digital Video Recorder component. Notice that a clip appears in the Recording window to indicate the recording activity. Press Stop when you are finished recording.

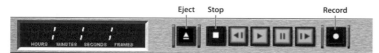

7   To immediately use the clip in Adobe Premiere Pro, click the Eject button at the top of the Digital Video Recorder. If you don't eject the clip, the program may have problems importing it. In Adobe Premiere Pro, choose File > Import, and navigate to the location where you created your Adobe OnLocation project. Available clips are in a folder called Ejected Clips. Select the file or files you want, and click Open. Your video is immediately available to edit, with no capture time or clip logging.

⚲ OnLocation Recording features

The digital recorder will actually start recording video five seconds before you click the Record button. This helps ensure you never miss a good scene. The amount of time this "pre video" is buffered can be adjusted in the menu options available through the field recorder.

If you want to break up a scene into multiple clips, clicking the Record button while already recording will start a new clip.

You can record direct to your hard drive and to tape with Adobe OnLocation. Simply follow the instructions to record direct to disk and also put a tape in your camcorder. The tape can become a backup or archive as needed.

Analyzing video with Adobe OnLocation scopes

Earlier in this lesson, you calibrated your camera so that focus, exposure, and white balance are correct. This is an important step, and the SureShot component is a very helpful tool in accomplishing that. But it's possible that changing conditions in the scene can alter color or exposure, so it's important to monitor your shoot continuously. Adobe OnLocation provides a powerful and useful set of components to help monitor video.

1   Close (power off) all components on the Adobe OnLocation desktop so you can add just the components helpful for monitoring the video signal.

2   Add the Field Monitor by choosing Component > 4:3 Field Monitor.

3   Add the Waveform Monitor by choosing Component > Waveform Monitor.

4   Add the Vectorscope by choosing Component > Vector Scope.

There are other components available for monitoring video, but the Waveform Monitor and Vectorscope are key tools for verifying a good video signal. Feel free to explore details of the other components in the Adobe OnLocation user guide.

5   Add the Digital Video Recorder by choosing Component > Digital Video Recorder.

Waveform Monitor

The Waveform Monitor represents luminance (or brightness) in a graphical form in real time as the video plays. The brightness value of each pixel in the video frame is represented by the waveform graph. The higher the graph, the brighter the pixel. A well-exposed scene has brightness values across the scale. It is easy to see that pixels that are all dark would make a dark video, or that pixels that are all bright would make a bright video. But it is also important to understand that having brightness values across the scale gives a feeling of depth to the image. Having good brightness values across the scale is called *range*. Let's take a look at some examples of good range and bad range using the waveform monitor as a tool.

1 Open the Lesson 3 Adobe OnLocation project by choosing File > Open Project, and then navigate to where you stored the lesson files. Open the Lesson 3.dvr file; you will notice three clips in the Digital Video Recorder recorded by Adobe OnLocation. They are similar clips, each recorded with different exposure settings.

2 Select the clip named normal.avi. As you play it, observe the Waveform Monitor. The luminance or brightness values have a nice range, from 7.5 (the normal low range for black) to 100 (the normal high range for white). This clip is an example of a scene that is properly exposed.

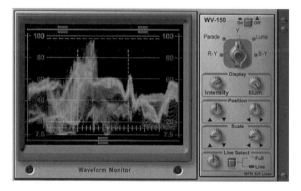

3 Select the clip named dark_loud.avi. When you play this clip, notice that the waveform does not extend to 100—all the brightness values are clumped at the bottom. While the image is not overly dark, it is uninteresting because of the limited range of luminance values. When you see a waveform like this, you should consider adjusting the exposure on the camera or changing the lighting to provide more range of luminance.

Observing the waveform monitor while you make lighting changes is a good way to know when you have it right.

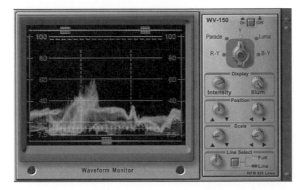

4   Select the clip named light_thin.avi. When you play this clip, notice that the waveform is pushed to the top with very few dark values. Again, the limited range of luminance makes this image uninteresting. This is another case where adjusting the lighting or camera exposure would make a much nicer image.

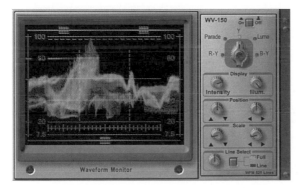

Vectorscope

While the waveform monitor is helpful for analyzing brightness, the Vectorscope is useful for analyzing color. The Vectorscope is a round graph with "no color" represented in the center and a high value of color represented on the outer edge. The color wheel is represented in quadrants around the circle of the Vectorscope. Starting at 11 o'clock and going clockwise are Red, Magenta, Blue, Cyan, Green, and Yellow. The further the graph extends to the edge, the higher the saturation of that color.

The Vectorscope can be very helpful in white-balancing, since a shift in color is very easy to see.

Play the sample clips that are included in the Lesson 3 Adobe OnLocation project. Notice that the Vectorscope shows a graph pointing towards red. This is the predominant color in this scene.

Showing the right colors onscreen

There are many dials on the scopes and field monitor for adjusting color and brightness values. These are for calibrating your computer monitor to match the scene. They do not modify the video in any way. They are only for adjusting the components to match difference in computer displays. Double-clicking these dials will reset them to default values. Typically, the default values are correct.

If you change resolutions on your computer monitor, it is possible to "lose" a component offscreen. If this happens, you can restart Adobe OnLocation while holding down the Ctrl and Shift keys to reset the default desktop.

Analyzing audio with Adobe OnLocation scopes

So far we have been focusing on video (no pun intended). But audio is half of any good production, so let's take a look at one of the audio components included with Adobe OnLocation: the Audio Spectrum Analyzer. It not only shows you the amplitude (loudness) of your audio, but also the amplitude across frequencies. This is very useful for isolating potential microphone problems.

1   Add the Audio Spectrum Analyzer to the desktop by choosing Component > Audio Spectrum Analyzer.

2   Play the clip named normal.avi, and observe the levels represented in the right half of the Audio Spectrum Analyzer. Since this is a stereo clip, you can see the left and right channels represented as it plays. Notice that there are good levels across most of the frequency range. This is an example of a good audio file. If you position the pointer over a line in the graph, the frequency of that line will be displayed. Also note that the two Master meters did not peak (turn red) as you played this file. The overall volume is good—but it's not too loud.

Master meter

3   Play the clip named dark_loud.avi. Notice this clip peaks or "clips" on the Master meter, as shown by the illuminated top red bar. This audio is too loud at some points, which causes clipping, making the loud sections sound very flat. In this case, you should turn down the audio to the camera, or reposition the microphone.

4   Play the clip named light_thin.avi. Notice the overall level or volume is OK, but it sounds very thin, like the actor is talking through a bad phone. This is represented visually by the frequencies being cut off, or very low. This could be caused by a high-pass filter being used incorrectly in the recording session. This would be very difficult to correct in post-production. It is much easier to fix at the scene when detected with these monitoring tools.

Using these video and audio monitoring tools can save you hours in post-production trying to correct problems. Adobe OnLocation can be a real time-saver in preventing problems and helping you produce high-quality video and audio.

Review

▶ Review questions

1   Why should you take time to white-balance your camera?

2   What is the value of recording direct to disk?

3   Which does the waveform monitor indicate: color or brightness?

4   How could you use the Vectorscope to check white balance?

5   What does it mean when the Master audio meters peak at red?

▶ Review answers

1   You white-balance your camera to make sure the color hue you are recording is accurate. It takes much longer to fix in post-production.

2   Recording direct to disk saves a lot of time because you don't have to capture clips, which is a serial process.

3   The waveform monitor indicates luminance (or brightness).

4   The Vectorscope indicates color. So, the absence of color would be represented as a dot in the center of the scope. If you point the camera at a white card and see the Vectorscope indicate a shift to one color, that's an indication that your white balance is off.

5   When the Master meters illuminate red at the high end of the scale, it's an indication that the volume of the audio is too loud. Red on the master meters causes clipping in those sections of the audio.

preferences

assets

Bridge

settings

Adobe Premiere Pro CS3 is eminently customizable and adaptable. It accepts just about any moving or still image you throw at it. All you need to do is adjust the project settings and preferences. Managing media is more efficient in Adobe Premiere Pro CS3, thanks to new flexible bins and the improved Adobe Bridge.

4 Selecting Settings, Adjusting Preferences, and Managing Assets

Topics covered in this lesson:

- Selecting project settings
- Adjusting user preferences
- Importing assets
- Taking a closer look at still images
- The basics of the Project panel
- New Bin features
- Working with assets in Adobe Bridge

Getting started

Typically, you won't have to give more than a passing glance to project settings and preferences. Nevertheless, it's good to know the options available to you. You'll learn how to manage your assets from within the Project panel and delve into Adobe Bridge—a full-scale asset browser that works with all products and file types in Adobe Creative Suite 3 Production Premium.

Selecting project settings

The basic rule of thumb when selecting project settings is to match the settings to your source material and not to the final output. Maintaining the original quality of source material means you'll have more options later. Even if your goal is to create a low-resolution video to play on the Internet, wait until you *finish* editing, and then reduce the *output* quality settings.

It's possible you might have a mix of source media—widescreen and standard, for example. The best approach here is to set up your project to match the majority of footage it will contain or to match the look you want to achieve. For example, choose a widescreen setting for a project that contains mostly widescreen videos but also some standard-definition video that you'll place in a "pillar box"—a black frame within the 16:9 aspect ratio widescreen.

Two types of settings

Adobe Premiere Pro has two settings: project settings and preferences. Their similarities can lead to some confusion. For example, both contain General and Capture categories. The Project Settings menu is also called the Custom Settings tab in the New Project dialog box.

Project settings apply to your current project. Your first step before creating a new project is to select that project's settings. Once you start a project, you can't change many of the project settings.

Preferences, on the other hand, generally apply to all projects, and you can change them at any time.

We'll start with a brief look at project settings, simply to check out the various options for project settings and consider under what circumstances you'd use them.

1 Start Adobe Premiere Pro CS3.

The startup screen appears. The Recent Projects list should be populated with the projects you worked on in the previous three lessons. In this case, you will be starting out fresh.

2 Click New Project to open the New Project dialog box.

This dialog box offers five folders with preset project settings that match virtually all the types of source media you'll work with.

3 Click the Custom Settings tab highlighted in the next figure.

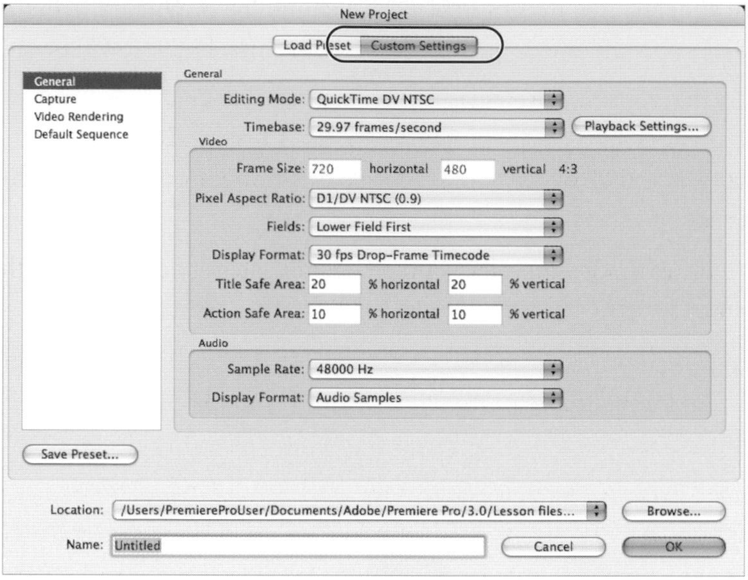

Custom settings—project settings—overview

When you start a new project, you can review and change project settings on this Custom Settings tab. You should do so only if none of the available presets match the specifications of your source media.

Later, you can open Project Settings from within the Adobe Premiere Pro workspace. The interface is virtually identical to the Custom Settings tab. The only difference is that the Project Settings menu does not have the file location and name section at the bottom.

Since some settings can't be changed after a project is created, confirm all project settings on the Custom Settings tab before starting a project.

Project settings are organized into four categories, listed on the left side of the tab: General, Capture, Video Rendering, and Default Sequence. Click each in turn. Here are some brief explanations (refer to Adobe Premiere Pro Help for further details):

• **General**—Adjust these settings to match the specifications of the most significant source media in your project. Usually, the editing mode you select from the top menu determines most of the settings in this window. Several editing modes are described as presets in the next section.

• **Capture**— The editing mode you select in the General category auto-selects the correct capture format, so this is essentially a redundant category.

• **Video Rendering**—If you select DV or HDV in the General category, there are no preview options. Preview options appear only if you choose desktop editing mode or use a third-party editing mode.

• **Default Sequence**—Each time you add a sequence to a project, Adobe Premiere Pro displays a menu that lets you select the number of video tracks and the number and type of audio tracks. When it appears, you will generally accept the default values. This category lets you set those defaults.

♡ Custom preset for new projects

You can create a customized new project preset: Simply make your choices in the four categories, and then click the Save Preset button. Give your customized project settings preset a name, and click OK. It appears in the New Project > Load Preset menu.

If you are editing standard DV or Native HDV, it is not necessary to use a custom preset. In this case, choose one of the standard presets on the Load Preset tab.

Checking out the new project presets

4   Click the Load Preset tab.

5   Open each of the available presets, and click through them. Note the explanation of each preset in the New Project Description area:

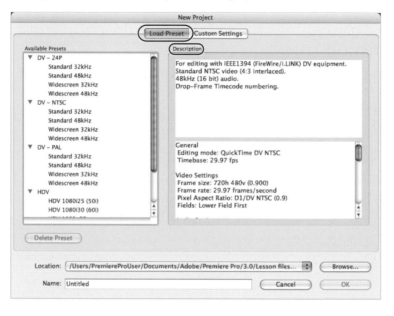

- **DV-24p**—This preset was created for use with 24p DV cameras like the Panasonic AG-DVX100 and Canon XL224p. It's sometimes used for film that has been shot at the film-standard 24 frames per second and transferred to DV.

- **DV-NTSC**—What most Adobe Premiere Pro users work with. NTSC is the TV display standard for North and South America and Japan.

- **DV-PAL**—The TV display standard for most of Western Europe and Australia.

- **HDV**—A compressed HD-style format that records to standard DV cassettes.

- **Mobile & Devices**—For editing video from mobile devices and other low-bandwidth video.

Adjusting user preferences

Preferences are different from project settings in that you typically set preferences once and have them apply to all your projects. You can change preferences and have them take immediate effect at any time.

Preferences include such things as default transition times, timing and number of auto saves, Project panel clip label colors, file folder location for captured video, and the user interface brightness (you adjusted this in Lesson 1).

You should be in the New Project dialog box, with the Load Preset tab selected.

If you continued past this point and are already in the Adobe Premiere Pro workspace, and you selected a DV preset that matches your source material, fine. Otherwise, return to the New Project dialog box by selecting File > New > Project.

1   Select a DV preset that matches your source material (probably DV-NTSC—Standard or Widescreen—48kHz).

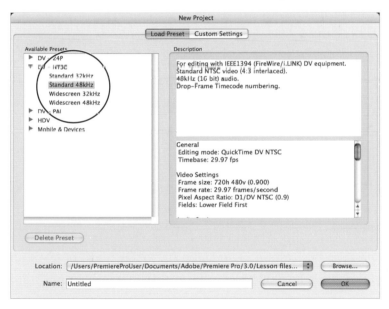

2   Click Browse, and navigate to the Lesson 04 folder.

3   Give your project a name—such as *Lesson 4 [your name]*—and click OK.

That takes you to the Adobe Premiere Pro CS3 user interface.

4   Choose Edit > Preferences > General in Windows or Premiere Pro > Preferences > General in Mac OS.

Note: You can select any of the Preferences submenus. All choices take you to the Preferences dialog box, with the appropriate category selected. You can easily move from one category to another by clicking a category submenu name in the list on the left.

5   Click each Preferences category name in turn to check out the options. You will encounter some fairly obscure possibilities here.

Preferences categories

These rarely come into play until you have used Adobe Premiere Pro for a while, and most are self-explanatory. You can look up specifics in Adobe Premiere Pro Help, but here's a brief run-through:

• **General**—Primarily sets default times for audio and video transitions, still-image duration, and preroll/postroll for camcorders during capture.

• **Audio**—Automation Keyframe Optimization is relevant when you use the Audio Mixer to change volume or panning. Selecting Thinning and a Minimum Time Interval of greater than 30 msec makes it easier to edit the changes later.

- **Audio Hardware**—Sets the default audio hardware device.

- **Audio Output Mapping**—Specifies how each audio hardware device channel corresponds to an Adobe Premiere Pro audio output channel. Generally the default settings will work fine.

- **Auto Save**—Sets the frequency and number of Auto Saves. To open an auto-saved project, choose File > Open Project, navigate to the Premiere Pro Auto Save folder, and double-click a project.

- **Capture**—Sets four basic capture parameters.

- **Device Control**—Preroll (which you can set in General Preferences) and Timecode Offset (usually used only during analog video capture).

- **Label Colors**—Lets you change the default Project panel media link label colors.

- **Label Defaults**—Assigns specific label colors to different media types.

- **Media**—Use this to empty the cache folders.

- **Scratch Disks**—Set file-folder locations for seven items, including captured video and preview files. The default location for all such files is your current project file folder.

- **Titler**—Specifies the characters to be used for font and style samples in the Adobe Titler frame.

- **Trim**—Adjusts how many frames and audio units are trimmed if you select the Large Trim Offset (a quick way to chop off chunks of video) in the Trim frame.

- **User Interface**— Sets the interface brightness. You saw this in Lesson 1.

Any changes you make in the preferences take effect immediately and remain in effect the next time you start Adobe Premiere Pro. You can change them again at any time.

Note: *When you finish reviewing the various options, click Cancel, or click OK if you made any changes that you want to keep.*

Importing assets

In Lesson 1, your project started with links to assets that had already been placed in the Project panel. Adding those links to the Project panel—importing assets, in Adobe Premiere Pro parlance—is easy. But there are a few issues to keep in mind. This lesson will cover the how-tos of importing, and the issues you're most likely to encounter.

In this mini-lesson you will import all four standard media types: video, audio, graphics, and still images. You will see two importing methods, and take a look at the properties of audio and graphic files.

You can continue where you left off, or open Lesson 4-1.prproj from the Lesson 04 folder.

You should see the standard Adobe Premiere Pro opening workspace. All the frames should be empty except for the Sequence 01 item in the Project panel and in the Timeline.

1   Choose File > Import.

2   Navigate to the Lesson 04 folder, select the audio clip, the graphic file, the two stills, and the video, as shown in the following figure, and then click Open (Windows) or Import (Mac OS).

3   Double-click inside the Project panel, in the empty space below the newly added clips.

Note: This is a different and faster way to open the Import dialog box (Windows) or the Choose Object dialog box (Mac OS). You could also use the keyboard shortcut Ctrl+I (Windows) or Command+I (Mac OS).

You will import files from a different file folder, demonstrating that you don't have to keep all your assets in the same place. The Project panel simply lists links to your assets, wherever they may be.

4   Navigate to the Lesson 04/Photoshop Images folder, select PS layered image.psd, and then click Open (Windows) or Import (Mac OS).

For the Photoshop CS3 file, an Import Layered File dialog box appears.

5   Choose Sequence from the Import As menu, and click OK.

You could have selected Footage and then had the option of merging all the layers into a single graphic or selecting a specific layer. Choosing Sequence does two things:

•   Adds a file folder to your Project panel with all the Photoshop CS3 layers listed as separate clips

•   Creates a new sequence with all the layers on separate video tracks

6   Right-click (Windows) or Control-click (Mac OS) 32khz audio file.wav in the Project panel, and choose Properties from the context menu.

Note: The Source Audio Format is 32000 Hz – 16 bit – Stereo and the Project Audio Format is 48000 Hz – 32 bit floating point – Stereo. Adobe Premiere Pro up-converts all audio to the project setting, thereby ensuring no quality is lost during editing. Floating point data allows for even more precise and smoother edits.

7   Close the Properties window.

Image and graphics issues

Adobe Premiere Pro can import just about any image and graphic file type. You've already seen how it handles Photoshop CS3 layered files—giving you the option to import the layers as separate graphics within a sequence, as single layers, or by merging the entire file into one graphic clip.

What's left to cover is how Adobe Premiere Pro handles Adobe Illustrator® CS3 files and image files. You'll start this lesson where you left off. If you need to start fresh, just open Lesson 4-2.prproj from the Lesson 04 folder.

Note: You may be prompted with a dialog box asking where a particular file is. This will happen when the original files were saved on a hard drive other than the one you're using. You'll need to tell Adobe Premiere Pro where the file is: In this case, navigate to the Lesson 4 folder and select the file that the dialog box is prompting you for.

1　Right-click (Windows) or Control-click (Mac OS) illustrator file.ai in the Project panel, and choose Properties from the context menu.

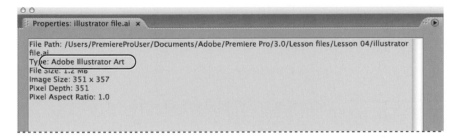

This file type is Adobe Illustrator Art. Here's how Adobe Premiere Pro deals with Illustrator CS3 files:

• Like the Photoshop CS3 file you imported in step 4, this is a layered graphic file. However, Adobe Premiere Pro doesn't give you the option to import Illustrator CS3 files in separate layers. It merges them.

• It also uses a process called *rasterization* to convert the vector (path-based) Illustrator art into the pixel-based image format used by Adobe Premiere Pro.

• Adobe Premiere Pro automatically *anti-aliases*, or smooths edges of the Illustrator art.

• Adobe Premiere Pro converts all empty areas into a transparent alpha channel, so that clips below those areas on the Timeline can show through if you choose.

2　Close the Properties window.

Edit Illustrator files in Illustrator

If you right-click (Windows) or Control-click (Mac OS) illustrator file.ai again, you'll note that one option is Edit Original. If you have Illustrator installed on your computer, selecting Edit Original will open this graphic in Illustrator, ready to edit. So, even though the layers are merged in Adobe Premiere Pro, you can go back to Illustrator, edit the original layered file, save it, and the changes will immediately show up in Adobe Premiere Pro.

3   Convert the Project panel into a floating window by holding down Ctrl (Windows) or Command (Mac OS) and dragging the panel by its drag handle.

4   Expand the Project panel's floating window as wide as you can, and click the PS layered image folder triangle to display all the Photoshop CS3 graphic layers.

5   Drag the scroll bar along the bottom of the Project panel, noting all the various descriptive columns and types of media they apply to.

In particular, note the *Video Info* for the two JPEG images. These are image resolutions, and are much larger than standard DV: 720x480. You'll see how Adobe Premiere Pro deals with that in the next steps.

6   Drag the Project panel back to its original frame next to the Effects tab.

Note: If you have trouble re-docking that floating window back in its frame, choose Window > Workspace > Reset Current Workspace to get it into place.

7   Drag the two still images—crew.jpg and closeup.jpg—to the Video 1 track in the Timeline.

8 Press the backslash (\) key. That is the keyboard shortcut to expand the Timeline view to match the length of the clips in it. Your Timeline should look like the next figure.

9 Drag the current-time indicator (CTI) within the two clips.

Note: As you drag the CTI, look in the Program Monitor. You will see only a portion of each image because it is larger than the project preset dimensions. Both clips have resolutions that are much larger than the standard DV screen size. By default, Adobe Premiere Pro centers them in the screen and displays them in their original resolution. The next step explains how to view them in their entirety, without changing the aspect ratio of the images.

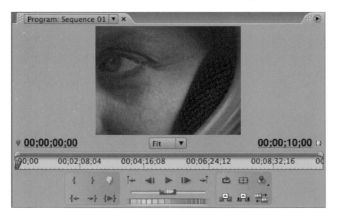

10 Right-click (Windows) or Control-click (Mac OS) the first clip—crew.jpg—in the Timeline, and choose Scale To Frame Size to turn on that feature.

Now, you see the entire image.

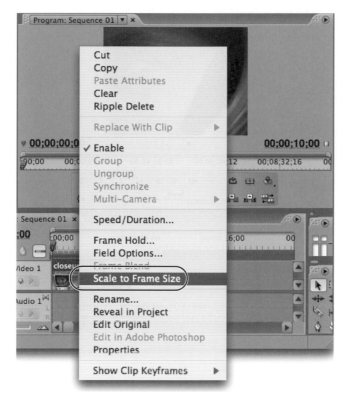

Note: If you want all your images to be automatically scaled to the project frame size, you can set that as a preference in the General preferences category. The option must be set before you import the images for it to take effect.

11 You can also manually scale the image from its full resolution using the Motion tool in the Effect Controls panel. The benefit of this method is that it allows you to pan or zoom up to the full image resolution. Select the closeup.jpg image on the timeline.

12 Expand the Motion effect in the Effect Controls panel.

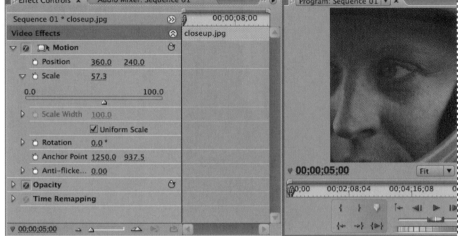

13 Expand the Scale parameter and adjust it larger or smaller. Watch the effect it has on the image. You can manually scale the image to any size you like. In a later lesson, we will look at keyframing this parameter to create animation.

Image tips

Here are a few tips for importing images:

- You can import images up to 4,096x4,096 pixels.

- If you don't plan to zoom or pan, try to create files with a frame size at least as large as the frame size of the project—720x534 for NTSC DV (see the Square Versus Rectangular Pixels tip). Otherwise, you have to scale up the image and it will lose some of its sharpness.

- If you plan to zoom or pan, try to create images such that the zoomed or panned area has a frame size at least as large as the frame size of the project.

💡 **Square versus rectangular pixels**

TV sets display rectangular pixels—slightly vertical rectangles (.9 aspect ratio) for NTSC and slightly horizontal for PAL. PC monitors use square pixels. Images created in graphics software typically are square. Adobe Premiere Pro adjusts them to display properly by squashing and interpolating the square pixels to keep the images' original aspect ratios and to display them properly on TV sets. So when you create graphics or images with square pixels, create them with your TV standard in mind: 720x534 for NTSC (that resolution will become 720x480 after Premiere Pro squashes the square pixels into rectangles) and 768x576 for PAL (for other standards, including high definition, see "About square-pixel footage" in Adobe Premiere Pro Help).

Managing media in the new bins

The Project panel is a means to access and organize your assets—video clips, audio files, still images, graphics, and sequences. Each listed media asset is a link. The files themselves remain in their file folders, while the assets are stored in *bins*. Bins behave like folders as a way to organize and categorize your assets visually within Adobe Premiere Pro.

Importing and logically arranging your assets in the Project panel is simple. You can create new bins and bins inside of bins. Adobe Premiere Pro CS3 has introduced new bin features to make organizing even easier.

In this lesson you will check out some of the Project panel options, and then rearrange the clips you have been working with. If you need to start fresh, open Project 4-2.

1   Click the Icon View button in the lower left corner of the Project panel (highlighted in the next figure).

That changes the Project panel display from a list to thumbnails and icons.

2   Expand the Project panel by dragging its right edge to the right so you can see all seven items.

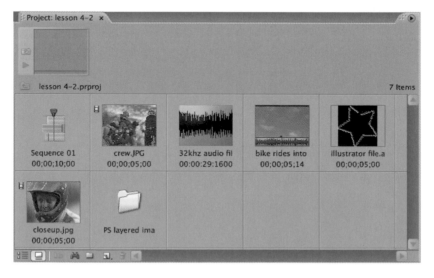

3   Click 32khz audio file.wav to select it, and then click the Play button on the thumbnail viewer (highlighted in the next figure).

You can click any other asset and play it. The Play button will be unavailable (dimmed) for still images and graphics.

4   Click bike rides into frame.mov, and drag the slider under the thumbnail viewer a few seconds into the clip.

5   Click the Poster Frame button next to the Preview screen to create a new thumbnail image for that clip.

Note: *The new thumbnail appears immediately in the Project panel. The thumbnail image has an audio display in it, indicating this is a video clip with audio.*

6 Click the New Bin button to create a new file folder.

The new bin appears in the Project panel with its default name—*Bin 01*.

7 Change its name from Bin 01 to *Audio,* and press Enter or Return.

8 Create another bin, and name it *Stills.*

9 Drag the audio clip onto the Audio bin thumbnail.

10 Drag the two JPEG stills and the Illustrator file into the new Stills bin.

11 Return to the list view (click the List View button to the left of the Icon View button).

12 Click somewhere in the Project panel to deselect any bin that might be selected.

Note: You need to deselect at this point so that the bin you're about to add won't be a subfolder inside another folder. There are instances when you might want to use subfolders to help organize the Project panel.

13 Click the New Bin button to create a new bin. Name it *Sequences.*

14 Open the PS Layered image bin, and drag the PS layered image Sequence into the Sequences bin.

15 Create one more bin named *Movies,* and drag the movie file into that bin.

16 Click somewhere in the Project panel to deselect any bin that might be selected.

17 Drag Sequence 01 into the Movies bin as well. It is useful to organize your project assets in this type of bin structure. You may come up with your own way of organizing, but organizing by asset type, as demonstrated here, is a good way to start.

18 Click twice on Name at the top of the file link list in the Project panel to put all the asset links and bins in alphabetical order. Your Project panel should look like the following figure.

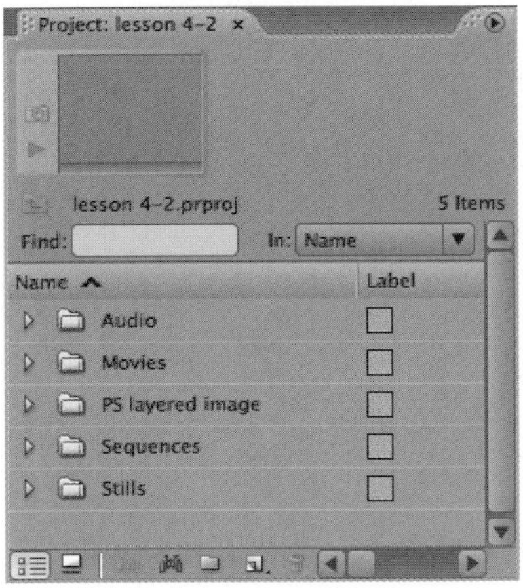

New bin features

Adobe Premiere Pro CS3 has introduced some new bin features that are helpful when you have a lot of assets. It is possible to have thousands of assets (movie clips, image clips, audio clips and so on) in your bins. The new features are very helpful in finding, moving, and organizing assets.

Multiple bins open at once

In Adobe Premiere Pro CS3, you can open multiple bins at the same time in their own window or docked to a panel. This makes it very easy to drag clips between two bins.

1 Double-click the Stills bin you just created. Notice it opens in its own window.

2 Practice dragging clips from this new window to other bins and back.

3   Dock the new Stills bin with another panel, to try a different method of organizing your bins.

4   Close the Stills bin by clicking the "x" on its tab. Notice the Stills bin still exists in the main Project panel.

Find

Adobe Premiere Pro CS3 has significantly improved the searching capability within the Project panel. The Find tool is located near the top of the Project panel.

1   If your workspace has gotten messy, open the Lesson 4-3.prproj project.

2   Type the word *bike* in the Find box. Notice that the Movies bin automatically expands to reveal the movie clip with the word *bike* in it.

3   Type the letters *ps* in the Find box. Notice that any bin containing a file with *ps* in its name is expanded.

This new feature is very simple, yet amazingly powerful in finding just the right clip quickly and easily.

4   When you're finished, clear all text in the Find box so all the files are visible.

Working with assets in Adobe Bridge

Adobe Bridge CS3 simplifies the everyday tasks of asset management by giving you a powerful way to browse and search your digital assets; view and edit metadata (file information such as contents, copyright status, origin, and history of documents); and add, rename, move, and delete files and folders.

Right-click (Windows) or Control-click (Mac OS) an asset in the Project panel, and choose Reveal in Bridge. Bridge starts, and displays the contents of the Lesson 04 folder.

Note: You can also start Bridge by choosing File > Browse. In that case, it will display the contents of the program's main file folder: Premiere Pro/3.0.

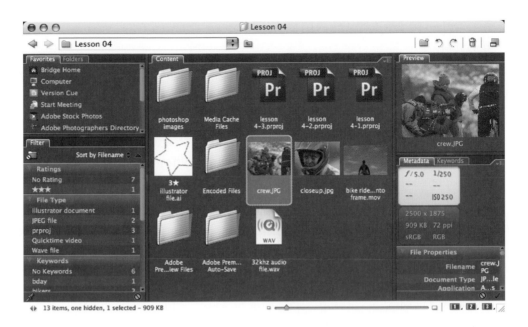

The Adobe Bridge window is made up of several parts:

• **Favorites panel**—Lists the folders you want quick access to. It's located on the left side of the Bridge window.

• **Folders panel**—Lists the folder hierarchy to help you navigate to the correct folder. It's located on the left side of the Bridge window, along with the Favorites panel.

• **Preview panel**—Displays a thumbnail of the selected file. The panel is located on the right side of the Bridge window.

• **Metadata panel**—Contains metadata—text embedded in the file—for the selected file. Access its tab in the lower right corner of the Bridge window.

• **Keywords panel**—Helps you organize your images by attaching keywords to them.

• **Content panel**—Displays thumbnail previews of the items in the current folder, along with information about those items.

The bottom of the Bridge window displays status information and contains a button for toggling the display of all but the Content panel, a slider for setting the size of thumbnails, and buttons for specifying the type of display in the Content panel.

Managing files and folders in Bridge

Bridge lets you easily drag files and move them between folders. You can use standard operating-system-level commands to cut, copy, paste, or delete files. You can also create and delete folders.

Drag files into Bridge by selecting one or more files on the desktop, in a folder, or in another application that supports the drag-and-drop feature, and then dragging them into the Content panel in Bridge. The files are moved from their former folder into the one displayed in Bridge.

You can specify how you want to view files and folders in the Content panel, such as how big thumbnails should be, whether file information should be displayed, what type of files should be shown, and the order in which they should appear.

Follow these steps to get a basic feel for Adobe Bridge:

1   Drag the Thumbnail slider at the bottom of the Bridge window to adjust the size of thumbnails.

2   Click the bike rides into frame.mov thumbnail to select it.

3   Click the Play button in the Preview panel to view this video.

Note: Bridge can play or display virtually any media asset.

4 Click the Horizontal Filmstrip workspace button (labeled "2") in the lower right corner of the Bridge window, to display thumbnails in a scrolling list along with an extra-large thumbnail of the currently selected item.

5 Choose View > Sort, and note the many sorting options.

Note: Selecting Manually will return the thumbnails to the last order in which you dragged the files.

6 Choose View > Slideshow to view thumbnails as a slide show that takes over the entire screen.

This is useful when you want to work with large versions of all the graphics files within a folder. Instructions on how to use the slide show appear when you press the keyboard shortcut H.

7 Press Esc to exit the slide show.

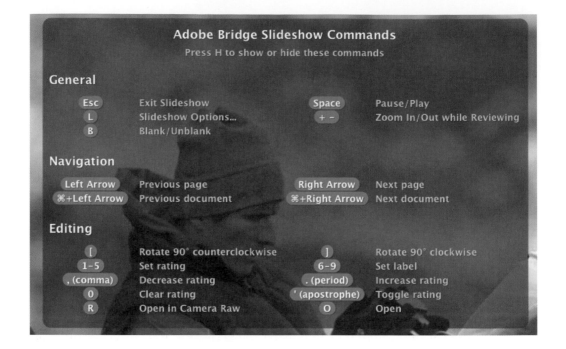

Using labels, ratings, and keywords to organize files

Labeling files allows you to quickly sort a large group of files. Labels are colors that you assign to individual files or groups of files. You can also rate files by assigning from 0 to 5 stars. Finally, you can assign keywords to files to help you identify files based on their content. Here's how to do all three tasks:

1 Return to the thumbnail view by clicking the Default workspace button (labeled "1") in the lower right corner of the Bridge window.

2 Select the crew.jpg and closeup.jpg files (they should be next to each other in the thumbnail view).

3 Select Label, and notice the five predefined status choices. Select Approved as the status.

4 Notice that the two JPEGs now have green status labels under their thumbnails.

Note: If you don't see any labels, the thumbnail images may be too small. Move the slider on the bottom a bit to the right to enlarge the icons; the labels should then be displayed.

Here are two other Label functions:

- To remove labels from files, choose Label > No Label.
- To sort by label color, choose View > Sort > By Label.

💡 Using labels to purge assets

Suppose you've just imported a large number of files and are viewing them in Bridge. As you review each new file, you can assign those you want to keep a green label. After this initial pass, you can use the Filter panel to view and work on just those files you've labeled green. Then you can discard the rest.

5   Click the illustrator file.ai thumbnail to select it.

6   Click one of the dots representing the number of stars you want to give the file.

Note: *If you cannot see the small dots under the thumbnail, increase the size of the thumbnail.*

💡 Rate new files to prioritize them

Suppose you've just imported a large number of images and are viewing them in Bridge. As you review each new image, you can rate them in priority from best to worst. After this initial pass, you can view only files you've rated with 4 or 5 stars, and work on those.

7   Return to the standard Bridge view by clicking the Default workspace button in the lower right corner of the window. Click the Keywords tab to open that panel.

8　Open the Keywords panel menu, choose New Keyword, and then type *Lesson 4*.

9　Click the newly added Lesson 4 keyword set to select it.

10　Open the panel menu again, choose New Sub Keyword, and type *Bikers*.

11　Select the bike movie file and the biker image, and select the box next to Bikers in the Keywords panel.

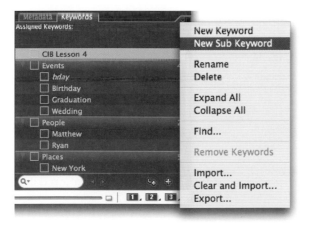

12　Locate the Filter panel. Notice the information the Filter panel has accumulated about your collection of files. It has set up categories based on file type, date, aspect ratio, labels, ratings and keywords. Click the keyword Bikers to have Bridge filter your files for you.

13 Notice you can combine filter items by selecting multiple filters. While the keyword Bikers is selected in the Filter panel, you can also click the JPEG file filter. Now only the JPEG file with the keyword Bikers is displayed. Combined with the rating and keyword tools, filtering is a powerful way to manage large numbers of files.

14 Click the Clear filter button in the lower right corner of the Filter panel to remove all filters.

Note: Take a look at the other Find parameters. This is a very helpful tool.

Here are some other Keyword functions:

• To remove keywords from a file, select the file, and then deselect the box next to the keyword or keyword set you want to remove.

• To rename a keyword or keyword set, select the keyword or keyword set, and choose Rename from the panel menu. Type the new name over the old name in the panel, and press Enter or Return.

• To move a keyword to a different keyword set, drag the keyword into the set you want.

• To delete a keyword, select the keyword, and then click the Delete Keyword button at the bottom of the panel, or choose Delete from the panel menu.

Adding and editing metadata

Depending on the selected file, the following types of metadata appear in the Metadata panel of Adobe Bridge:

• **File Properties**—Characteristics of the file, including the size, creation date, and modification date.

• **IPTC Core**—Information about the file, such as creator, address, description, date created, captions, and copyright information.

• **Camera Data**—Information assigned by digital cameras with an EXIF (Exchangeable Image File Format) feature. EXIF information includes the camera make/model, aperture and shutter speed settings when the picture was taken, and the date.

• **Audio**—Data associated with the audio source such as artist, album, and encoding.

- **Video**—Video-specific data such as frame rate, aspect ratio, field order, and tape-logging information.

To edit metadata, select a file, click in the metadata box you want to change, and type the information. When done, click the Apply icon (check mark) in the lower right corner of the Metadata panel.

Review

▶ **Review questions**

1 What is the principal difference between project settings and preferences?

2 What is the basic rule of thumb when selecting a project setting preset?

3 Describe two ways to import assets.

4 Adobe Premiere Pro handles Photoshop CS3 and Illustrator CS3 layered graphic files differently. Explain the differences.

5 What is the advantage of importing high-resolution photos?

6 In Bridge, how do you add a color label to a file, and why would you use these labels?

▶ **Review answers**

1 Project settings apply to the current project and you select them before opening the project. They primarily refer to the specifications of your source media. Preferences apply to any project and you can change them at any time. They have more to do with overall functionality of your workspace.

2 Select a preset that matches your source media. For most users, that would be DV-NTSC Standard 48 kHz.

3 Choose File > Import or double-click in an empty space in the Project panel.

4 Adobe Premiere Pro lets you import Photoshop CS3 files in one of three ways: as a sequence with individual layers on separate video tracks, on an individual-layer basis, or as a merged file. Adobe Premiere Pro imports Illustrator CS3 layered graphics only as merged files. It rasterizes and anti-aliases Illustrator vector-based art.

5 You can pan and zoom in on them and maintain a sharp-looking image. To see images at their full resolution, right-click (Windows) or Control-click (Mac OS) them in the Timeline and deselect Scale To Frame Size.

6 Click a file, choose Label, and select a color. This can come in handy when you are reviewing a lot of media files and want to sort them into categories.

storyboard

Rolling

Overlay

Extract

Snap

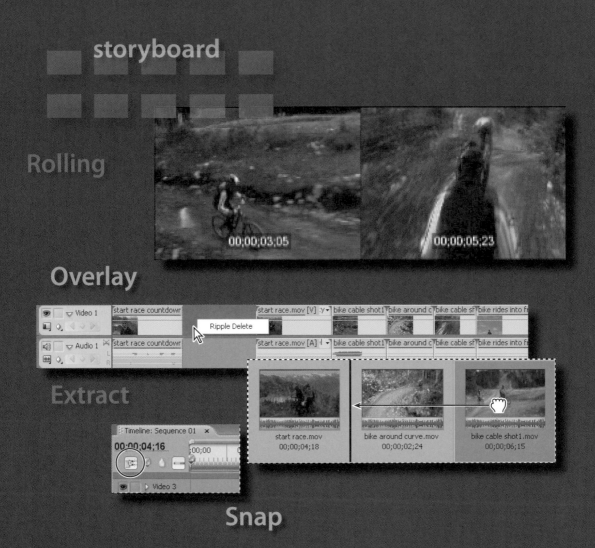

You will see very few transitions like dissolves or wipes in the video-editing world. Watch any TV news program, and virtually every edit in every story is a cut edit with no transitions. There is an art to creating cuts-only videos, and Adobe Premiere Pro CS3 gives you a full palette of cut edit tools and techniques.

5 Creating Cuts-only Videos

Topics covered in this lesson:

- Using a storyboard to build a rough cut
- Editing clips on the Timeline
- Moving clips to, from, and within the Timeline
- Working with Source Monitor editing tools
- Adjusting clips in the Trim panel
- Using other editing tools

Getting started

You create a video by first laying down a cuts-only version. Later, you can apply transitions, effects, titles, and motion, and work on compositing. Whether or not you use those extra effects, there is a real art to building a cuts-only video. You want to create a logical flow to your clips, make matching edits, and avoid jump cuts.

Adobe Premiere Pro offers several means to those ends. Depending on your circumstances, you might work in the Trim panel, use the Ripple Edit tool, or move clips on the Timeline using the Source Monitor or keyboard modifiers. We will review all those techniques in this lesson.

Using a storyboard to build a rough cut

You've seen storyboards. Film directors and animators frequently use walls of photos and sketches to visualize story flow and camera angles.

Storyboards also help after the fact. In the case of Adobe Premiere Pro, you can arrange clip thumbnails in the Project panel to get a basic feel for how your finished video will work. Then you can move all those clips to the Timeline for more precise editing.

This approach can come in handy by revealing gaps in your story—places that need fleshing out with more video or graphics. It's also a way to note redundancy and to quickly place a whole bunch of ordered clips on a sequence. When you are confronted with a Project panel loaded with clips, storyboards can help you see the big picture.

After creating your storyboard, you can place several clips in a sequence on the Timeline at one time.

1   Start Adobe Premiere Pro.

2   Click Open Project, navigate to the Lesson 05 folder, and double-click Lesson 5-1.prproj.

Note: This is a DV-NTSC Standard 48kHz project.

3   Double-click in an empty space in the Project panel (or choose File > Import), and import all the assets (except the project files) from the Lesson 05 folder.

4 Create a new bin named *Storyboard* in the Project panel (click the New Bin button).

5   Double-click the new Storyboard bin icon to open it in its own window. This will make it easy to move clips into this bin.

6   In the main bin, select all the movie clips (do not select the audio clip or sequence 1).

7   Right-click (Windows) or Control-click (Mac OS) one of the selected clips (you need to click the clip name or you will deselect all the clips) to bring up the context menu, and choose Copy.

Note: *Choosing Copy when you've highlighted multiple clips will copy the entire collection of clips.*

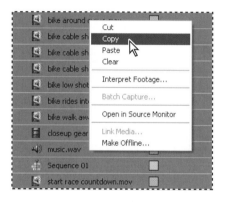

8   Select the Storyboard bin (so it is the active window) and choose Edit > Paste. All ten video files show up in the Storyboard bin. They remain in the main Project panel as well, because you copied them rather than dragging them.

Note: *The reason you have copied and pasted the video files into the separate Storyboard bin is because you will delete some of them during this lesson. This way, you delete them from the Storyboard bin, but not from the Project panel.*

9   Click the Icon View button in the Storyboard bin to switch to icon view.

10 Click the panel menu icon, and then choose Thumbnails > Large.

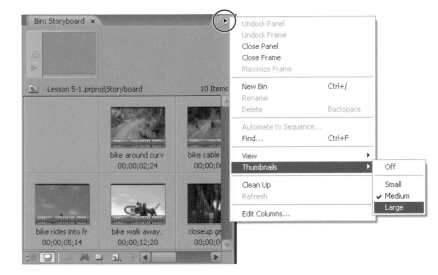

11 Resize the Storyboard bin so you can see all the thumbnails.

Arranging your storyboard

In this section, you will learn how to arrange thumbnails into a logical order. You will see one person's opinion of what constitutes a logical order, but before that, complete the following steps to see what you can come up with on your own. Keep in mind that you will trim some clips later to make the edits work more smoothly.

In turn, view each clip in the Preview Monitor by clicking the clip to select it and then clicking the Preview Monitor Play button.

Decide which clips do not work in this sequence and settle on an order for the remaining clips. Take some time working on this before continuing with this lesson. Selecting an order for clips is something you will do time after time.

Note: Some of the videos are a little dark and can be hard to view critically in the Project panel Preview Monitor. In those cases, double-click on a clip and view it in the Source Monitor.

Here's one person's opinion about a logical lineup:

- start race countdown.mov
- start race.mov
- bike cable shot1.mov
- bike around curve.mov
- bike cable shot3.mov
- bike rides into frame.mov
- bike walk away.mov

…leaving out the following clips, which don't work in this sequence:

- closeup gears.mov (let's keep it about the race)
- bike cable shot2.mov (too similar to bike cable shot 1.mov)
- bike low shot.mov (it's a cool shot, but a different biker)

Here's how to create the recommended sequence:

1   Remove the videos that do not work by selecting them and pressing the Delete key to remove them from the Storyboard bin.

Note: These clips will remain in the top-level view of the Project panel.

> 💡 **No word wrap**
>
> *The Project panel icon view does not have the equivalent of word wrap. Removing clips leaves gaps in the icon view. Newly added clips generally run past the right side of the panel, and when you resize the panel, the clips don't move to accommodate the change. To remedy these issues, open the panel menu and choose Clean Up.*

2   Drag the remaining clips to put them into the order indicated.

To move a clip, simply drag it to a new location. The pointer changes and a black vertical line indicates the new location for placement.

Note: As you drag clips, you will leave gaps. Use Clean Up to remove those gaps.

Your storyboard should look like the next figure.

Automating your storyboard to a sequence

Now you're going to move your storyboard clips to the Timeline, placing them there contiguously, in sequential order. Adobe Premiere Pro calls this *Automate To Sequence.* Here's how you do it:

1   Make sure the current-time indicator (CTI) is at the beginning of the Timeline. Automate To Sequence places the clips starting at the CTI location.

2 With the Storyboard bin window active, choose Edit > Select All to highlight all the clips (you can also marquee-select or use the Shift-click method).

3 Click the Automate To Sequence button in the lower left corner of the Project panel (highlighted in the next figure).

Note: You can also choose Automate To Sequence from the panel menu.

4 The newly opened Automate To Sequence dialog box has several options. Set the dialog box with the settings as shown in the figure on the next page. The options include:

• **Ordering**—Sort Order puts clips on a sequence in the order you established in the storyboard. Selection Order places them in the order you selected them if you Ctrl-clicked (Windows) or Command-clicked (Mac OS) individual clips.

• **Placement**—Places clips sequentially on the Timeline as opposed to at unnumbered markers (something we haven't covered).

• **Method**—The choices are Insert Edit or Overlay Edit, both of which will be discussed later in this lesson. Because here you are placing the clips on an empty sequence, both methods will do the same thing.

• **Clip Overlap**—Overlap presumes that you'll put a transition such as a cross-dissolve between all clips. The goal in this lesson is to create a cuts-only video; that is, a video with no transitions. Set Clip Overlap to zero.

• **Apply Default Audio/Video Transition**—Because you'll opt for no transitions, make sure these options are unselected.

• **Ignore Audio/Video**—The clips you are currently using have no audio, so these options are unavailable.

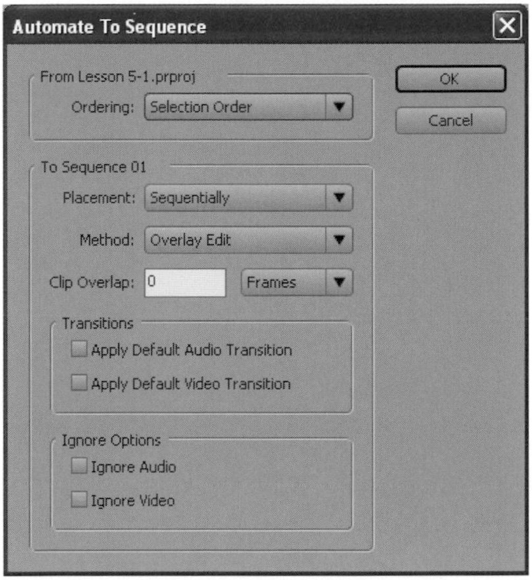

Automate To Sequence [X]

From Lesson 5-1.prproj

Ordering: [Selection Order ▼]

[OK]
[Cancel]

To Sequence 01

Placement: [Sequentially ▼]

Method: [Overlay Edit ▼]

Clip Overlap: [0   ] [Frames ▼]

Transitions
☐ Apply Default Audio Transition
☐ Apply Default Video Transition

Ignore Options
☐ Ignore Audio
☐ Ignore Video

4   Click OK. This places your clips in order on the sequence in the Timeline.

5   Drag the Project panel out of the way and play the Timeline by clicking inside the Timeline to activate it and then pressing the spacebar.

Note: View this sequence critically. Several edits are jump cuts or feel awkward. Some clips are too long. The next task is to fix those flaws.

Editing clips on the Timeline

You will use a variety of editing tools to improve this storyboard rough cut:

- Trim a clip by dragging its end.

- Use the Ripple Delete command to remove a gap between clips.

- Use the Ripple Edit tool to save a step when you lengthen or shorten a clip.

You can start where you left off in Lesson 5-1 or start fresh by opening Lesson 5-2.prproj from the Lesson 05 folder.

Trimming a clip

1   If your workspace has gotten messy, choose Window > Workspace > Reset Current Workspace to return it to the default.

2   Click the List button in the Project panel (lower left corner) to switch back to that view.

3   Click in the Timeline to select it and press the backslash key (\) to expand the view of the clips to full Timeline width.

4   Expand that view a bit more (zoom in) by pressing the equal sign (=) key twice.

This expands the width of the clips to help you make a more accurate edit. Your Timeline should look like the next figure.

Note: All the clips on the timeline may still be in a selected state from the Automate To Sequence operation. Click in any blank area in the sequence to deselect the group of clips.

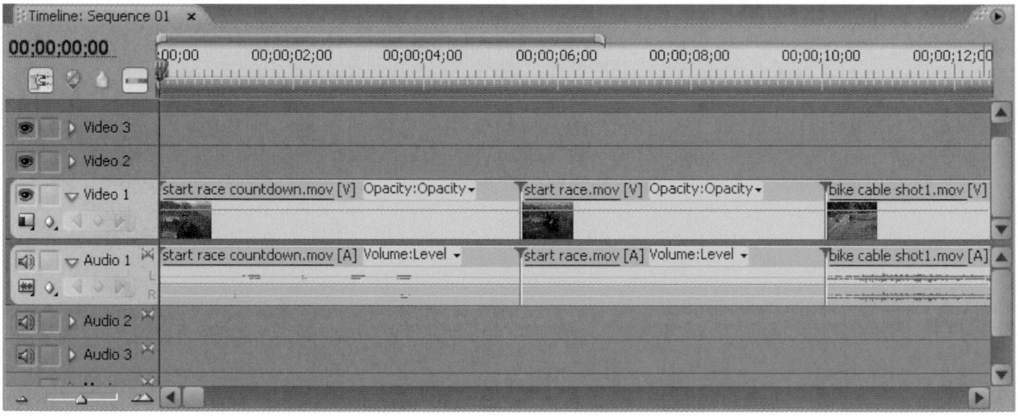

5   Hover the pointer over the right side of the first clip until you see the left-facing Trim bracket (⊣+), which is shown in the next figure.

Note: As you move your pointer around, you might notice that it changes into a Pen Keyframe tool (◆+). That happens when you hover the pointer over the thin yellow Opacity line. You'll work with the Opacity effect in upcoming lessons on compositing.

6   Drag the bracket to the left about one second, to just after the actor says "Go." Use the timecode pop-up display in the Timeline and the Program Monitor display for reference. Release the mouse button. The purpose is to remove the extra time after the actor says "Go."

Note: This trim edit leaves a gap between the two clips on the Timeline. You'll remove this gap later.

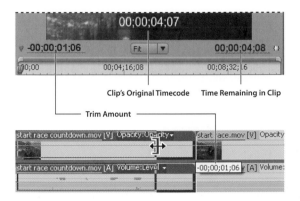

Step farther back using History

You will make multiple edits and, therefore, a few mistakes. You know you can back up one step at a time by pressing Ctrl+Z in Windows or Command+Z in Mac OS (or by choosing Edit > Undo). You can also use the History panel to move back several steps at once—even as far back as the original Automate To Sequence.

7   The second clip, start race.mov, needs to have the beginning trimmed to remove the time during the countdown. We don't want to watch the countdown twice. For this clip, use the program monitor and CTI to help locate the spot to trim. Scrub the CTI to the point where the bikers start moving. That is at 00;00;08;20 on the timeline. (you can read this time at the lower left area of the Program Monitor).

8   Leave the CTI at this point on the timeline.

9   Drag the left edge of the start race.mov clip to the right until the left edge reaches the CTI line.

The edge of the clip should snap to that CTI (see the Snap feature sidebar). Release the mouse button.

Snap feature

Adobe Premiere Pro has a tremendously useful feature called snap. It's a default setting, and in only a few instances will you want to turn it off. With snap turned on, as you drag a clip toward another clip, it will jump to the edge of the adjacent clip to make a clean, unbroken edit. With Snap turned off, you'd have to slide the new clip very carefully next to the other clip to ensure there is no gap.

Snap is also useful when making precise edits. Using the Selection tool to trim a clip can be a bit clumsy, as you might have noted in step 6 of this mini-lesson. Snap allows you to trim to the CTI very easily.

Locate the frame you want trim to by dragging the CTI through your sequence to that frame's location (use the Right Arrow and Left Arrow keys to move to the specific frame). Use the Selection tool and drag the edge of the clip toward the CTI line. When it gets near the line, it will snap to the CTI, and you'll have made a frame-specific edit. You can use this technique in all sorts of circumstances.

If you want to toggle the snap feature off or on, click the Snap button in the top left corner of the Timeline (highlighted below).

Closing the gaps—Ripple Delete command

Trimming the two clips has left a gap in the sequence. You'll remove them using the Ripple Delete command.

1   Right-click (Windows) or Control-click (Mac OS) the gap between the first and second clips, and then choose Ripple Delete (your only "choice").

The Ripple Delete command removes the gap by sliding all the material after the gap to the left.

Using the Ripple Edit tool

A way to avoid creating those gaps in the first place is to use the Ripple Edit tool (highlighted below). It's one of the eleven tools in the Tools panel.

Use the Ripple Edit tool to trim a clip in the same way you used the Selection tool in Trim mode. The two differences are that the Ripple Edit tool does not leave a gap on the sequence and the display in the Program Monitor gives a clearer representation of how the edit will work.

When you use the Ripple Edit tool to lengthen or shorten a clip, your action ripples through the sequence. That is, all clips after that edit slide to the left to fill the gap, or slide to the right to accommodate a longer clip.

2   Click the Ripple Edit tool (or press B on your keyboard).

3   Hover the tool over the right edge of the bike cable shot 1.mov clip until it turns into a large, left-facing square bracket (⊹).

Note: *The Ripple Edit pointer is larger than the Selection tool's Trim pointer.*

4 Drag it to the left one second and 8 frames (00;00;01;10 from the right edge of the clip, as seen in the lower left area of the Program Monitor as you drag the Ripple Edit tool). This is to cut the video just as both bikers are out of the frame.

Watch the moving edit position on the right half of the Program Monitor. Your goal is to move that clip until the biker's head position moves just off the bottom of the frame.

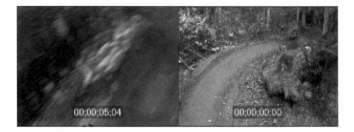

5 Release the mouse button to complete the edit. The remaining part of the clip moves left to fill the gap, and the clips to its right slide along with it. Play that portion of the sequence to see if the edit works smoothly.

6 Trim away about half the length of the last clip (bike walk away.mov), as it is a bit long. Use the Selection tool (switch to it by clicking it or by pressing V on your keyboard). Hover the Selection tool over the right edge of the clip and drag it to the left, removing about half the length of the clip.

7 View your sequence. It should flow fairly smoothly.

8 To polish your cuts-only video, you need to add a soundtrack. Drag the music.wav file from the project bin to the Audio 2 track on the same sequence as your video clips. Position it all the way to the left of the sequence.

9 Hover over the right end of the music.wav file until the Selection tool changes to the Trim tool, and drag it to the left to match the length of the video.

10 Play the sequence now by pressing the spacebar or Enter or Return to see the difference a music soundtrack makes to a video. If you would like to compare your project to the finished Classroom in a Book version, open and play Lesson 5-3.prproj.

Note: Don't worry that the soundtrack suddenly ends. You will learn ways to fade audio in a later lesson.

Moving clips to, from, and within the Timeline

One of the beauties of Adobe Premiere Pro is how easy it is to add clips anywhere in the project, move them around, and remove them altogether.

There are two ways to place a clip in the Timeline (whether you drag it from the Project panel or from another location in the Timeline):

- **Overlay**—The newly placed clip and its audio replace what was on the sequence.

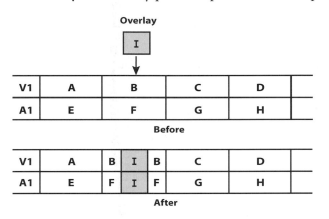

- **Insert**—The first frame of the newly placed clip cuts the current clip, and without covering up anything, slides the cut segment and all clips after it to the right. This process requires using a keyboard modifier—in this case, the Ctrl (Windows) or Command (Mac OS) key.

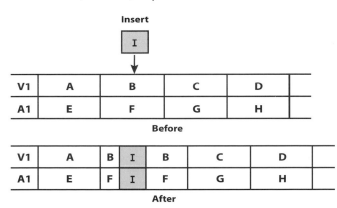

And there are two ways to move a clip from a location in the Timeline:

- **Lift**—Leaves a gap where the clip used to be.

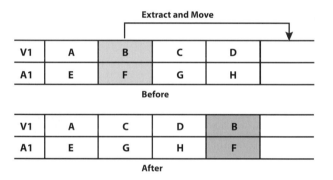

- **Extract**—Works like a ripple edit in that other clips move over to fill the gap. This move also requires a keyboard modifier—holding down the Ctrl (Windows) or Command (Mac OS) key *before* clicking the clip to be removed.

Adding and moving clips on the Timeline

You'll start by setting up a new sequence with three clips on it.

1   Continue with the Lesson 5-2.prproj project, or open the Lesson 5-3.prproj project.

2   Choose File > New > Sequence.

Note: The New Sequence dialog box displays the default values for numbers and types of tracks from the Default Sequence category of project settings. You can change the default values by choosing Project > Project Settings > Default Sequence.

3 Name the sequence *Bike Race Seq,* and click OK.

New Sequence	⊠

Sequence Name: Bike Race Seq   [OK]   [Cancel]

Tracks
  Video
        Video: 3 tracks

  Audio
        Master: Stereo ▼

        Mono: 0   Mono Submix: 0

        Stereo: 3   Stereo Submix: 0

        5.1: 0   5.1 Submix: 0

4 Select three video clips from the project panel—bike around curve.mov, bike cable shot1.mov, and bike cable shot2.mov—and drag them to Video 1 track on the newly created bike race sequence in the Timeline.

5 Press the backslash key (\) to expand the view.

Overlay edit example

6 Drag the movie clip bike cable shot3.mov from the Project panel to the Timeline so its first frame is approximately in the middle of the second clip.

Note: *The Program Monitor shows two images. The left view is the new Out point of the first clip that will precede the new clip. The right view is the new In point of the next clip that will follow the newly placed clip.*

7 Drop bike cable shot3.mov on the sequence.

That is an overlay edit. It covers the video and audio that was there before. It does not change the length of the sequence.

Insert edit example

8 Press Ctrl+Z (Windows) or Command+Z (Mac OS) to undo the previous edit.

9 Drag bike cable shot3.mov to the same place, but this time hold down Ctrl (Windows) or Command (Mac OS) *before releasing* the mouse button.

Notice that bike cable shot3.mov slices the first clip in two, sliding the second half of the second clip and all subsequent clips to the right and inserting bike cable shot3.mov on the Timeline.

That is an insert edit. Your sequence is now longer.

Note: As you hold bike cable shot3.mov over the first clip in the sequence, press and release the Ctrl or Command key and note that the Program Monitor switches back and forth. It shows only one image for an insert edit—where you will cut clip one—and two images for an overlay—the new Out point for clip one and the new In point for clip two.

Lift-and-move edit example

10 Press Ctrl+Z (Windows) or Command+Z (Mac OS) to undo the previous edit.

11 Drag bike cable shot3.mov from the Project panel to the end of the third clip to create a four-clip sequence. Press the backslash key (\) to see all the clips. Then press the minus key (-) to zoom out one level, to give yourself room to move clips around.

12 Drag the second clip to the end of the four clips on the Timeline.

That is a lift-and-move edit. There is a gap where the second clip used to be, and the end of the sequence extends beyond its former length.

Note: No keyboard modifier is needed as you place the clip at the end of the sequence, because nothing comes after it.

Extract-and-move edit example

13 Press Ctrl+Z (Windows) or Command+Z (Mac OS) to return to the original position.

14 Press Ctrl (Windows) or Command (Mac OS), and then drag the second clip to the end of the sequence.

This is an extract-and-move edit. Because you held down Ctrl (Windows) or Command (Mac OS) while removing the clip from its former position, you created the equivalent of a ripple delete. The sequence length does not change.

Extract-and-overlay edit example

15   Press Ctrl+Z (Windows) or Command+Z (Mac OS) to return to the original position.

16   Press the S key to turn off the snap feature (or click the Snap button in the upper left corner of the Timeline).

17   Press Ctrl (Windows) or Command (Mac OS), and then drag the first clip to the center of the third clip, *release* Ctrl or Command, and then drop the clip there.

That is an extract-and-overlay edit. Clips slide over to fill the gap left by the removed clip (the keyboard modifier turned what would have been a lift into an extract). The sequence length is shorter.

Note: If you had not used the keyboard modifier when removing the clip from its original location, that would have left a gap there—a lift-and-overlay edit.

Extract-and-insert edit example

18   Press Ctrl+Z (Windows) or Command+Z (Mac OS) to return to the original position.

19   Press Ctrl (Windows) or Command (Mac OS), and drag the first clip to the center of the third clip. Continue holding down Ctrl or Command, and drop the clip there.

That is an Extract and Insert. Clips slide over to fill the gap left by the removed first clip, and the clips after the insert edit point slide to the right. The sequence length remains unchanged.

💡 **Modifier-key feedback**

As you drag a clip from the Project panel to a sequence, or from one place on a sequence track to another, Adobe Premiere Pro displays a text message at the bottom of the user interface reminding you of modifier-key options.

Working with Source Monitor editing tools

In the beginning of this lesson, we assembled clips on the Timeline by creating a storyboard and then automating the storyboard to the Timeline. We also practiced dragging clips from a bin directly to the Timeline. Both of these methods (or workflows) are valid. Now we will look at one of the most common workflows for assembling clips onto the Timeline. It may seem awkward at first, but if you practice this method you may find it to be the fastest, most efficient way to edit. It's helpful to trim clips before moving them from the Project panel to the Timeline. Do that by double-clicking a clip in the bin to open it in the Source Monitor.

1 Continue with the Lesson 5-3.prproj project or open the Lesson 5-4.prproj project.

2 Drag a marquee around all four clips in the Lesson 5-3 sequence in the Timeline, and then press Delete.

💡 **Selecting multiple clips**

Another way to select more than one clip in the Timeline is to Shift+click the clips, one at a time.

3 Double-click the clip start race countdown.mov to open it in the Source Monitor.

Note: You also can drag the clip from the Project panel and drop it on the Source Monitor.

4 Move the Source Monitor's CTI to 00;20, just before the actor starts counting. This is where you want this clip to start. You want to remove the frames where he is just staring blankly.

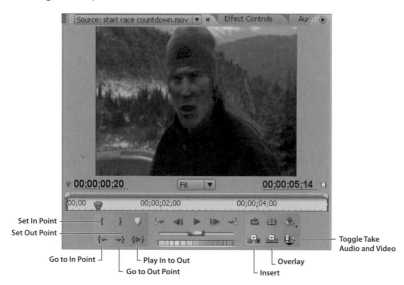

5 Click the Set In Point button.

Note: The Set In Point button is the same as that used in the Capture panel. It also has the same keyboard shortcut: I.

6 You need to trim extra footage off the end of this clip as well. Move the Source Monitor CTI to just after the actor says "Go," which is at 04;00.

7 Click the Set Out Point button.

8 Navigate back and forth between the In and Out points by clicking Go To In Point (or pressing Q) and Go To Out Point (or pressing V). Play that entire segment by clicking the Play In To Out button. Notice that the portion of the clip we want to keep is identified in blue under the Source Monitor.

9 Move the Timeline CTI to the beginning of the sequence.

10 Check to see that the Video 1 and Audio 1 track headers (highlighted in the next figure) are selected—*targeted,* in Adobe Premiere Pro parlance. If not, click in one or both to highlight them (their corners also become rounded).

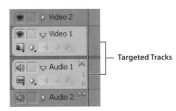

— Targeted Tracks

11 Click the Source Monitor Insert button to place this clip at the CTI line in the empty Bike Race Seq sequence.

Note: Clicking either Insert or Overlay will place the clip at the Timeline CTI.

12 Notice that the clip is sent to the timeline with the beginning and ends trimmed because of the In and Out points we set in the Source Monitor for this clip.

Note: Notice that the sequence CTI is automatically moved to the end of the clip on the timeline. This is so that when you send the next clip from the Source Monitor it will be placed right after the first clip.

13 Double-click the clip start race.mov in the Project panel to open that clip in the Source Monitor.

14 Click the Source Monitor tab to display a list of currently open clips.

All clips viewed in the Source Monitor show up in this list. You can access them here and remove all, or one at a time, by selecting Close All or Close.

15 Play the start race.mov clip in the Source Monitor, and look for edit points. The beginning of this clip is a different angle of the same countdown in the previous clip. Let's remove the beginning of this clip; it's redundant. Set the In point just as the bikers start down the hill. That is at about 03:02.

16 See that the Timeline CTI is at the end of the first clip (it goes there automatically after either an insert edit or an overlay edit). Click the Insert button on the Source Monitor to send this clip to the Timeline. The keyboard shortcut for this insertion is the comma (,) key.

Play the Timeline to see how that edit works.

17 Use the Source Monitor to create In and Out points for the rest of the clips you used to create the movie during the storyboard section of this lesson.

Note: *You can use the Source Monitor to send just the video or just the audio to the Timeline. Use the Toggle Take Audio And Video icon in the lower right of the Source Monitor to control this.*

The more you practice this method, the more natural it will be. Practice using keyboard shortcuts for setting In and Out points, and sending to the Timeline (insert or overlay), and you will get faster and faster at editing. This is the preferred method (or workflow) for many professional editors.

Adjusting clips in the Trim panel

The Trim panel is a very useful tool. Its value is its large preview monitors, precise controls, and informative timecode displays.

Rolling-edit and rippling-edit behaviors

You apply the Ripple Edit tool to only one clip. It changes the length of your project, because the rest of the project slides over to accommodate the change. A rolling edit does not change the length of your project. It takes place at an edit point between two clips, shortening one and lengthening the other.

1   Continue with the Lesson 5-4.prproj project.

2   Marquee-select the clips in the bike race sequence, and then press Delete.

3   Drag clips bike cable shot1.mov and bike cable shot3.mov to the Bike Race Seq sequence to Video 1 track in the Timeline. You worked with these clips earlier in this lesson.

4   Place the CTI at the edit point between the two clips.

5   Click the Trim button (▦—shortcut: T) in the lower right corner of the Program Monitor.

This opens the Trim panel.

6   Hover the pointer over the left preview screen until it turns into a left-facing Ripple Edit pointer (➧).

7 Trim the right edge of clip (the Out point) by dragging it left to about one second (watch the Out Shift timecode below the center of the left screen).

8 Use the same method to trim the right clip's In point to the right to about one second (use the In Shift timecode beneath the center of the right screen).

9 Click the precision trimming tools—the –1 and +1 numbers (highlighted in the next figure)—to trim or lengthen the clips one frame at a time until you have the exact edit point you want. Look for the point on the left clip where the biker's helmet just leaves the bottom of the frame at 00;00;05;06.

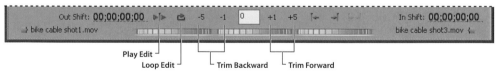

Trim panel editing tools

Note: *Click in the left or right preview screen to make it active (so the precise trim tools apply to it). You can tell which preview screen is active by the thin blue line beneath it.*

10 Click the Play Edit button in the Trim panel to review your work.

11 Hover the pointer between the two preview screens. It turns into the Rolling Edit tool ✛ (highlighted in the next figure).

12 Drag the Rolling Edit tool left and right to change the Out and In points of the left and right clips, respectively. Notice how both clips move and the clips are in sync.

13 Close the Trim panel by clicking the Close button in its corner.

Using other editing tools

The Tools panel has lost weight in Adobe Premiere Pro. Previous versions packed 18 tools into an even smaller space than the current Tools panel. Now, it has only 11. The reason context-sensitive tools. In particular, the Selection tool changes to other tools depending on its location in the Timeline and elsewhere.

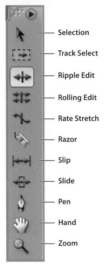

The Tools panel's editing tools

Here's a brief rundown of the tools (keyboard shortcut letters shown in parentheses):

- **Selection** (V) ⬚—Multipurpose, all-around aid. You use it frequently to drag, drop, select, and trim clips.

- **Track Select** (A) ⬚—Not to be confused with the Selection tool, the Track Select tool enables you to select all clips to the right of wherever you position it on a video or audio track. You can Shift-click to select other tracks. After they've been selected, you can slide them, delete them, cut/paste them, or copy/paste them.

- **Ripple Edit** (B) ⬚—You've worked with this many times already. A ripple edit trims a clip and shifts subsequent clips in the track by the amount you trimmed.

- **Rolling Edit** (N) ⬚—A rolling edit trims adjacent Out and In points simultaneously and by the same number of frames. This effectively moves the edit point between clips, preserving other clips' positions in time and maintaining the total duration of the sequence. You just did this in the Trim panel.

- **Rate Stretch** (X) ↖—You can stretch or shrink a clip, putting it in slow motion or speeding up the action.

- **Razor** (C) ✎—Razor slices a clip or clips in two. It can be useful when you want to use different effects that can't both be applied to a single clip, such as different speed settings.

- **Slip** (Y) ↦—By dragging with the Slip tool, you can change a clip's starting and ending frames without changing its duration or affecting adjacent clips.

- **Slide** (U) ⇹—A slide edit shifts a clip along the timeline while trimming adjacent clips to compensate for the move. As you drag a clip left or right with the Slide tool, the Out point of the preceding clip and the In point of the following clip are trimmed by the number of frames you move the clip. The clip's In and Out points (and hence, its duration) remain unchanged. We'll cover the Slide tool later in the book, along with the Slip tool.

- **Pen** (P) ✒—Use this to add, select, move, delete, or adjust keyframes on a sequence as well as create and adjust curves in the Titler, Effect Controls panel, and Program Monitor. You use the keyframes to change audio volume levels and panning, alter clip opacity, and change video and audio effects over time.

- **Hand** (H) ✋—Use the Hand tool to scroll an entire sequence by grabbing a clip and sliding it and the rest of the sequence to one side. It works the same as moving the scroll bar at the bottom of the Timeline.

- **Zoom** (Z) ⚲—This works like the Zoom In and Zoom Out buttons in the lower left corner of the Timeline and the viewing area bar at the top of the sequence above the time ruler. Default is Zoom In (⚲). Hold down Alt (Windows) or Option (Mac OS) to change that to Zoom Out (⚲). When you want to expand the view of a set of clips in the sequence, drag the Zoom tool around those clips.

Review

▶ **Review questions**

1   How can storyboards help you create your project?

2   What is the difference between a trim and a ripple edit?

3   You want to drag a clip from the Project panel and place it between two clips in a sequence without covering them up. How do you do that?

4   How do you move a clip from one position on a sequence to another without covering up other clips and at the same time automatically filling the gap left by the removed clip?

5   How do you use the Source Monitor to do an overlay, video-only edit?

6   What can you accomplish using the Trim panel's Rolling Edit tool?

▶ **Review answers**

1   Storyboards can give you an overall feel for the flow of your project, reveal gaps, help you weed out weaker shots, and avoid redundancy.

2   Trims leave gaps where the trimmed video used to be (or, if you lengthen a clip using the Trim tool, they cover that portion of the next clip). Ripple edits automatically fill gaps by sliding the clips following the edit to the left (filling the space left by the edit) or to the right (to compensate for a lengthened clip).

3   Use an insert edit. Before you drop the clip between the two clips in the sequence, hold down the Ctrl (Windows) or Command (Mac OS) key to switch from an overlay edit to an insert edit.

4   Hold down Ctrl (Windows) or Command (Mac OS) as you extract the clip, and hold down Ctrl (Windows) or Command (Mac OS) again as you place the clip in its new position.

5   Change the Toggle Take Audio And Video button to the video-only filmstrip icon, position the Timeline CTI where you want to make the edit, target the audio and video tracks, and click the Overlay button in the Source Monitor.

6   Once you find a matching edit between two clips, you can fine-tune that edit using the Rolling Edit tool. It'll help you find just the right place to make a seamless edit.

Cross Dissolve

Page Peel

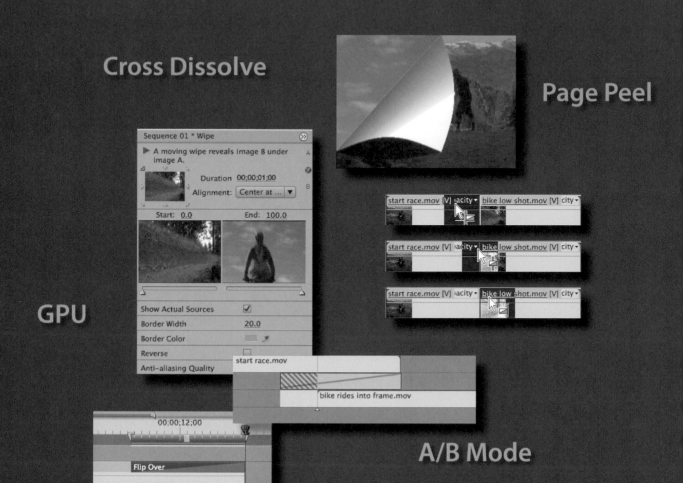

GPU

Sequence 01 * Wipe

▶ A moving wipe reveals image B under
image A.

Duration 00;00;01;00
Alignment: Center at ... ▼

Start: 0.0   End: 100.0

Show Actual Sources   ☑
Border Width   20.0
Border Color
Reverse
Anti-aliasing Quality

start race.mov [V] acity ▼ | bike low shot.mov [V] city ▼

start race.mov [V] acity ▼ | bike low shot.mov [V] city ▼

start race.mov [V] acity ▼ | bike low shot.mov [V] city ▼

start race.mov

bike rides into frame.mov

00;00;12;00

Flip Over

A/B Mode

transitions

*Transitions can make a video move
more smoothly or snap the audience
to attention. Some transitions are
whimsical, others draw attention to a
portion of the scene, and still others
create a frantic mood. Adobe Premiere
Pro CS3 has nearly 80 transitions that
are easy to use and customize. Fun
stuff—but try to use restraint.*

6 | Adding Video Transitions

Topics covered in this lesson:

- Using transitions with restraint
- Experimenting with transitions
- Changing parameters in the Effect Controls panel
- Fine-tuning transitions

Getting started

Applying transitions between clips—dissolves, page wipes, spinning screens, and many more—is a nice way to ease viewers from one scene to the next or to grab their attention.

There's an art to adding transitions to your project. Applying them starts simply enough: a mere drag-and-drop process. The art comes in their placement, length, and parameters, such as colored borders, motion, and start/end locations.

Most transition work takes place in the Effect Controls panel. In addition to the various options unique to each transition, that panel displays something called an A/B timeline. This feature makes it easy to move transitions relative to the edit point, change the transition duration, and apply transitions to clips that don't have sufficient head or tail frames.

Using transitions with restraint

Once you discover the cornucopia of transition possibilities that Adobe Premiere Pro offers, you will be tempted to use them for every edit. They can be great fun.

Despite that, it is highly recommended that you use restraint.

Watch some TV news stories. Most use cuts-only edits. It's unlikely you'll see any transitions. Why? Time is a factor, but more and more stations these days have ready access to nonlinear editors (NLEs) such as Adobe Premiere Pro, and it takes almost no time to add a transition by using an NLE.

The principal reason for the dearth of transitions is that they can be distracting. If a TV news editor uses one, it's for a purpose. Their most frequent newsroom editing-bay use is to take what would have been a jarring edit—such as a major jump cut—and make it more palatable. An oft-heard newsroom phrase applies: "If you can't solve it, dissolve it."

That's not to say transitions don't have their place in carefully planned stories. Consider the Star Wars movies with all their highly stylized transitions, like obvious, slow wipes. Each of those transitions has a purpose. George Lucas purposely created a look reminiscent of old serialized movies and TV shows. Specifically, they send a clear message to the audience: "Pay attention. We're transitioning across space and time."

Adding whimsy

Transitions can lighten up a story. Here are a few examples:

- Start on a tight hand-shot of someone cutting a deck of cards, and make a Swap transition—one image slides to one side and another slides over it—to another card-related shot.

- Start with a tight shot of a clock (analog, not digital) and use the aptly named Clock Wipe—a line centered on the screen sweeps around to reveal another image—to move to another setting and time.

- Get that James Bond, through-the-bloody-eye effect with the Iris Round transition.

- Take a medium shot of a garage door and use a Push—one image moves off the top while another replaces it from below—to transition to the next shot of the garage interior.

• With some planning and experimentation, you can videotape someone pushing against a wall while walking in place and use that same Push transition (after applying a horizontal direction to it) to have that person "slide" the old scene off screen.

Adding visual interest

Transitions can give your video some pizzazz:

• Take a shot of a car driving through the frame and use a Wipe, synchronized with the speed of the car, to move to the next scene.

• Transition from a shot of driving rain or a waterfall by using the Slash Slide transition, in which streaks, like driving rain, slice through an image, revealing another image behind it.

• Use the Venetian Blinds transition as a great way to move from an interior to an exterior.

• A Page Peel transition works well with a piece of parchment.

During this lesson, feel free to experiment with all that Adobe Premiere Pro has to offer.

Trying some transitions

Adobe Premiere Pro contains nearly 80 video transitions (plus two audio transitions, covered later in the book). Some are subtle, and some are "in your face." The more you experiment with them, the more likely you are to use them well.

Applying a transition between two clips starts with a simple drag-and-drop process. That might be enough for many transitions, but Adobe Premiere Pro gives you a wide variety of options for fine-tuning transitions. Some transitions have a Custom button that opens a separate dialog box with sets of options unique to each. And most offer tools that allow you to position the transition precisely.

First, you'll be introduced to some of the transitions in Adobe Premiere Pro. Then you'll see some others that offer extra options.

1 Start Adobe Premiere Pro, and open the Lesson 6-1.prproj project.

2 Choose Window > Workspace > Effects.

This changes the workspace to the preset that the Adobe Premiere Pro development team created to make it easier to work with transitions and effects.

3   Drag the three MOV video clips from the Project panel to the Video 1 track, and press the backslash key (\) to expand the view.

Note: There are little triangles in the upper right and upper left corners of the clips (highlighted in the next figure). They indicate that the clips are at their original, full length. For transitions to work smoothly, you need handles—*some unused head and tail frames to overlap between the clips. Trimming both clips will give you those handles.*

4   Select the Ripple Edit tool (or press B on the keyboard) and drag the end of the first clip to the left to shorten it by about two seconds (note the time in the pop-up display).

5   Use the Ripple Edit tool to drag the beginning of the second clip to the right about two seconds into the clip.

6   Press the backslash key (\) to expand the Timeline view.

Note: Since you used the Ripple Edit tool, these two trims should have no gap. If there is a gap, right-click (Windows) or Control-click (Mac OS), and choose Ripple Delete.

7   Create handles at the end of the second clip and beginning of the third clip in the same way. Use the Ripple Edit tool to drag the end of the second clip two seconds to the left, and drag the beginning of the third clip two seconds to the right.

8   The Effects panel should be docked with the Project panel. Select the Effects panel by clicking it, and then open the Video Transitions > Dissolve bin.

9   Drag Cross Dissolve to the edit between the first two clips on the sequence, but don't release the mouse button just yet.

Note: Cross Dissolve has a red box around it, indicating it's the default transition.

10 While still holding down the mouse button, move the pointer to the left and right, and note how the pointer and the highlighted rectangle on the clips change (see next figure). You can place the transition such that it ends at the edit point, is centered on the edit point, or starts there.

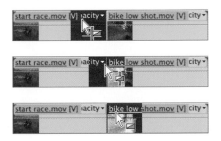

11 Place the transition at the middle of the edit point, and drop the transition there.

12 Put the CTI ahead of the transition, and press the spacebar to play it.

The transition has a one-second duration by default.

> ### Changing the default transition and duration
>
> *There are two primary uses for the default transition: when automating a storyboard to a sequence or as a quick means to add a transition by using the keyboard shortcut (Ctrl+D in Windows or Command+D in Mac OS). To set a different default transition, select the transition you want to use, open the Effects panel menu, and choose Set Default Transition. A red box will appear around that transition. You can change the default duration by choosing Default Transition Duration, which opens the General Preferences dialog box.*

13 Open the 3D Motion bin under the video transitions, and drag Flip Over to the beginning of the first clip. Note that the only placement option is to have the transition start at the edit point.

One very cool characteristic of transitions in Adobe Premiere Pro is that you can use them at the beginning or end of a clip. This is called a *single-sided transition* (*double-sided transitions* go between clips).

14 Press Home to move the CTI to the beginning of the timeline and play the transition. This is a slick way to start a video.

> ### 💡 Transitions on any track
>
> *Adobe Premiere Pro lets you place transitions between two clips (or at the beginnings or ends of clips) on any track in a sequence. Older versions of Premiere limited transitions to the Video 1 track. One very cool use of single-sided transitions is to put them in clips on higher tracks so they gradually reveal or cover up what's below them in the Timeline. We're using only a single track in these lessons to simplify things and because transition behavior on the Video 1 track is the same as on any other track.*

15 Drag the Flip Over transition to the end of the third clip.

16 Click the Effect Controls tab to open the Effect Controls panel. (It may already be visible.)

17 Click the Flip Over transition rectangle at the end of the clip in the Timeline to switch on the display of its parameters in the Effect Controls panel.

18 Select the Reverse option (highlighted in the next figure) to have the Flip Over flip in the opposite direction at the end of the clip.

19 Open the Page Peel bin and drag the Page Peel transition to the Cross Dissolve transition between the two clips. That replaces Cross Dissolve with Center Peel. Play that transition.

Note: The next step calls for the use of a GPU (graphics processor unit). If your computer does not have a GPU with enough horsepower to handle the GPU effects in Adobe Premiere Pro, they will not show up in the Effects panel. In that case, skip the next step. Note that GPU transitions are not currently available for Macintosh.

20 (Windows only) Open the GPU Transitions bin and drag the Center Peel transition on top of the Page Peel transition already on the timeline. Play that transition.

Note: There is also a Center Peel transition in the Page Peel folder in the Windows version. They behave very differently.

21 Test out some other transitions. It's a good idea to try at least one from every bin.

Note: There are dozens of transitions to choose from. If you know the name of a transition, you can type the beginning of that name in the Contains text box to find a single transition quickly.

Sequence display changes

When you add a transition to a sequence, a short red horizontal line appears above that transition (highlighted in the next figure). That red line means that this portion of the sequence must be rendered before you can record it back to tape or create a file of your finished project.

Rendering happens automatically when you export your project, but you can choose to render selected portions of your sequence to make those sections display more smoothly on slower computers. To do that, slide the handles of the work area bar (highlighted below) to the ends of the red rendering line (they will snap to those points) and press Enter or Return. Adobe Premiere Pro will create a video clip of that segment (tucked away in the Preview Files folder with an indecipherable file name) and will change the line from red to green.

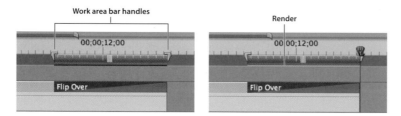

Note: The work area bar may cover all clips on the timeline by default. Pressing Enter or Return will render any areas that require rendering that are within the In and Out points of the work area bar. By adjusting the length of the work area bar, you can control what areas of the project are rendered.

Changing parameters in the Effect Controls panel

Up to this point you've seen the default action of each transition you've tested. That just scratches the surface of their possibilities. Tucked away in the Effect Controls panel is a passel of parameters, unique to each transition.

You'll start with the Cross Dissolve transition, and then move on to most of the transitions that were used earlier in this lesson. Here's how you adjust transition characteristics:

1   Continue where you left off in Lesson 6-1, or open the Lesson 6-2 project.

2   Drag the Cross Dissolve transition from the Effects > Video Transitions > Dissolve bin to the beginning of the first clip.

3   Click the transition rectangle in the upper left corner of the clip in the sequence to display its parameters in the Effect Controls panel.

4   Select the Show Actual Sources option (highlighted in the previous figure) and drag the sliders beneath the Start and End preview screens.

You can use those sliders to have the transition start partially faded up, and end less than completely faded up.

5   Change the duration in the Effect Controls panel to 2 seconds, and play the transition in the Timeline.

Note: Another way to change the duration of the transition is to drag the edge of the transition on the timeline: Drag the right edge of the transition left and right with the standard Selection tool to adjust its length.

6   Play the transition at different lengths to see the effect.

7   Drag the Push transition from the Slide Transitions bin to the edit between the first and second clips.

Play it in the Timeline and notice the direction that it pushes.

8   Change the direction to go from top to bottom by clicking the North To South triangle (highlighted in the next figure).

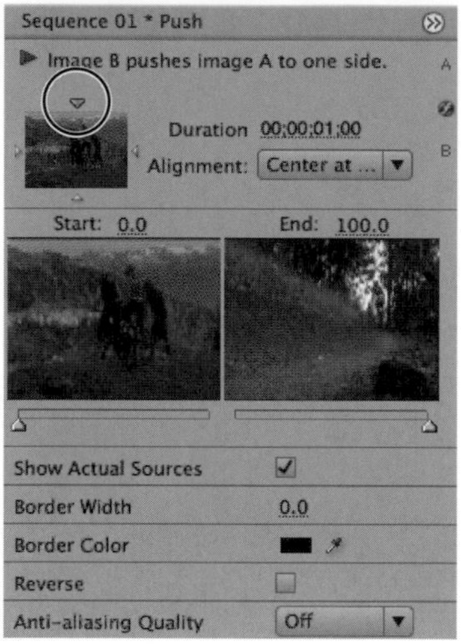

9   Apply the Wipe transition (Wipe bin) between the second and third clips.

Note that there are three new options: Border Width, Border Color, and Anti-aliasing Quality.

10   Change the Border Width to 20.

11   Click the upper left direction triangle to change the direction to Northwest To Southeast.

12   Click the Eyedropper tool (highlighted in the figure on the next page) and click the clouds in the sky to choose a light blue.

13 Set Anti-aliasing Quality to High. Play that transition.

14 Apply the Iris Round transition (Iris bin) at the end of the last clip. Notice that when you drop a new transition on top of an old transition, it replaces the old transition. This transition has a new option; a small positioning circle.

15 Select the Reverse option to make the Iris close rather than open.

16 Move the End slider (under the End Preview screen) to the left so you can see how the transition will look as it finishes.

17 Move the positioning circle in the Start screen to make the transition finish on the biker's face (watch the position of the transition change in the End screen).

Note: You can also watch the end position in the Program Monitor. You need to drag the Timeline CTI through the transition to view it.

18 When you settle on a location, return the End slider all the way back to the right. Play the transition.

Using the A/B mode to fine-tune a transition

Because the developers of Adobe Premiere Pro initially created it from the ground up, they had the opportunity to make some fundamental decisions. One was to no longer include A/B editing in the Timeline.

A/B editing is old-school, linear, film-style editing. Film editors frequently use two reels of film: an A-roll and a B-roll, which are usually duplicates made from the same original. The two-reel approach permits cross-dissolves from the A track to the B track.

The advantage of A/B editing in older versions of Premiere was that it let you more easily modify transition positioning and start and end points than you could on single-tracks NLEs.

Here's the good news for both A/B and single-track editing camps: Adobe Premiere Pro includes all of that functionality in its Effect Controls panel.

Working with the Effect Controls panel's A/B feature

The Effect Controls A/B editing mode splits a single video track into two subtracks. What would normally be two consecutive and contiguous clips on a single track are now displayed as individual clips on separate subtracks, giving you the option to apply a transition between them, to manipulate their head and tail frames—or handles—and to change other transition elements.

1   Continue where you left off in Lesson 6-2, or open Lesson 6-3.

2   Click on the Push transition that is applied between clips one and two to display its parameters in the Effect Controls panel.

3   Open the A/B timeline in the Effect Controls panel by clicking the Show/Hide Timeline View button (⊗) in the upper right corner.

Note: You might need to expand the width of the Effect Controls panel to make the Show/Hide Timeline View button available. Also, the Effect Controls timeline may already be visible. Clicking the Show/Hide Timeline View button in the Effect Controls panel toggles it on and off.

4   Drag the border (pointer illustrated in the next figure) between the A/B timeline and the transition parameters section to expand the view of the timeline.

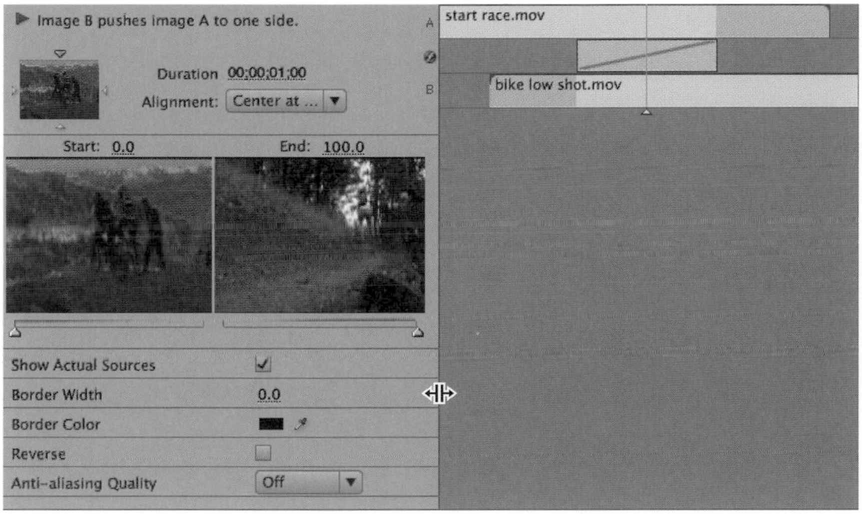

5   Hover the pointer over the white edit line at the center of the transition rectangle (shown in the next figure).

That's the edit point between the two clips, and the pointer that appears there is the Rolling Edit tool (‡)—the same Rolling Edit tool you encountered in the Trim panel.

6   Drag the Rolling Edit tool left and right, and note how the changing Out point of the left clip and the changing In point of the right clip show up in the Program Monitor.

Note: As was the case when you used the Rolling Edit tool in the Trim panel, moving it left or right does not change the overall length of the sequence.

7   Move the pointer slightly to the left or right of the edit line and notice that it changes to the Slide tool (↔).

8   Use the Slide tool to drag the transition rectangle left and right.

Note: That changes the start and end points of the transition without changing its overall length (default duration: 1 second). The new start and end points show up in the Program Monitor, but unlike using the Rolling Edit tool, moving the transition rectangle by using the Slide tool does not change the edit point between the two clips.

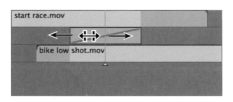

9   Click the Alignment menu, and click through the three available options: Center At Cut, Start At Cut, and End At Cut.

Note: The transition rectangle moves to a new location as you make each change. These three locations mimic the options when you drag a transition to the Timeline. Also, if you manually change the transition location, the Custom Start alignment option becomes available.

10   Drag an end (it doesn't matter which end) of the viewing area bar to the edge of the A/B timeline.

As shown in the next figure, that expands your view of the two adjacent clips so you can see the beginning of the left clip and the end of the right clip.

Viewing area bar

11 Drag the right and left edges of the transition to lengthen it.

Two other ways to change transition duration

You can also change the duration value by typing a new time or by clicking the duration time and dragging left or right to decrease or increase its value.

Note: *As you lengthen the transition, the viewing area bar shrinks, thereby allowing you to drag its ends yet again to expand the area viewed in the A/B timeline.*

Dealing with inadequate (or no) head or tail handles

Eventually you will want to place transitions at edit points where you don't have adequate head or tail handles (footage beyond the In or Out point of your clip). This might be because you paused the camcorder too soon or didn't get it started fast enough. You might want to add a transition to ease what would be an abrupt cut edit. Adobe Premiere Pro deals elegantly with that.

1 Open the Lesson 6-4 project. Notice that the two clips on the timeline have no "heads or tails." You can tell this because of the little triangles in the corners of the clips: the triangles indicate the very ends of the clips.

2 Using the standard Selection tool, drag the right edge of the last clip to the left, and release. Notice the little triangle at the end of that clip is no longer visible. Stretch the clip back to its full length.

3   Drag the Dissolve transition to that edit point between the two clips.
You will get the "Insufficient Media" alert. Click OK.

4   Click the transition to display it in the Effect Controls panel, and note that the transition rectangle has parallel diagonal lines running through it, indicating the lack of head or tail frames.

5   Lengthen the transition to about 3 seconds by dragging the right and left edges of the transition rectangle.

Note: The A and B clips retain their light blue color, indicating there are no head or tail frames available for overlap.

6   Drag the CTI slowly through the entire transition, and watch how it works:

- For the first half of the transition (up to the edit point), the B clip is a freeze frame while the A clip continues to play.

- At the edit point, the A clip becomes a freeze frame and the B clip starts to play.

- When played at regular speed (at the default one-second duration), few viewers would notice the freeze frames.

When only one clip has no head or tail handles

In this lesson's example, both the A and B clips have no head or tail handle frames. Frequently only one clip has no head or tail room. In those cases, Adobe Premiere Pro forces placement of the transition to start or end at the edit point, depending on which clip lacks extra frames for the overlap.

You can override that by dragging the transition into the clip lacking extra frames. The next figure shows examples of both circumstances with the transition centered. The diagonal lines indicate that freeze frames will take the place of the head or tail frames.

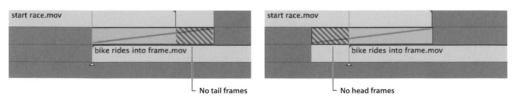

The transition on the left has no extra tail frames. The one on the right has no extra head frames.

Audio transitions

Transitions are not just for video. Adding a cross-fade transition to the end of an audio clip is a really fast way to add a fade in or fade out to an audio clip.

1   Still in the Lesson 6-4 project, play the timeline, and notice the abrupt start and end volume of the soundtrack.

2   Click the Crossfade bin inside the audio transitions bin in the Effects panel.

3   Drag the Constant Power transition to the beginning of the audio clip in Audio Track 1. Play the timeline, and notice the transition has created a fade in to the music soundtrack.

4   Position the CTI on the timeline at the end of the music clip, and press Shift+Ctrl+D in Windows or Shift+Command+D in Mac OS. This is the keyboard shortcut to add the default audio transition to the edit point near the CTI—a very fast way to add a fade in or fade out to an audio track.

5   Drag the length of the audio transition to be longer or shorter, and listen to the effect when you play the timeline.

Transitions are fun and interesting to add to your project. However, overuse of transitions is the common giveaway of an amateur video. When choosing a transition, make sure it adds meaning to your project rather than showing off how many editing tricks you know. Watch your favorite movies and TV shows to learn how the pros use transitions.

Review

▶ Review questions

1   How do you change the default transition duration?

2   How do you track down a transition by name?

3   How do you replace a transition with another one?

4   You apply a transition, but it doesn't show up in the Effect Controls panel. Why not?

5   Some transitions start as small squares, circles, or other geometric shapes, and then grow to reveal the next clip. How do you get those transitions to start with *large* geometric shapes that shrink to reveal the next clip?

6   Explain three ways to change the duration of a transition.

7   What is an easy way to fade audio at the beginning or end of a clip?

▶ Review answers

1   There are two ways to change the default transition duration. 1: Choose Edit > Preferences > General (Windows) or Premiere Pro > Preferences > General (Mac OS) and change the Video Transition Duration from the default 30 frames (one second) to whatever length you want. 2: In the Effects panel, choose Default Transition Duration from the panel menu. That too opens the General Preferences dialog box.

2   Start typing the transition name in the Contains text box in the Effects panel. As you type, Adobe Premiere Pro displays all effects and transitions (audio and video) that have that letter combination anywhere in their names. Type more letters to narrow down your search.

3   Drag the replacement transition on top of the transition you're rejecting. The new one automatically replaces the old one.

4   Click on the newly placed transition to select it. That displays its parameters in the Effect Controls panel.

5   Simple. Select the Reverse option in the Effect Controls panel. That switches the movement from starting small and ending fullscreen to starting fullscreen and ending small.

6   Drag the edge of the transition rectangle in the Timeline, do the same thing in the Effect Controls panel A/B timeline, or change the Duration value in the Effect Controls panel.

7   An easy way to fade audio in or out is to apply an audio crossfade transition to the beginning or end of a clip.

Title Styles ×

KozukaMinchoStd Slant Lime 28

Styles

Titler

strokes

Gears of Progress

supers

Director
Producer
Actors
Videographer

The Adobe Premiere Pro Titler is a multi-faceted, feature-rich text and shape creation tool. You can use it to build text—of any size, color, or style—with borders, beveled edges, shadows, textures, and sheens. Your Titler-designed text and objects can run superimposed over video as static titles, rolling credits, or as standalone clips.

7 Creating Dynamic Titles

Topics covered in this lesson:

- Strengthen your project with supers

- Changing text parameters

- Building text from scratch

- Putting text on a path

- Creating shapes

- Making text roll and crawl

- Text effects: sheens, strokes, shadows, and fill

Getting started

Onscreen text helps tell your story. Your message can be reinforced through supers (superimposed text), giving a location or an interviewee's name and title, onscreen bulleted points, opening titles, and closing credits.

Text can present information much more succinctly and clearly than narration. It can also reinforce narrated and visual information by reminding viewers about the people in your piece and the message you're trying to convey.

The Adobe Premiere Pro Titler offers you a full range of text- and shape-creation options. You can use any font on your computer. Your text and objects can be any color (or multiple colors), any degree of transparency, and a multiplicity of shapes. Using the Path tool, you can place your text on the most convoluted curved line you can imagine. The Titler is an engaging and powerful tool.

Its infinite customizability means that you can create a look unique to your productions.

Strengthen your project with titles

Consider this opening sequence: a telephoto shot of scorched desert sand with rippling heat distorting the scene. Dry, desiccated, lifeless sagebrush. A lizard slowly seeking shade beneath a small stone. And a small plume of dust in the distance. Attention-getting stuff.

Now a narrator intones, "The summer heat beats down on the Bonneville Salt Flats." Effective. But even better is a title: Bonneville Salt Flats. Then, as the plume of dust moves toward the camera, another super: Speed Trials—Summer 2005. Then a rocket-shaped vehicle screams through the scene.

Rather than interrupt the building suspense with a sonorous narrator, save him for later. Instead, simply use titles to set up your story.

Here are other instances in which text can be an effective alternative to voice-overs:

• Instead of using a voice-over to say, "Sue Smith, vice president of manufacturing for Acme Industries," put that information in a super at the bottom of the screen.

• Instead of narrating a collection of statistics, use bulleted points that pop up onscreen with each new item.

Text strengthens your project.

Changing text parameters

In this lesson you start with some formatted text and then change its parameters. This approach is a good way to get a quick overview of the powerful features of the Adobe Premiere Pro Titler. Later in this lesson you'll build basic text from scratch.

1 Start Adobe Premiere Pro, and open the Lesson 7-1 project.

2 Double-click Lesson 7-1 Start Text in the Project panel.

That opens the Titler with a title already loaded over a video frame. Here's a quick rundown on the Titler's panels:

- **Titler main panel**—The screen where you build and view text and graphics.
- **Title Properties**—Text and graphic options such as font characteristics and effects.
- **Title Styles**—Preset text styles. You can choose from several libraries of styles.
- **Title Actions**—Use to align, center, or distribute text and groups of objects.
- **Title Tools**—Define text boundaries, set text paths, and select geometric shapes.

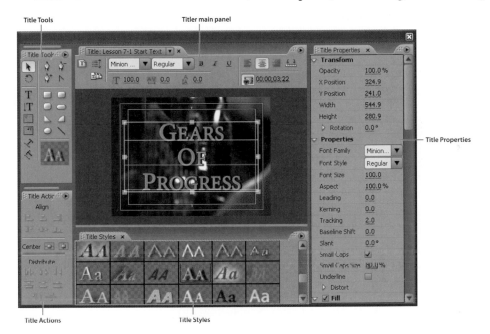

3   Click several different thumbnails in the Title Styles panel.

They instantly change your text to the new style. When done, return to the original style selection: Info Bronze (shown in the next figure).

Note: Styles are fonts with preset properties such as bold, italic, size, and slant, as well as effects such as fill color and style, stroke, sheen, and shadow.

4 Click the Font Browser menu in the Titler. Note the current font is Minion Pro.

5 Scroll through the fonts and note that as you select a new font you see immediately how it'll work with your text.

Note: With all the clicking and testing, you might have deselected the text. If there is no bounding box with handles around the text, select the text by clicking the Selection tool (upper left corner) and clicking anywhere in the text.

6 Click the Font Family menu in the Title Properties panel on the right of the Titler.

7 Change the font family to Times New Roman and in the Font Style menu below that, change the font style to Bold Italic.

The changes show up immediately in the Titler screen.

8 Change the font size to 125 by dragging the Font Size number or typing the new value.

9 Deselect Small Caps. Your screen should look like the next figure.

Note: Small Caps puts all selected objects into uppercase. Any size to less than 100% shrinks all but the first character of each word.

Title-safe margin

10 Change the Aspect to 80% to shrink the horizontal scale of the text so it fits within the width of the title-safe margin, defined by the smaller of the two rectangles (noted in the previous figure).

Note: NTSC TV sets cut off the edges of a video signal. Keeping text within the title-safe margin (also called the title-safe zone) ensures viewers will see all of your text.

11 Click the Vertical Center and Horizontal Center buttons in the Title Actions panel.

12 Change Leading to –10 to shrink the distance between the lines of type so the text appears above the bottom of the title-safe margin.

13 Click Info Bronze to change the text back to its original style.

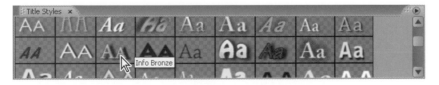

14 Drag the Titler floating window to the right—far enough to be able to see the Project panel.

15 In the Project panel, double-click Lesson 7-1 Finish Text to load it in the Titler.

16 Switch between the two titles by using the panel menu in the Titler main panel. Your text should look similar to Lesson 7-1 Finish Text.

17 Close the Titler by clicking the little x in the upper right corner (Windows) or the close button (Mac OS).

Note: Adobe Premiere Pro automatically saves your updated Lesson 7-1 Start Text in the project file. It does not show up as a separate file on your hard drive.

18 Drag Lesson 7-1 Start Text from the Project panel to the Video 2 track on the Timeline, trim it so it fits above the video clip, and drag the CTI through it to see how it looks over that video clip.

19 Delete the title from the timeline.

Note: You can apply transitions to titles to fade them up or move them on or off the screen.

💡 Using titles in other projects

You are likely to create title templates for location names and interviewee supers, that you can use in multiple projects. However, Adobe Premiere Pro does not automatically save titles as separate files. To make a title available for use in another project, select the title in the Project panel, choose File > Export > Title, give your title a name, choose a location, and click Save. Later, you can simply import that title file the same way you import any other asset.

Extra credit: Other title properties options

Double-click Lesson 7-1 Start Text to reopen the Titler, and then check out four other text-related options. First select the text by using the Selection tool, and then adjust these properties:

- **Kerning**—Adjusts spacing between selected character pairs.

- **Tracking**—Adjusts spacing for a group of characters.

- **Baseline Shift**—Specifies the distance of the characters from the baseline—the thin white line running through the bottoms of each line of characters. Raise or lower selected type to create superscripts or subscripts.

- **Distort**—Stretches text along its x and y axes.

Building text from scratch

The Titler offers three approaches to creating text, each offering both a horizontal and vertical text-direction option:

- **Point text**—Builds a text bounding box as you type. The text runs on one line until you press Enter or Return or choose Word Wrap from the Title menu. Changing the shape and size of the box changes the shape and size of the text.

- **Paragraph (area) text**—You set the size and shape of the text box before entering text. Changing the box size later displays more or less text, but does not change the shape or size of the text.

- **Text on a path**—You build a path for the text to follow by clicking points in the text screen to create curves, and then adjusting the shape and direction of those curves.

The Titler text tools. Selecting a tool from the left or right side determines whether the text will orient horizontally or vertically.

Since Adobe Premiere Pro CS3 automatically saves text to the project file, you can switch to a new or different title and not lose whatever you've created in the current title. That's what you'll do now.

1   If the Titler is open, move the Titler floating window so you can see the main menu.

2   Choose File > New > Title to open the New Title dialog box (Ctrl+T in Windows or Command+T in Mac OS).

3   Type *Bike Title* in the Name box, and click OK.

Note: Before version 2.0, Adobe Premiere Pro saved all titles as independent files separate from the project file. You can import titles created in older versions of Adobe Premiere Pro just as you import any asset. When you save the project, the imported titles are saved with the project, not as separate files. The old files remain unchanged.

4   Drag the timecode (to the right of the Show Video button) to change the video frame displayed in the text screen.

This can come in handy if you want to position text relative to the video contents or check how the text looks over your video.

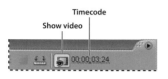

5   Click the Show Video button to hide the video clip.

💡 **Checkerboard pattern signifies transparency**

The background now consists of a grayscale checkerboard, which signifies a transparency. That is, if you place text created in the Titler on a video track above other video clips, the video on lower tracks will be visible wherever you see that checkerboard. You can also create text or geometric objects with some transparency. In that case, you'll see the checkerboard through an object, which means the video will show through but will appear as if it's covered with smoked or tinted glass.

6   Click the Birch White 80 style (the third style of this style group).

7   Click the Type tool (**T**)—shortcut T—and click anywhere in the Titler screen.

The Type tool creates point text.

8   Start typing. For the purposes of this exercise, type *Changing Gears*.

Note: *If you continue typing, you will note that point text does not wrap. Your text will run off the screen to the right. To make it wrap when it reaches the title-safe margin, choose Title > Word Wrap. To begin a new line, press Enter or Return.*

9   Click the Selection tool (the black arrow in the upper left corner of the Title Tools panel). That puts handles on the text bounding box.

Note: In this case, the Selection tool keyboard shortcut, V, won't work, because you are typing inside a text bounding box.

10   Drag the corners and edges of the text bounding box and note how the text changes size and shape accordingly.

11   Hover the pointer just outside a corner of the text bounding box until a curved line pointer (↰) appears. Then drag to rotate the bounding box off its horizontal orientation.

> 💡 **More than one way to move a box**
>
> *Instead of dragging bounding box handles, you can change values in the Transform settings (in the Title Properties panel). Either type new values or position your pointer on a value and drag left or right. Your changes show up immediately in the bounding box.*

12   Click anywhere within the bounding box (the Selection tool is still active) and drag the angled text and its bounding box around the Titler screen.

13   Edit that text by double-clicking anywhere in the text and typing.

You can drag to select text you want to remove or replace.

14   Delete all the text by clicking the Selection tool, which puts handles on the text bounding box indicating the entire frame is selected, and pressing Delete.

15   Click the Area Type tool (▣) and drag a text bounding box into the Titler screen that nearly fills the title-safe zone.

The Area Type tool creates paragraph text.

> ### Turning off safe margins
>
> *You can turn off the title-safe margins or action-safe margins by opening the Titler panel menu (or choosing Title > View) and then choosing Safe Title Margin or Safe Action margin, respectively.*

16 Start typing. This time, type enough characters to go beyond the end of the bounding box.

Unlike point text, area text remains within the confines of the bounding box you defined. It wraps at the bounding box borders. Press Enter or Return to go down a line.

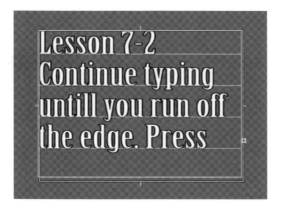

17 Click the Selection tool and change the size and shape of the bounding box.

The text does not change size. Instead, it adjusts its position on the bounding box baselines. If you make the box too small for all your text, the extra text scrolls below the bottom edge of the bounding box. In that case, a small plus sign (+) appears near the lower right corner outside the bounding box.

18 Double-click within the text to edit it.

19 Switch to the Selection tool, click anywhere in the text bounding box, and press Delete to remove the text.

𝒬 **Vertical text**

While you're testing your text, try the vertically oriented Vertical Type tool and Vertical Area Type tool. They create text with each character standing on top of the next one.

Putting text on a path

The Path Type tool is both elegant and tricky. It enables you to build paths that are simple or complex, straight and/or curved, for your text to follow.

If you've worked with the Pen tool in Adobe Photoshop or Adobe Illustrator, you know how to use the Path Type tool. You define a path by creating a number of points in the Titler screen and dragging handles at each point to define curves.

1 Select the Path Type tool (✧).

2 Click and drag anywhere in the Titler screen.

That creates an anchor point with handles. You'll use those handles to define the curve's characteristics. If you only click without dragging, you won't add handles. It's tricky to add them later.

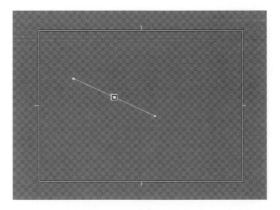

3 Click and drag somewhere else to create another anchor point with handles.

The Titler automatically creates a curved path between the two anchor points.

Note: You can add as many anchor points as you choose. Each new point outside the confines of the current bounding box expands the bounding box dimensions. Delete points by selecting the Delete Anchor Point tool (see next figure) and clicking on an anchor.

4   Click the Pen tool (✒).

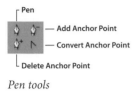

Pen tools

5   Hover that pointer over the handles (your pointer changes to a black arrow, as shown in the next figure) and drag the handles.

Make them longer, shorter, or just move them around to see how they work.

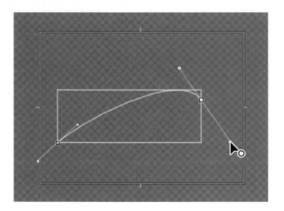

6   Drag the anchor points to lengthen or shorten the path.

7   Click anywhere inside the newly created bounding box.

That places a blinking text insertion point at the beginning of the curved line.

8   Type some text. Your Titler screen should look something like the next figure.

If you're having trouble with the Pen tool, double-click Lesson 7-2 Text in the Project panel and work with it.

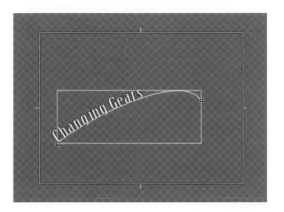

You will want to practice creating path text if you want to master the technique, but for now just try to get a basic idea of how it works.

Creating shapes

If you've created shapes in graphics-editing software such as Photoshop or Illustrator, you know how to create geometric objects in Adobe Premiere Pro.

Simply select from the various shapes in the Title Tools panel, drag and draw the outline, and release the mouse button.

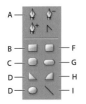

Shape drawing tools. **A.** *Pen* **B.** *Rectangle* **C.** *Rounded Corner Rectangle* **D.** *Wedge* **E.** *Ellipse*
F. *Clipped Corner Rectangle* **G.** *Rounded Rectangle* **H.** *Arc* **I.** *Line*

1 Press Ctrl+T in Windows or Command+T in Mac OS to open a new title. Type *Shapes* in the Name box in the New Title dialog box, and click OK.

2 Select the Rectangle tool (R) and drag in the Titler screen to create a rectangle.

Note: *Not all shape tools have keyboard shortcuts.*

3   Click different title styles while the rectangle is still selected. Notice that title styles affect shapes as well as text. Click the first style (Caslon Pro 68) for a simple style with no shading, outlines, or shadows.

4   Shift-drag in another location to create a square.

Note: Pressing Shift creates shapes with symmetrical properties: circles, squares, and equilateral triangles. To maintain the aspect ratio while resizing a shape you've already made, hold down the Shift key before making the change.

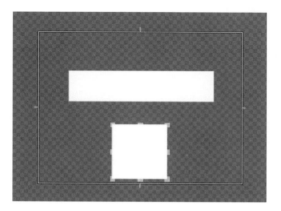

5   Click the Selection tool, drag it in the Titler screen to marquee-select the two objects, and press Delete to make a clean slate.

6   Select the Rounded Corner Rectangle tool and Alt-drag (Windows) or Option-drag (Mac OS) to draw from the center of the shape.

The center remains in the spot where you first clicked, and the figure changes shape and size around that point as you drag.

7   Choose the Clipped Corner Rectangle tool, and Shift+Alt-drag (Windows) or Shift+Option-drag (Mac OS) to constrain the aspect ratio and draw from the center.

8   Select the Arc tool (A) and drag diagonally across the corner points to flip the shape diagonally as you draw.

9   Click the Wedge tool (W) and drag across, up, or down to flip the shape horizontally or vertically as you draw.

Note: *To flip the shape after you've drawn it, use the Selection tool to drag a corner point in the direction you want it to flip.*

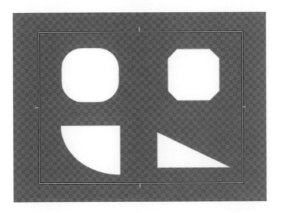

10 Marquee-select those four objects, and press Delete to make another clean slate.

11 Select the Line tool (L) and drag to create a single line.

12 Select the Pen tool and click to create an anchor point (don't drag to create handles).

13 Click again in the Titler screen where you want the segment to end (or Shift-click to constrain the segment's angle to a multiple of 45 degrees). This creates another anchor point.

14 Continue clicking the Pen tool to create additional straight segments. The last anchor point you add appears as a large square, indicating that it is selected.

15 Complete the path by doing one of the following:

• To close the path, move the Pen tool to the initial anchor point. When it is directly over the initial anchor point, a circle appears underneath the pen pointer (highlighted in the next figure). Click to make the connection.

- To leave the path open, Ctrl-click (Windows) or Command-click (Mac OS) anywhere away from all objects, or select a different tool in the Title Tools panel.

Experiment with the different shape options. Try overlapping them and using different styles. The possibilities are endless.

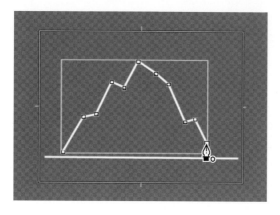

Making text roll and crawl

Using the Titler, you can make rolling text for opening and closing credits and crawling text for items such as headline bulletins.

1 Choose Title > New Title > Default Roll.

2 Name it *Rolling Credits,* and click OK.

3 Type some text.

Create placeholder credits as in the following figure, pressing Enter or Return after each line. Type enough text to more than fill the screen vertically.

Note: *With rolling text selected, the Titler automatically adds a scroll bar along the right side that enables you to view your text as it runs off the bottom of the screen. If you select one of the Crawl options, that scroll bar will appear at the bottom to enable you to view text running off the right or left edge of the screen.*

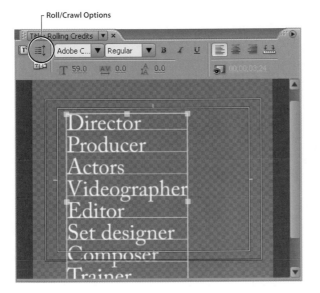

4   Click the Roll/Crawl Options button (highlighted in the previous figure).

You have the following options (shown in the next figure):

- **Still**—Changes the credits to a still title.

- **Roll**—Should be selected already, because this title was created as rolling credits.

- **Crawl Left, Crawl Right**—Indicates the crawl direction (rolling text always moves up the screen).

- **Start Off Screen**—Controls whether the credits start completely off the screen and roll on, or begin with the uppermost text item at the top or side of the screen.

- **End Off Screen**—Indicates whether the credits roll completely off the screen.

- **Pre-Roll**—Specifies the number of frames before the first words appear on screen.

- **Ease-In**—The number of frames at the beginning to gradually increase the speed of the roll or crawl from zero to its full speed.

- **Ease-Out**—The number of frames to slow down the roll or crawl at its end.

- **Post-Roll**—The number of frames that play after the roll or crawl ends.

Roll/Crawl Options

Title Type
- ○ Still
- ⦿ Roll
- ○ Crawl Left
- ○ Crawl Right

OK

Cancel

Timing (Frames)
- ☐ Start Off Screen   ☐ End Off Screen

| Preroll | Ease-In | Ease-Out | Postroll |
| 0 | 0 | 0 | 0 |

5   Select Start Off Screen and End Off Screen, and type *5* for Ease-In and Ease-Out.

6   Close the Titler.

7   Drag your newly created Rolling Credits to the Video 2 track of the Timeline above the video clip (if another title is there, drag this one directly on top of it to do an overlay edit).

Note: The default length of rolling or crawling credits is 5 seconds. If you change the length of the credits clip, that changes the speed. A longer clip length means slower rolling credits.

8   With the sequence selected, press the spacebar to view your rolling credits.

Note: If you're having trouble with rolling or crawling text, open the Lesson 7-3 project to work with the credits as described here.

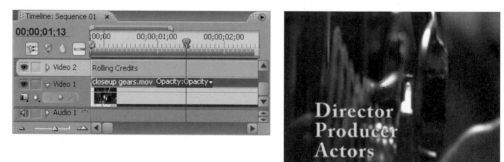

Text effects: Sheens, strokes, shadows, and fill

Reverse engineering can be a good learning tool. So in this mini-lesson you will deconstruct one of the many built-in templates that come with Adobe Premiere Pro to learn how to work with Titler's effects..

Unlike styles, templates are a combination of background graphics, geometric shapes, and placeholder text. They are organized into themes with enough variety for just about any circumstance.

They are tremendously useful. You can easily customize graphic themes to suit your needs or build your own templates from scratch and save them for future projects.

1 Choose Title > New Title > Based On Template.

Note: You can also open the Titler and choose Title > Templates to get to the same Templates screen.

2 Open as many template folders and click through as many templates as you like.

3 Open the Lower Thirds folder, select Lower Third 1024, and click OK.

Note: This is a good template to experiment with because it has a full range of effects, including four-color gradient, reduced opacity (transparency), sheen, stroke, and shadows.

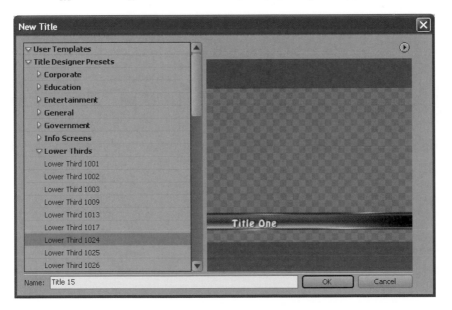

4 Click the Selection tool (V) and move it over the template.

Bounding boxes appear, delineating the three components of this title: *Title One* text, a brown and yellow rectangle, and a black rectangle superimposed over the right side of the brown and yellow rectangle.

5 Drag each bounding box in turn up the screen so you can see the template's three components.

Your Titler screen should look something like the next figure.

Note: If you have trouble selecting the components, double-click the Lesson 7-4 project in the Project panel to open a disassembled version of the template.

6 Drag the top edge of the brown and yellow rectangle to expand it.

That selects it and displays its characteristics in the Titler Properties panel.

7 Collapse the Transform and Properties areas in the panel to make some room.

8 Expand Fill, Sheen (in the Fill section), Strokes, and Outer Strokes (no inner strokes are used in this template).

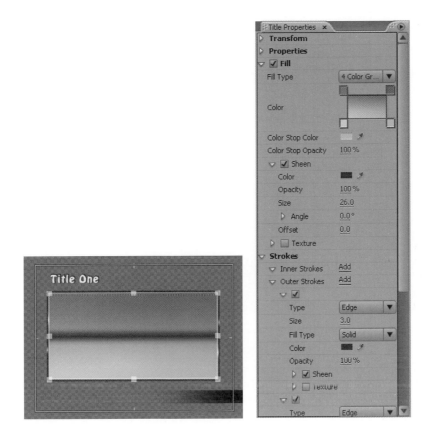

9 Open the Fill Type pop up menu for Fill and select each option in turn to see what they do. When done, return to 4 Color Gradient as shown in the figure above.

10 Double-click one or two of the four color-stop boxes around the 4 Color Gradient display to open the Color Picker. Select new colors.

Note: Each color is slightly different from the other three, and the colors at the top are slightly darker than the bottom colors. This gives this rectangle extra depth.

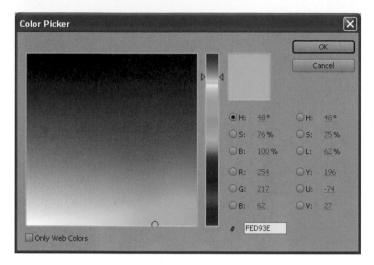

💡 Lift a color from your video

Instead of using the Color Picker to change the color stop color, use the Eyedropper tool to select a color from your video. Click the Show Video button at the top of the Titler main panel, move to a frame you want to use by dragging the timecode left or right, drag the Eyedropper tool into your video scene, and click in a color that suits your needs.

11 Change the color-stop opacities by clicking each Color Stop box, and changing its opacity setting.

Note: You can change the opacity (transparency) of any color applied to any object or text, be it fill, sheen, or stroke. You can give a geometric shape or text a solid-color stroke border and convert its fill color to 0% opacity to display only its edges.

12 Click the Sheen color box and change its color, opacity, size, angle, and offset.

Note: Sheen is a soft-edged color that typically runs horizontally through shapes or text. In this case, it's the brown, horizontal line that runs through the entire rectangle.

13 Click the two Outer Stroke disclosure triangles to expand the parameters.

Strokes are outer or inner borders on text or graphic objects. They have the same collection of properties available for text and other Titler objects. In this case, both strokes are 3 points wide and they fall adjacent to one another.

14 Change the size of the two outer strokes to 25 points each. As shown in the next figure, that more clearly displays the sheen applied to these borders.

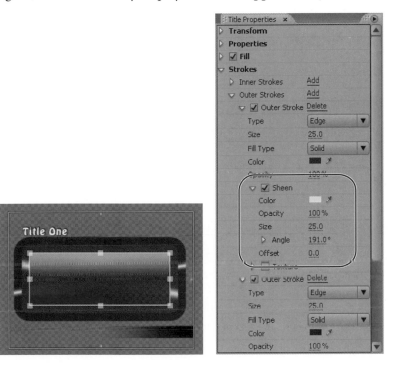

💡 Sheen artistry

Take a look at the sheen properties for both outer strokes. Note that the angles are 191 degrees and 351 degrees (270 and 90 degrees are horizontal). That is, each sheen appears just a bit above the center line on one side and a bit below the center line on the other. If the sheens were to run through the entire box, they'd form an X. This is a clever bit of visual artistry. Before you expanded the rectangle, the sheens were on the top and bottom edges. In this taller mode, they are along the sides. To see how that works, drag the rectangle's bounding box top edge up and down and watch the sheens move along the edges.

15   Click the word *Add* next to Inner Strokes. That opens the Inner Stroke property.

16   Check the Inner Stroke box to turn on its parameters and experiment with this new stroke by changing its Size, Fill Type, Color, and Opacity settings.

Note: Adding a sheen or a shadow to an object is just as easy. Just select the object in the Titler screen, check the appropriate properties box, and adjust the parameters.

17   Click the Title One text to select it, and then open its Shadow properties.

Title One doesn't have an obvious shadow because the shadow size is only 2 points. It's more like an outer stroke.

18   Change all the characteristics to see how the Shadow feature works.

Take a look at the example in the next figure. Everything is self-explanatory, with the exception of Spread. Increasing the Spread value softens the shadow.

19   Select the black gradient rectangle in the drawing area of the title and take a look at its 4 Color Gradient style.

All the color stops are black. This template's designer set an opacity of 0 percent (completely transparent) to the color stops on the left side and 100 percent (opaque) to the stops on the right side. In that way, the black rectangle's opacity gradually changes to give text appearing on it a more dramatic look.

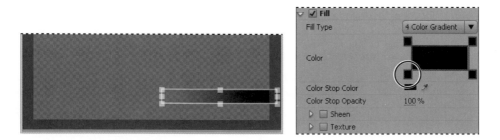

Experiment with effects

You can learn a lot by experimenting with effects. Open a new title, select a style, and draw an object. Do this with several distinctly different styles. Then open the Fill, Strokes, and Shadow properties, and make lots of changes to each object.

Create some new outer and inner strokes. Add sheens. Check a Texture box, and add any graphic image or Photoshop CS3 file to add some real pizzazz to your text and object.

The more you play with the Titler, the more you'll come to appreciate its depth and creative possibilities.

Review

▶ Review questions

1 What are the differences between point text and area (or paragraph) text?

2 Why display the title-safe margin?

3 What's the difference between a style and a template when using the Titler?

4 Describe two ways to change a font.

5 How do you create a circle in a square?

6 How do you apply a stroke or a sheen?

▶ Review answers

1 You create point text with the Type tool. Its bounding box expands as you type. Changing the box shape changes the text size and shape accordingly. When you use the Area Type tool, you define a bounding box, and the characters remain within its confines. Changing the box's shape displays more or fewer characters.

2 NTSC TV sets cut off the edges of the TV signal. The amount lost varies from set to set. Displaying the title-safe margin and keeping your text within its borders ensures that viewers will see all of your title.

3 A style can be applied to characters or objects you create in the Titler. Templates give you a starting point to create your own full-featured graphic or text backgrounds.

4 With the text object selected, either click the Font pop-up menu and select a new font, or click the Font Browser menu in the Title main panel and view the fonts before choosing.

5 Hold down the Shift key as you draw using the Rectangle tool. Then hold down Alt+Shift or Option+Shift when using the Ellipse or Rounded Rectangle tool and click in the center of the square to place the center of the circle there. (You could drag a circle inside the square later, but this is more elegant.)

6 Select the text or object to edit and check its Stroke (Outer or Inner) or Sheen box. Then start adjusting parameters, and they will show up on the object.

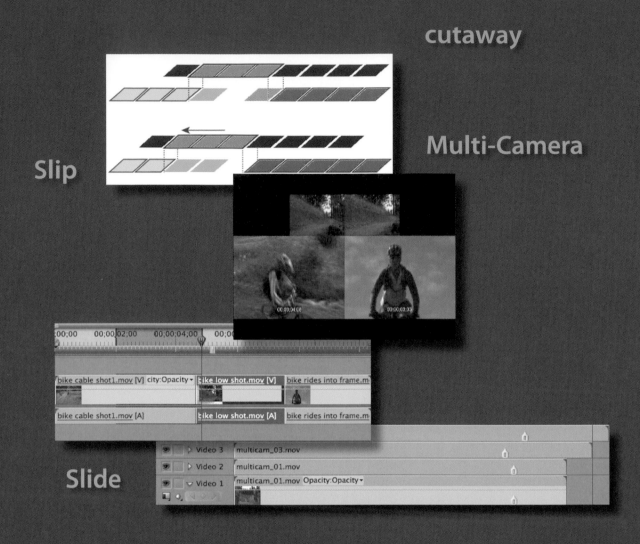

cutaway

Slip

Multi-Camera

Slide

Time to take a break from single-topic lessons and delve into some specialized editing tools and techniques. In this lesson, you will use editing tools that can save you a lot of time. Generate custom transitions to match whatever mood you want to create.

8 | Applying Specialized Editing Tools

Topics covered in this lesson:

- Timesaving editing tools

- Slicing and moving clips

- Custom transitions

Getting started

In this lesson, you try out three specialized editing tools—Rolling Edit, Slip, and Slide—and two Program Monitor buttons—Lift and Extract. All can simplify certain tasks. Using the Track Select tool, you will move entire timelines or portions of timelines with ease. You will learn about transitions that require the use of graphics.

Then you will dive into multi-camera editing. If you ever have a multi-camera video shoot, this feature will save you a lot of time in switching between camera angles

Timesaving editing tools

You use the first three tools—Rolling Edit, Slide, and Slip—for a variety of situations, including when you want to preserve the overall length of your program. They come in handy for precisely timed projects such as 30-second advertisements. You've seen the Rolling Edit tool in action in the Trim panel.

You've worked with extract edits and lift edits by using the drag-and-drop method. In this mini-lesson, you will use the Program Monitor's Extract and Lift buttons to remove selected groups of frames—even when they're spread out over one or more clips.

In some cases, it can be easier to make individual edits and forgo these specialized tools, but it's good for any video editor to know how to use all five of them:

- **Rolling edit**—Rolls the cut point between two adjacent clips, shortening one and lengthening the other (thereby retaining the overall length of the project).

- **Slide edit**—Slides the entire clip over two adjacent clips, shortening and lengthening those adjacent clips without changing the selected clip's length or In and Out points.

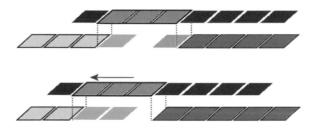

The slide edit changes the In and Out points of adjacent clips while retaining the original clip's edit points.

- **Slip edit**—Slips a clip under two adjacent clips. Slip changes a clip's starting and ending frames without changing its duration or affecting adjacent clips.

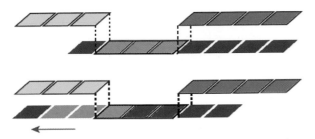

The slip edit changes the In and Out points of the selected clip while retaining the adjacent clip's edit points.

Note: *Though Slip and Slide tools are typically employed on the center clip of three adjacent clips, each tool functions normally even if the clip is adjacent to a clip on one side and a blank space on the other. For the Rolling Edit, Slip, and Slide tools to work as expected, there need to be sufficient unused head or tail frames to make the edits.*

- **Extract edit**—Removes a selected range of frames and closes the gap by moving the following clips to the left.

- **Lift edit**—Removes a selected range of frames and leaves a gap.

Making rolling, slide, and slip edits

1   Start Adobe Premiere Pro, and open the Lesson 8-1.prproj project.

2   Open Sequence 01 in the Timeline, if it is not already open.

There are three clips already on the timeline, with enough head and tail frames to allow the edits you're about to make.

3 Select the Rolling Edit tool (keyboard shortcut N) in the Tools panel.

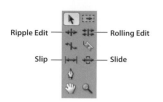

4 Drag the edit point between Clip A and Clip B (the first two clips on the Timeline), using the Program Monitor split screen to find a better matching edit.

Try rolling the edit point to the left 00;26 (26 frames). You can use the Program Monitor timecode or the pop-up timecode (both shown in the next figure) in the Timeline to find that edit.

Note: *To facilitate making a precise, frame-specific edit, expand the view of the Timeline by pressing the equal sign (=) key.*

The Rolling Edit tool changes the Out and In points of adjacent clips.

5   Select the Slide tool (U) and position it over the middle clip.

6   Drag the second clip left or right.

This is just to demonstrate the edit. You don't need to find a specific edit point.

7   Take a look at the Program Monitor as you perform the slide edit.

The two top images are the In point and Out point of Clip B. They do not change. The two larger images are the Out point and In point of the adjacent clips—Clip A and Clip C, respectively. These edit points change as you slide the selected clip over those adjacent clips.

Note: *As you move the clip, you will eventually run out of head or tail frames, and the timecodes will stop changing in the Program Monitor.*

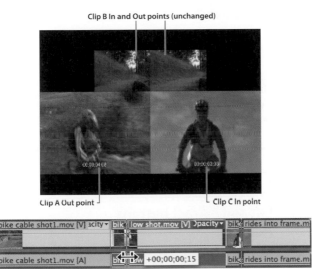

The Slide tool moves a clip over two adjacent clips.

8   Select the Slip tool (Y) and drag Clip B left and right.

9   Take a look at the Program Monitor as you perform the slip edit.

The two top images are the Out point and In point of Clips A and C, respectively. They do not change. The two larger images are the In point and Out point of Clip B. These edit points change as you slip Clip B *under* Clips A and C.

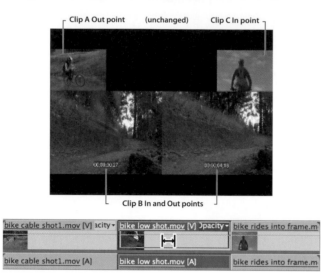

The Slip tool moves a clip under two adjacent clips.

Note: *Try both the Slide and Slip tools on Clips A and C. Both editing tools work on the first or last clips in a sequence.*

Using the Program Monitor's Lift and Extract buttons

1 Click the History tab, and then click New/Open to undo all the rolling, slide, and slip edits you just made.

2 Move the Timeline CTI to about midway on the first clip.

3   Drag a viewing area bar handle (highlighted in the next figure) in the Program Monitor so its CTI is roughly centered. This is simply to make it easier to set In and Out points.

4   Use the jog disk and the Step Forward and Step Back controls in the Program Monitor to advance the CTI to where the second bike lands after the jump. This should be at 00;00;02;00.

5   Click the Set In Point button (I) in the Program Monitor.

6   Drag the Program Monitor CTI within the second clip—to find a matching edit—at about 00;00;04;25.

7   Click the Set Out Point button (O).

As shown in the next figure, your Timeline now has a light blue highlighted zone between the In and Out points, and a gray area in the time ruler with In and Out point brackets at each end.

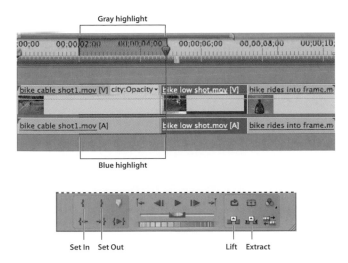

Note: The Lift and Extract buttons look the same until you get really close to the screen. As shown above, Extract has tiny triangles indicating that adjacent clips will fill the gap left by the edit.

8   Click the Lift button.

That deletes those selected frames and leaves a gap.

9   Press Ctrl+Z (Windows) or Command+Z (Mac OS) to undo that edit.

10   Click the Extract button.

That performs the equivalent of a Ripple delete. Play this edit to see how, by clicking only one button, you edited two clips.

Using graphics with transitions

In Lesson 6, we skipped a transition that requires the use of graphics files: The Gradient Wipe transition. Gradient Wipe lets parts of Clip A and Clip B be displayed together using a custom mask, and gradually moves from one scene to the next using a smooth animation. It's like other wipe transitions, but in this case you control the shape of the edges. Clip B shows through the black area, whereas Clip A shows through the white area (you can select the Reverse option in Effect Controls to swap that function). Also, in this case, Adobe Premiere Pro does see things as gray. As the transition progresses, the gray areas darken, and more of Clip B shows through, until at the end of the transition only clip B is onscreen.

1   Create a new sequence by clicking File > New > Sequence and name it *Transitions Seq.*

2   Click the New Item button at the bottom of the Project panel (highlighted in the next figure), and choose Color Matte.

Note: You will use two color mattes—solid color, screen-size graphics—to get a better feel for how these transitions work.

3   Drag the triangles along the color slider to a color you like, click in the screen to pick a shade, and click OK.

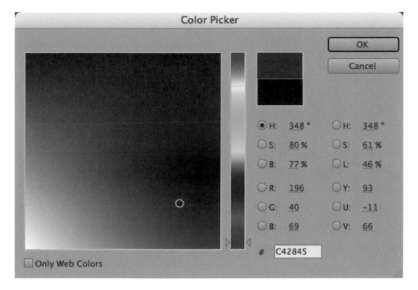

4   Give your color a descriptive name, and click OK.

5   Follow that process again to make another matte with an obviously different color.

💡 Color mattes are useful objects

Now that you know how to make color mattes, consider using them in your projects. For instance, use them if you want a simple color background for text or for pictures-in-pictures. You can tint videos by laying a color matte over a clip and reducing its opacity. We'll look at that kind of compositing later in the book.

6   Drag both color mattes to the new sequence you just created, and press the backslash key (\) to expand your view.

7   Drag Gradient Wipe (from the Wipe transition bin) to the edit point.

Note: The Gradient Wipe Settings dialog box should appear. If not, click the transition rectangle in the Timeline to view its parameters in the Effect Controls panel, and then click Custom.

Gradient Wipe Settings

Select Image

Softness: 10

Cancel   OK

8   Click Select Image, and then double-click Gradient Wipe-1.jpg, and note that it is a simple diagonal gradient.

9   Adjust the softness of the transition's edges by dragging the Softness slider, and then click OK.

10   Drag the CTI through the transition, and note that Clip B increasingly shows through Clip A.

11   Make sure the transition is selected by clicking on it and then select Reverse in the Effect Controls panel and see how that transition works.

12   Click Custom, and try Gradient Wipe-2.jpg. As shown in the next figure (on the right), it uses multiple gradients.

Note: Gradient Wipe can use very elaborate wipes. All you need is basic graphics-creation software. The graphics used in this lesson were made with Adobe Photoshop CS3 because it's so easy to create gradients with it.

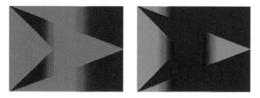

Two Gradient Wipe transitions.

Creating the initial multi-camera sequence

1   Open the Lesson 8-2.prproj project.

2   Double-click multicam_01.mov to open it in the Source Monitor.

3   Move the Source Monitor CTI to where the bikers slap hands after the race, which is at 00;00;16;16.

You will use this as your clapper slate to set the sync point on all four clips.

4   Right-click (Windows) or Control-click (Mac OS) in the Source Monitor time ruler and choose Set Clip Marker > Next Available Numbered.

This adds a little marker triangle behind the Source Monitor CTI (you'll need to drag the CTI out of the way to see that marker).

Note: You can put markers on clips or sequences. You use markers for a variety of purposes, most frequently to mark DVD chapter points in sequences. In this case, you will have Adobe Premiere Pro move the four clips so the markers you place on their sync points all line up vertically.

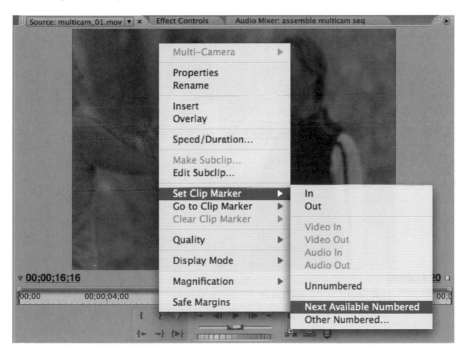

5   Check that the Video 1 track header is targeted (highlighted). If not, click it as needed to target the track, and move the CTI to the beginning of the sequence.

6   Click the Overlay button (Insert will work in this case too) in the Source Monitor to drop multicam_01.mov on Video 1 in the sequence.

Note: All four multicam clips were recorded at the same time, so using the hand slap near the ends of the clips is a good way to sync them all up. Since they are at four different angles, you might have to look closely on some clips to see the exact frame where their hands touch.

7   Repeat the sync point location process, including adding the clip marker, for multicam_02. We selected 00;00;16;29 as the sync point. Add the marker to the clip as you did on the first clip.

8   Click the Video 2 header to target that track, move the CTI to the beginning of the sequence, and click the Overlay button in the Source Monitor.

Your sequence should look like the next figure. Note the marker icons (🔖) in the clips. You will line up those markers in a few steps.

Note: If you clicked the Insert button instead of Overlay, that would have moved the clips in Video 1 to the right.

9   Repeat that process for multicam_03.mov, targeting the Video 3 track, moving the Timeline CTI to the beginning before clicking the Overlay button.

10   Repeat the marker setting and overlay process for multicam_04.mov, except there is no Video 4 track on the timeline, so you can't target a track to overlay it to. Instead of moving the clip with the Overlay button, you can drag it to the timeline. Click somewhere in the Source Monitor window and drag to the gray blank space above Video 3 track and drop it. Adobe Premiere Pro creates the Video 4 track.

Your sequence should look like the next figure. Notice that the markers do not line up. That is OK; we'll take care of that next. If you had trouble marking your clips, open the Lesson 8-3 project to start at this point.

Note: Video clips placed above track 4 will not be available for multi-camera editing.

11 Marquee-select the four clips.

12 Check whether the Video 1 track is targeted (highlighted). If not, click its header to target it (it's not necessary, in this case, to target an audio track).

13 Choose Clip > Synchronize, select Numbered Clip Marker (Marker 0 is the only choice), and then click OK. The clips align to the marker on the clip in Video 1.

All the markers are lined up vertically. The beginning of the clips above Video 1 were trimmed because they all had more video before the sync point than the clip in Video 1.

Note: There are other syncing options. If the timecode had not been changed from the original footage, you could have foregone creating all the markers and selected Timecode.

Switching multiple cameras

Now you will nest that synced and trimmed sequence in another sequence, switch on the multi-camera function, and edit this four-camera shoot.

1 Choose File > New > Sequence, and name it *Multi-cam*.

2 Drag Sequence 01 from the Project panel to the beginning of the Video 1 track on the Multi-cam sequence. This is called nesting a sequence in a sequence.

3 Click the Video 1 track header to target it, click the nested sequence video clip to select it, and then choose Clip > Multi-Camera > Enable.

Note: The Multi-Camera > Enable command will be unavailable unless you have the video track selected.

4   Choose Window > Multi-Camera Monitor.

That opens the five-screen Multi-Camera Monitor.

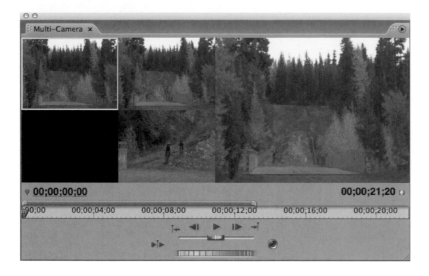

5   Click the Play button and watch this video to get a feel for when to make your edits.

Note: After making your edits, you can go back and change them in the Multi-Camera Monitor or on the Timeline.

6   Move the CTI back to the beginning, click Play, and start clicking any of the four screens on the left side to switch among those cameras.

A red box appears around the selected camera each time you make an edit.

Note: You can also press the number keys 1-4 to switch among the four cameras.

7   Use the playback controls to review your edited sequence.

Note that at each edit point, a yellow box appears on that camera shot.

8   Close the Multi-Camera Monitor.

You can always return to it by selecting it from the Program Monitor panel menu.

9   Take a look at the sequence in the Timeline.

As shown in the next figure, it has multiple cut edits. Each clip's label starts with [MC #]. The number represents the video track used for that edit.

[MC 4] assemble multi | [MC 1] assemble mult | [MC 3] assemble multicam seq [V] Opacity:Opacity ▾

Finalizing multi-camera editing

To change an edit in the Multi-Camera Monitor:

1   Open the Multi-Camera Monitor by choosing Window > Multi-Camera Monitor.

2   Click the Go To Previous (or Next) Edit Point buttons, or use the Page Up or Page Down key to move to an edit.

Go to Previous/Next Edit Point

3   Click a different camera to change that edit.

Changing an edit in the Timeline

1   Right-click (Windows) or Control-click (Mac OS) the clip you want to change.

2   Choose Multi-Camera from the context menu, and click on the camera number.

Multicam tips

•   You can use any of the timeline editing tools to change the edit points of a multicam sequence.

•   You can replay the multicam sequence with the Multi-Camera Monitor from any point to re-edit the project.

•   You can switch back to the sequence where the original clip is and apply effects or color correction (we will talk about color correction in a later lesson), and the effect will ripple to the multicam sequence.

•   If you don't have a good visual clue in the video to sync multiple clips, look for a clap or loud noise in the audio track. It is often easier to sync video by looking for a common spike in the audio waveform.

Note: This example of multicam footage did not include any audio.

Review

▶ **Review questions**

1 What's the basic difference between a slide edit and a slip edit?

2 What's going on when you use the Rolling Edit, Slip, or Slide tool and the clip frames stop moving in the Program Monitor and you can't move the edit point any farther?

3 Is it necessary to have the custom gradient file imported into Adobe Premiere Pro to use it in the Gradient Wipe transition?

4 Describe four ways to set sync points for multi-camera clips.

▶ **Review answers**

1 You slide a clip *over* adjacent clips, retaining the selected clip's original In and Out points. You slip a clip *under* adjacent clips, changing the selected clip's In and Out points.

2 You've reached the end of the line—the beginning or end of the original clip. There are no additional head or tail frames to enable you to move the edit any farther.

3 No. The custom gradient can exist anywhere on your computer. It is not necessary to import it into an Adobe Premiere Pro bin.

4 Clip start, clip end, timecode, and markers. You used markers in the Lesson 8-3 project. If you had access to the original session videotapes, you could have used Timecode or their clapper slate.

interpolation

video effects

velocity

keyframes

Adobe Premiere Pro CS3 features more than 140 video effects—a mind-boggling collection of fantastic visual effects such as lightning, spotlights, and strobe lights. You can use video effects to change color attributes, adjust brightness and contrast, and simulate lens flare. Most effects come with an array of parameters, all of which you can animate—have change over time—by using precise keyframe controls. The possibilities are endless.

9 | Adding Video Effects

Topics covered in this lesson:

- Sampling some basic video effects
- Manipulating keyframes and effect parameters
- Adding keyframe interpolation and velocity
- Keyframing some advanced effects

Getting started

Video effects let you add visual flair or repair technical issues. Video effects can alter the exposure or color of footage, distort images, or add artistic style. You can also use effects to rotate and animate a clip or adjust its size and position within the frame.

Adding video effects is easy: drag to a clip or select the clip and drag the effect to the Effect Controls panel. You can combine as many effects as you like on a single clip, which can produce surprising results. Moreover, you can use a nested sequence to add the same effects to a collection of clips.

Virtually all the video effect parameters are accessible within the Effect Controls panel, making it easy to set the behaviors and the intensity of those effects. You can add keyframes independently to every attribute listed in the Effect Controls panel to make those behaviors change over time. In addition, you can use Bezier curves to adjust the velocity and acceleration of those changes.

It is not practical to explain the more than 140 video effects included with Adobe Premiere Pro CS3. Rather, we'll look at a representative sample of what's available and learn how to use the various types of parameters you'll encounter. To really get a feel for the possibilities of Adobe Premiere Pro, you'll need to do some experimenting.

Sampling some basic video effects

In this lesson, you will work with several effects, each offering something new in terms of its parameters or settings.

1   Start Adobe Premiere Pro, open the Lesson 9-1 project, and switch to the Effects workspace (choose Window > Workspace > Effects).

2   You might need to click the Effects tab next to the Project panel to make it visible.

3   Open the Video Effects folder.

Note: There are many Video Effects categories. Some effects are difficult to categorize and could reside in multiple categories or in categories by themselves, but this taxonomy works reasonably well.

4   Click the Effects panel menu, and choose New Custom Bin.

That bin/folder appears in the Effects panel below Video Transitions.

5   Highlight the bin, and change its name to something like *My Favorite Effects*.

6   Open any Video Effects folder, and drag a few effects into your custom bin.

Note: The effects remain in their original folder and also appear in yours. You can use custom folders to build effect categories that match your work style.

7   Drag the Black & White video effect (Video Effects > Image Control) to the clip on the Timeline.

That immediately converts your full-color footage to black-and-white—or, more accurately, grayscale. It also puts that effect in the Effect Controls panel.

Note: There are three other effects in the Effect Controls panel: Motion, Opacity, and Time Remapping. These are fixed effects. Adobe Premiere Pro automatically makes them available for all video clips. If the clip has audio, you will also see the Volume fixed effect.

8   Toggle the Black & White effect off and on by using the button (⊘) in the Effect Controls panel. If the Effect Controls panel is not visible, click its tab.

Toggling an effect on and off is a good way to see how an effect works with other effects. This toggle switch is the only parameter available with the Black & White effect. The effect is either on or off.

💡 **Resolve jarring shifts to grayscale**

Moving between full-color and black-and-white clips can be jarring. So here's a fix: Use a Cross Dissolve between clips or within the grayscale clip. To put one within the clip in this lesson, select the Razor Edit tool (C), cut the clip in two places, drag the Cross Dissolve transition to those edit points, select the first and third clip segments in turn, and switch off the Black & White effect on both. Now your sequence shifts gradually from color to black and white, and back to color. Undo those edits by clicking the History tab and clicking Apply Filter.

9   Check that the clip is selected so that its parameters are displayed in the Effect Controls panel, click Black & White to select it, and then press Delete.

10   Drag Directional Blur (Video Effects > Blur & Sharpen) into the Effect Controls panel.

This is the other way to apply a video effect—select the clip in the Timeline to display it in the Effect Controls panel, and drag the effect to the Effect Controls panel.

💡 **Finding effects**

With so many video effects folders, it's sometimes tricky to locate an effect. If you know part or all of an effect's name, start typing it in the Contains text box at the top of the Effects panel. Adobe Premiere Pro immediately displays all effects and transitions that contain that letter combination, narrowing the search as you type.

11 Expand the Directional Blur's filter, and note there are options the Black & White effect did not have: Direction, Blur Length, and a stopwatch next to each option (the latter is to activate keyframing, which we will cover later in this lesson).

12 Set Direction to 90 degrees and Blur Length to 3, to simulate the scene being filmed with a slow shutter speed.

Note: *The specific options available in each effect vary; however, they all operate in a similar manner.*

13 Expand the Blur Length option, and move the slider in the Effect Controls panel. As you change that setting, it shows up in real time in the Program Monitor.

14 Open the Effect Controls panel menu, and choose Delete All Effects From Clip. (You cannot delete Motion, Opacity, Time Remapping, or Volume. These are fixed effects that are always there.)

This is an easy way to start fresh.

15 Drag Spherize (Video Effects > Distort) to the Effect Controls panel, and click its disclosure triangles to display its parameters.

Like the Motion fixed effect above it in the Effect Controls panel, Spherize has a Transform button (▱▸) that lets you directly control its location in the Program Monitor.

16 Move the Radius slider to about 130 so you can see the effect in the Program Monitor.

17 Click the word *Spherize* (the name of the effect) in the Effect Controls panel to switch on its Transform control cross hair in the Program Monitor, and drag the bulbous-looking effect around inside that screen.

Note: The Center Of Sphere parameters in the Effect Controls panel change as you do this.

18 Delete Spherize, drag Wave Warp (Video Effects > Distort) to the Effect Controls panel, and click its six disclosure triangles to display its eight parameters.

Note: Wave Warp has three menus. These are specific effect conditions that do not have numeric values associated with them, but even these are keyframeable; that is, you can switch from one discrete condition to another at any time in the clip's duration.

19 Make various selections from each of the three menus, and then adjust some of the other parameters.

Note: Eight parameters might seem like a lot, but that's about average for the video effects in Adobe Premiere Pro.

20 Play this clip.

This is one of the animated effects you'll find in Adobe Premiere Pro. While virtually all Adobe Premiere Pro video effects let you animate them over time with keyframes, Wave Warp and a few others have built-in animations that operate independently of keyframes.

21 Reset the Wave Warp back to its starting point by clicking the Reset button in its upper right corner.

Manipulating keyframes and effect parameters

Virtually all parameters for all video effects are keyframeable. That is, you can change the effect's behavior over time in myriad ways. For example, you can have an effect gradually change out of focus, change color, warp into a funhouse mirror, or lengthen its shadow.

1 Expand the display of the Effect Controls panel until its view is wide enough for the Show/Hide Timeline View chevron button (◉) to become active, and click that button to open the effects timeline. (Depending on your screen size, you might want to put the Effect Controls panel into a floating window.)

2 Delete the Wave Warp effect, and drag the Solarize In preset (Presets > Solarizes > Solarize In) to the Effect Controls panel.

3 Play the clip to see how this preset works. The clip starts at the maximum Solarize threshold value, and reduces to zero at the one-second point.

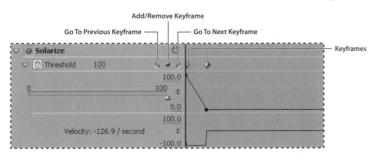

4 Drag the effect's second keyframe to the right and play the clip again.

It takes longer for the Solarize effect to resolve to the normal image. Keyframes are not permanently fixed; you can change their position without changing their value.

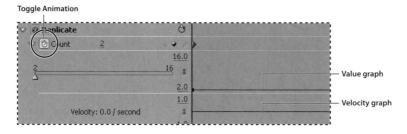

5 Delete the Solarize effect, drag Replicate (Video Effects > Stylize) to the Effect Controls panel, and click its single disclosure triangle to display its parameter.

6 Put the CTI at the beginning of the clip (with the Effect Controls panel active, press Home or Page Up).

7 Click the Toggle Animation stopwatch button (⏱), highlighted in the next figure. That does three things:

• Activates keyframing for the Replicate effect's Count parameter.

• Adds a keyframe at the CTI location and gives it Replicate's default starting value of two (a 2x2 grid of replicated clips).

• Displays two thin black lines in the Effect Controls timeline: the Value graph and the Velocity graph.

Toggle Animation

8 Drag the CTI to about the one-second point.

Locate the one-second point by looking in the Program Monitor or the Timeline time ruler. It's generally not easy to see an exact time in the Effect Controls timeline unless you really widen its viewing area.

9 Change the Replicate effect's Count parameter to 6.

Note: That automatically adds another keyframe at that point, because changing a parameter at a location without a keyframe automatically adds a new keyframe.

10 Drag the CTI to about the three-second point.

11 Click the Add/Remove Keyframe button (between the two keyframe navigation buttons).

That adds a keyframe with the same value as the previous keyframe. In this way, the effect will not change from the one-second to the three-second position.

12 Go to the end of the clip (press Page Down, and then press the Left Arrow key) to display the last frame of the clip.

Note: Pressing Page Down takes you to the frame following the last frame in a selected clip. That is by design. You use the keyboard shortcut Page Down to go to the start of the next clip, not the final frame of the current clip.

13 Change the Count value to 10.

Your Effect Controls panel should look like the next figure.

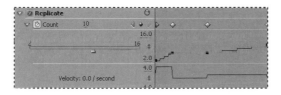

14 Play the clip, and note how the effect builds to a 6x6 grid, holds for two seconds, and then changes to a 16x16 grid at the end.

Now you'll use two methods to change two keyframe values.

15 Click the Go To Previous Keyframe button twice to move to the second keyframe.

16 Use the slider to change the Count value to 2. That's one simple way to change a keyframe's value.

17 Click the Go To Next Keyframe button to move to the third (of four) keyframes.

18 Hover the pointer over the corresponding keyframe on the Value graph (highlighted in the next figure). When it changes to the tiny Pen Tool pointer (▸₀), drag the keyframe as high as it will go, to change its value to 16.

This is the other way to change a keyframe's value.

Note: You can drag the keyframe only up or down. It will not allow you to move it left or right, to avoid inadvertently changing the keyframe's time position within the clip.

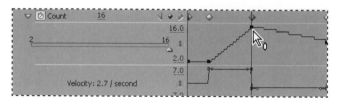

19 Drag bike title from the Project panel to the sequence after the video clip, position the CTI on it, and click it to display its parameters in the Effect Controls panel.

Note: If you don't move the CTI to the clip you're applying an effect to, you won't see that clip or its effect in the Program Monitor. Selecting a clip does not move the CTI to that clip.

20 Drag the Magnify effect to that clip or to the Effect Controls panel.

21 Set a keyframe at the beginning of the clip, with the Center value 30, 150.

Note: Make sure to activate keyframing in the Center option by clicking the Toggle Animation button.

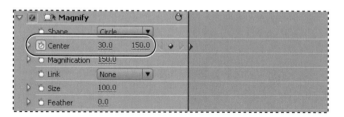

22 Set a keyframe near the end of the clip, with the Center value set to 700, 150.

23 Play this clip.

Note: Effects are great ways to animate or move a graphic or text over a video clip.

Extra credit: Combining effects

Open the Lesson 9-2 project to see multiple keyframed effects added to the bike title clip. Gaussian Blur, Lens Flare, and Basic 3D effects are applied to the same title clip, so you can deconstruct the file. Each effect is keyframed over time.

- Gaussian Blur provides an interesting entrance and exit for the title.

- Lens Flare moves across the letters, giving the illusion of light and movement.

- Basic 3D gives the title a swivel movement that enhances the Lens Flare effect.

See if you can recreate the effect from scratch.

Creating an effect preset

If you plan to reuse an effect with keyframes, save it as a preset. To do that, set your keyframes, parameters, and interpolation controls (these will be covered later), click the effect name in the Effect Controls panel, open the panel menu, choose Save Preset, give the preset a name, note whether to scale it to the clip length or anchor it to the clip In or Out point, and then click OK. It'll show up in the Presets folder.

Order counts

Clip-based (non-fixed) video effects work from bottom to top in the Effect Controls panel, with the most recently applied effect appearing at the bottom of the effect list. For example, if you apply the Tint effect and then apply Black & White, the clip will appear as grayscale. Black & White trumps Tint because it appears below Tint in the Effect Controls panel effect list. If you apply Black & White first, and then apply Tint, the clip will have the color you select in the Tint effect. Opacity and Motion, which are fixed effects, are always the final two effects applied—even when, in this case, you used a Motion preset and applied it first. If you want Motion to be applied in a different order, then use a clip-based motion effect, such as Basic 3D. You can drag effects up and down within the Effect Controls panel to change their order.

Adding keyframe interpolation and velocity

Keyframe interpolation changes the behavior of an effect parameter as it moves toward or away from a keyframe. The default behavior that you've seen so far is linear—constant velocity between keyframes. What generally works better is something that mirrors your experience or exaggerates it—gradual acceleration or deceleration or super-fast changes.

Adobe Premiere Pro CS3 offers two ways to control those changes: keyframe interpolation and the Velocity graph. Keyframe interpolation is the easiest—basically two clicks—while tweaking the Velocity graph can become a full-time occupation. To get a handle on this feature will take some time and practice on your part.

For the this lesson, we're going to use the Motion fixed effect. Its Position, Scale, and Rotation parameters all lend themselves to speed changes.

1   Open the Lesson 9-3 project.

2   Notice the bike title is over the bike cable shot2.mov clip. Click the bike title clip to select it.

3   Stretch the Effect Controls panel as wide as is practical. If you put it in a floating window, leave room to view the Program Monitor.

4   Open the Effect Controls panel's timeline (click the Show/Hide Timeline View chevron button).

5   Expand the Motion effect, and add Rotation keyframes in four places: the first and last frame, plus two more in between.

To do that, position the CTI at the beginning of the clip, click Rotation's Toggle Animation button (that adds a keyframe at the beginning of the clip with the default parameter value of zero), drag the CTI to the three other positions, and click the Add/Remove Keyframe button in each spot. Your Effect Controls panel should look like the following figure.

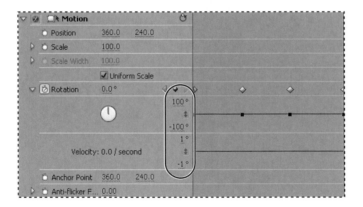

6   Look at the numbers highlighted in the previous figure. Expand the Rotation parameter if you haven't already.

•   **100 and −100**—Default values for the highest and lowest Rotation parameter settings. They will change to accommodate the actual high and low Rotation values once you change the keyframe settings.

- **1 and –1**—Default relative velocity values. Since you have not changed any parameters, the velocity is a straight line with a value of zero.

7 Change the Rotation value for the second, third, and fourth keyframes by using three separate methods (navigate to the keyframes by using the Go To Next/Previous Keyframe buttons):

- **Second keyframe**—Click the Rotation value, and type *2x* (two full clockwise rotations).

- **Third keyframe**— Drag the keyframe on the Value Graph to –1x0.0 degrees.

- **Fourth keyframe**—Drag the Rotation wheel left until the value displayed is –2x0.0 degrees (it's difficult to get that exact figure—it's OK if you end up at something like –2x0.0 degrees).

Once completed, your keyframes and graphs should look like the next figure. If the graph lines are clipped, click the Toggle automatic range rescaling button.

Toggle automatic rescaling button

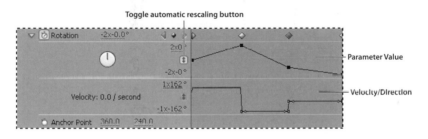

8 Drag the CTI through the clip and look at the Value and Velocity graphs and the numbers to the left of the graphs (shown in the previous figure):

- The top and bottom Value numbers have changed to 2x0 and –2x0 (two full rotations in both directions) to show the actual maximum and minimum parameter values. They remain unchanged as you move the CTI.

- The Value graph shows the parameters' values at any given time.

- The top and bottom Velocity numbers on the left side of the graph note the spread of the parameters' velocity in degrees per second.

- The Velocity graph shows the velocity between keyframes. The sudden drops or jumps represent sudden changes in acceleration—*jerks*, in physics parlance. Points on the graph above the middle of the Velocity graph area represent positive (clockwise) speeds and points below the center represent negative (counterclockwise) speeds. The farther the point or line is from the center, the greater the velocity (and you thought high school algebra was a waste of time).

9 Play that clip.

The text spins clockwise twice, spins faster going counterclockwise three times, and then slows down for one last rotation.

10 Right-click (Windows) or Control-click (Mac OS) the first keyframe, and then choose Ease Out.

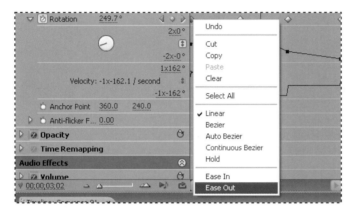

That does several things:

• The keyframe icon changes to an hourglass.

• The keyframe on the Value graph now has a Pen Tool handle and the graph has a slight curve.

• The keyframe on the Velocity graph has a similar Pen Tool handle and a more obvious curve. That curve shows the velocity change over time—its acceleration.

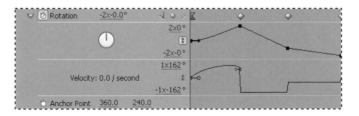

11 Play that portion of the clip. The effect looks more realistic as the motion "eases."

12 Right-click (Windows) or Control-click (Mac OS) the next three keyframes, and apply (in this order) the Bezier, Auto-Bezier, and Ease In interpolation methods. Here's a rundown on the Adobe Premiere Pro keyframe interpolation methods:

- **Linear**—The default behavior. A uniform rate of change between keyframes.

- **Bezier**—Lets you manually adjust the shape of the graph on either side of a keyframe. This allows for sudden acceleration changes into or out of a keyframe.

- **Continuous Bezier**—Creates a smooth rate of change *through* a keyframe. Unlike Bezier, if you adjust one handle, the handle on the other side of the keyframe moves in a complementary fashion to ensure a smooth transition through the keyframe.

- **Auto Bezier**—Creates a smooth rate of change through a keyframe even if you change the keyframe parameter value. If you choose to manually adjust its handles, it changes to a Continuous Bezier point, retaining the smooth transition through the keyframe.

- **Hold**—Changes a property value without a gradual transition (sudden effect change). The graph following a keyframe with the Hold interpolation applied appears as a horizontal straight line.

- **Ease In**—Slows down the value changes entering a keyframe.

- **Ease Out** Gradually accelerates the value changes leaving a keyframe.

Your Effect Controls timeline should look like the following figure (the value and velocity graph-limit numbers might differ, depending on the size of your Effect Controls panel).

Note: By adding these smooth curves, the parameter values change over the course of the effect such that they sometimes might be greater than the highest keyframe parameter value or less than the lowest keyframe parameter you set.

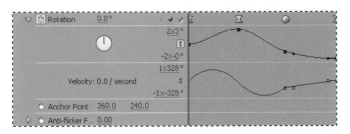

13 Play the entire clip and marvel (really) at how slick it looks.

Simply by adding keyframe interpolation, your Motion effect looks much more realistic.

14 Select the second keyframe—the Bezier hourglass—to activate it. Pen Tool handles appear on the Value and Velocity graph keyframes as well as on the two adjacent sets of keyframes. That's because changing one keyframe's interpolation handles can change the behavior of the keyframes next to it.

15 Drag the handle on the Velocity graph keyframe (highlighted in the next figure).

That creates a steep velocity curve, meaning the title will accelerate quickly, then decelerate quickly, but will still spin only twice between the first and second keyframe. You changed the velocity without changing the value.

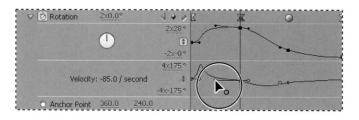

16 Select the third keyframe—the Auto Bezier circle icon—to activate it.

17 Drag the handle (highlighted in the next figure) and note that the circular keyframe icon immediately switches to an hourglass, because manually adjusting an Auto Bezier keyframe makes it a Continuous Bezier keyframe.

Note: *As you drag the left handle, the right handle moves in concert with it to keep the Value graph curve smooth through the keyframe.*

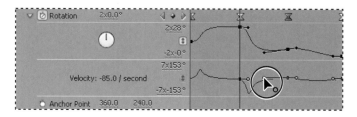

18 Click the Toggle Automatic Range Rescaling button (highlighted in the next figure) to un-constrain the curves.

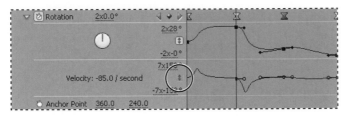

19 Adjust one or two handles, and note that the curves can extend beyond the boundaries of the Value graph and Velocity graph rectangles.

By activating Automatic Range Rescaling, you constrain the graph limits within the boundaries allotted in the Effect Controls panel. That's why the values to the left keep changing to let you know what the new upper and lower limits are.

Note: If you add another keyframe, it will have keyframe interpolation already applied to it. When you first add keyframes, you can grab their Value and Velocity graph handles and adjust the curves manually. Making any such adjustment will change the keyframe icon to the Bezier keyframe interpolation hourglass.

One additional velocity/interpolation issue

When working with Position-related parameters, the context menu for a keyframe will offer two types of interpolation options: Spatial Interpolation (related to location) and Temporal Interpolation (related to time). You can make spatial adjustments in the Program Monitor as well as the Effect Controls panel. You can make temporal adjustments on the clip in the Timeline and in the Effect Controls panel.

Those Motion-related topics are covered in Lesson 10.

Taking some fantastic effects for a test drive

This lesson combines hands-on, step-by-step tasks with experimentation. The purpose is to introduce you to three high-level effects, and to encourage you to explore further.

1 Choose Help > Adobe Premiere Pro Help.

2 Open Contents > Effect Reference > Gallery Of Effects > Gallery Of Effects.

There you will see examples of about a third of the video effects that come with Adobe Premiere Pro.

Note: The other headings under Effect Reference match bin names in the Effects panel.

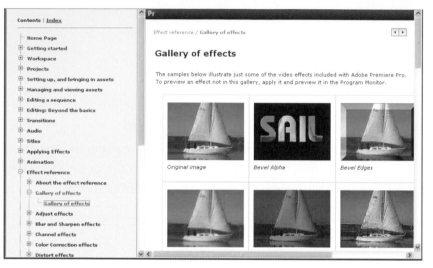

A portion of the Gallery of Effects in Adobe Premiere Pro Help.

3   Go back to the Effect Reference section of Help, click Generate Effects, and then click the Lightning effect.

This gives you an explanation of each parameter—25 in all!—in the Lightning effect. Every Adobe Premiere Pro video and audio effect has such a listing in Help.

4   Quit Help, return to the Adobe Premiere Pro workspace, and open Lesson 9-4.

5   Drag Lighting Effects (Video Effects > Adjust) to the clip in the Video 2 track.

6   Drag Texture 9.psd from the Project panel to the Video 3 track directly above the bike cable shot2.mov clip in the Video 2 track.

7   Right-click (Windows) or Control-click (Mac OS) the clip in Video 3, and deselect the Enable option.

Turning off Enable turns off the display of that graphic clip so it won't cover the clip below it in the sequence. You will use this graphic to add texture to a spotlight.

8   Select the bike cable shot2 clip in the Video 2 track to display its parameters in the Effect Controls panel.

9　Expand Lighting Effects to view all of its parameters.

10　Change the Bump Layer value to Video 3.

Note: Bump means texture. For this effect, you provide the texture by putting a graphic, image, or video clip on a video track above the clip to which you apply Lighting Effects.

11　Change Bump Channel to G (Green) or B (Blue).

Now the spotlight has a texture.

12　Experiment with the spotlight placement, angle, intensity, color, and so on.

Note: Lighting Effects has a Transform button which, in this case, lets you drag each of the five lights to different positions on the screen in the Program Monitor.

13　Delete Lighting Effects, and delete the texture clip from Track 3. Drag the Leave Color effect (Video Effects > Color Correction) to the bike cable shot2.mov clip. Set the CTI at the beginning of the clip.

14　Expand the Leave Color effect in the Effect Controls panel. This will present you with an eyedropper tool (next to the Color To Leave parameter—see figure on next page). Click the blue jacket of the lead rider in the Program Monitor to select the color blue.

15 Set the Amount To Decolor slider to 100%. This will decolor everything except the color you chose with the eyedropper.

16 Set the Tolerance slider to about 20%.

17 Render and play the clip to see the effect. The whole scene should be black-and-white, with the exception of the blue jacket.

Third-party plug-in providers

Now that you've got your feet wet, you're beginning to see what Adobe Premiere Pro is capable of. What might surprise you is that the dozens of effects that come with Adobe Premiere Pro only begin to tap its potential. There are hundreds of effects and transitions available online—some for free, most for retail purchase—from a broad spectrum of third-party providers.

To get a taste of all that is out there, visit *www.adobe.com*, go to the Adobe Premiere Pro page, and click Third-party Plug-ins. There you will see a list of effect packages, several of which contain dozens of effects. Most of those effects are deeply detailed and offer exciting possibilities. Check around a bit. Some third-party plug-in providers offer free trial packages or have demos of the effects online.

Review

▶ Review questions

1 What are the two ways to apply an effect to a clip?

2 List three ways to add a keyframe.

3 How do you make an effect start *within* a clip, rather than at the beginning?

4 Dragging an effect to a clip turns on its parameters in the Effect Controls panel, but you don't see the effect in the Program Monitor. Why not?

5 Describe two ways to change a keyframe's parameter setting.

6 How do you apply keyframe interpolation and adjust its settings?

▶ Review answers

1 Drag the effect to the clip or select the clip and drag the effect to the Effect Controls panel.

2 Move the CTI in the Effect Controls panel to where you want a keyframe and activate keyframing by clicking the Toggle Animation button; move the CTI and click the Add/Remove Keyframe button; and with keyframing activated, move the CTI to a position and change a parameter.

3 One of two ways, depending on the effect. Some effects, such as Fast Blur, have a zero setting where they do not change the clip's appearance. In that case, add a keyframe where you want the effect to start, and then set it to zero. Other effects are always "on" to some degree. In those cases, use the Razor Edit tool to cut the clip where you want the effect to start, and then apply the effect to the segment on the right.

4 You need to move the Timeline CTI to the selected clip to see it in the Program Monitor. Simply selecting a clip does not move the CTI to that clip.

5 Use the Go To Next/Previous Keyframe buttons and change the parameter value directly next to the parameter descriptor, or drag the corresponding keyframe on the Value graph up or down.

6 Apply keyframe interpolation through the context menu—right-click (Windows) or Control-click (Mac OS) a keyframe and select one of the keyframe interpolation methods such as Bezier or Ease In. Change the default settings by dragging the Bezier curve handles.

Motion

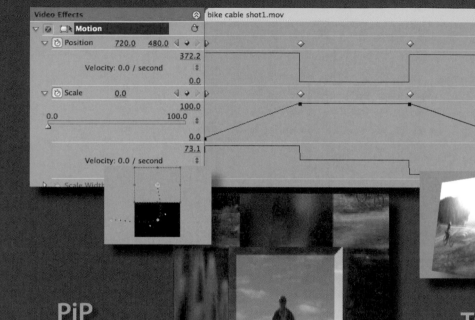

PiP

Transform

The Motion fixed effect is a handy feature that you will use frequently. It adds drama to static images and lets you change image sizes, fly them anywhere on (and off) the screen, and rotate them. You can further enhance motion characteristics by adding drop shadows and frames to your animated clips and building pictures-in-a-picture. Complementing Motion are several clip-based effects that have additional motion-oriented features such as skewing images and adding reflective glints.

10 | Putting Clips in Motion

Topics covered in this lesson:

- Applying the Motion effect to clips

- Changing clip size and adding rotation

- Working with keyframe interpolation

- Creating a picture in a picture

- Enhancing motion with shadows and beveled edges

- Other motion effects: Transform and Basic 3D

Getting started

You've seen the Motion effect in action already in this book. You used its Rotation feature to test keyframe interpolation and you've seen how it can zoom and pan still images.

As you watch TV advertisements, you're bound to see videos with clips flying over other images or clips that rotate onscreen—starting as small dots and expanding to full-screen size. You can create those effects by using the Motion fixed effect or several clip-based effects with motion settings.

You use the Motion effect to position, rotate, or scale a clip within the video frame. You can make those adjustments directly in the Program Monitor by dragging to change its position, or by dragging or rotating its handles to change its size, shape, or orientation.

You can also adjust Motion parameters in the Effect Controls panel and animate clips by using keyframes and Bezier controls.

Applying the Motion effect to clips

You adjust Motion effect parameters in the Program Monitor and the Effect Controls panel.

1   Open the Lesson 10-1 project.

2   Switch to the Effects workspace (Window > Workspace > Effects).

3   Open the View Zoom Level pop-up menu in the Program Monitor (highlighted in the next figure), and change the zoom level to 25%.

This will help you see and work with the Motion effect's bounding box.

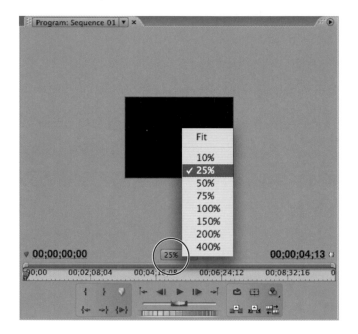

4   Expand the Program Monitor frame (if necessary) so there are no scroll bars in the screen. Your Program Monitor should look like the previous figure.

5   Play the clip in the timeline.

This is how the Motion effect you'll work on should look by the end of this mini-lesson.

6   Click the Motion disclosure triangle in the Effect Controls panel to display its parameters.

7 Click the Position Toggle Animation stopwatch button (highlighted in the next figure) to turn off its keyframes.

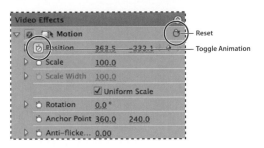

8 Click OK when prompted that the action will delete all keyframes.

9 Click the Reset button (to the right of Motion in the Effect Controls panel, highlighted in the previous figure).

These two actions return Motion to its default settings.

Examining Motion characteristics

1 Drag the CTI anywhere in the clip so you can see the video in the Program Monitor.

2 Click on the image in the Program Monitor screen.

That puts a bounding box with a cross hair and handles around the clip (as shown in the next figure) and activates the Motion effect in the Effect Controls panel. Clicking Motion or its Transform button (🖼️) in the Effect Controls panel will also activate the clip bounding box in the Program Monitor.

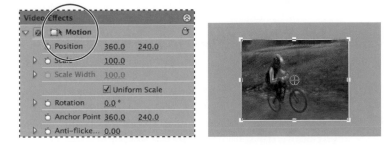

3 Click anywhere in the clip bounding box in the Program Monitor, drag this clip around, and note how the Position values in the Effect Controls panel change.

4 Drag the clip so its center is directly over the upper left corner of the screen, and note the Position values in the Effect Controls panel are 0, 0 (or close to that, depending on where you placed the center of the clip).

The lower right corner of the screen is 720, 480—the standard NTSC DV screen size.

Note: Adobe Premiere Pro uses something like an upside-down X/Y coordinate system for screen location. That coordinate system is based on a methodology used in Windows for so long that to change it now would create numerous programming headaches. The upper left corner of the screen is 0, 0. All x and y values respectively to the left of and above that point are negative. All x and y values respectively to the right of and below that point are positive.

5 Drag the clip completely off the screen to the left, as shown in the next figure.

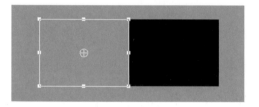

6 Fine-tune that adjustment by changing the Position values in the Effect Controls panel to -360, 240.

Since 360 is half of 720, this puts the right edge of the clip at the left edge of the screen frame.

7 Put the CTI at the beginning of the clip (press Page Up or Home), and add a Position keyframe there by clicking Position's Toggle Animation button.

8 Drag the CTI to the center of the clip, and change the Position values to 360, 240 (the center of the screen).

Changing the Position parameters adds a keyframe there.

9 Put the CTI at the end of the clip (press Page Down, and then the Left Arrow key).

10 Change the Position values to 360, -240.

That puts the clip completely above the screen and adds a keyframe.

11 Play the clip.

It moves smoothly onscreen, and then slides off the top. You have created a path (if you don't see the path, click the word *Motion* in the Effect Controls panel to switch on its display). Make note of a few things (highlighted in different colors in the next figure):

- It's a curved path. Adobe Premiere Pro automatically uses Bezier curves for motion.

- The little dots describe both the path and velocity. Dots close together represent a slower speed, dots farther apart represent a faster speed.

- The little four-point stars are keyframes.

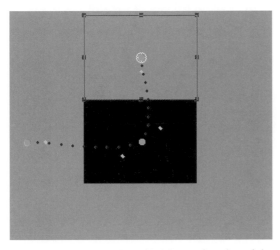

A clip motion path (color added for emphasis): Red dots represent the path (their spacing indicates relative velocity), cyan dots are keyframes, yellow dots are Bezier handles, and the magenta lines are the clip's bounding box.

12 Drag the center keyframe in the Program Monitor (the four-point star/square) down and to the left.

Notice that the dots get closer together to the left of the keyframe and farther apart to the right.

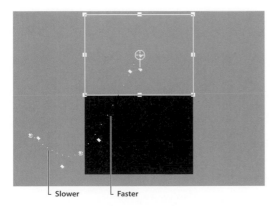

Slower   Faster

13 Play the clip. Note that it moves slowly until the first keyframe, and then speeds up.

Note: By moving the center keyframe, you changed its location and thereby the distance the clip traveled between it and its adjacent keyframes. But you didn't change the time between keyframes. So the clip moves faster between keyframes that are farther apart and slower for those closer to each other.

14 Drag the center keyframe again, this time down and to the right (use the next figure as a reference).

That creates a parabola with evenly spaced dots on both sides, meaning the velocity will be the same on both arms of the parabola.

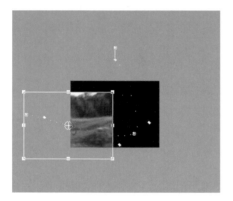

15 Drag the center keyframe in the Effect Controls panel first to the left, and then most of the way to the right.

Note: Now you are changing the time between keyframes, but not changing their physical location in the screen. The little path/velocity dots in the Program Monitor spread out or slide closer together, but the keyframes do not change locations.

16 Play this clip, and note how much slower it goes at the beginning and how much faster at the end.

It should behave the same way it did when you opened the lesson project.

Changing clip size and adding rotation

Simply sliding a clip around only begins to exploit the possibilities of the Motion effect. What makes the Motion effect so useful is the capability to shrink or expand the clip and to spin it.

For example, you can start a clip full-screen (or zoom in even farther) and then shrink it to reveal another clip. You can spin a clip onto the screen by having it start as a small dot and then spin it off the screen, having it grow as it moves away. You can also layer multiple clips, creating several pictures-in-a-picture.

Before you dive into this mini-lesson, look at Motion's six keyframeable options:

- **Position**—The screen location of the clip's anchor point (its center unless you change the anchor point).

- **Scale** (Scale Height, when Uniform Scale is deselected)—The relative size of the clip. The slider has a range from 0 to 100 percent, but you can set the numerical representation to increase the clip size to 600 percent of its original size.

Note: The percent refers to clip border perimeter, not clip area. So 50 percent is equal to 25 percent in terms of area, and 25 percent is equal to 6.25 percent in area.

- **Scale Width**—You must deselect Uniform Scale to make Scale Width available. Doing so lets you change the clip's width and height independently.

- **Rotation**—You worked with this in the Lesson 9-3 project. You can input degrees or number of rotations, for example 450° or 1x90. A positive number is clockwise and a negative number is counterclockwise. The maximum number of rotations allowed in either direction is 90, meaning that you can apply up to 180(!) full rotations to a clip.

- **Anchor Point**—The center of the rotation, as opposed to the center of the clip. You can set the clip to rotate around any point in the screen, including one of the clip's corners or around a point outside the clip like a ball at the end of a rope.

- **Anti-flicker Filter**—This feature is useful for images that contain high-frequency detail, such as fine lines, hard edges, parallel lines (moiré problems), or rotation. Those characteristics can cause flickering during motion. The default setting (0.00) adds no blurring and has no effect on flicker. To add some blurring and eliminate flicker, use 1.00.

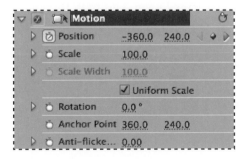

1 Open the Lesson 10-2 project, and open the Finished sequence.

2 Play the clip to see the animation.

This is how the Motion effect will look by the end of this mini-lesson.

3 Open the Practice sequence to start with the same clip but with no effects.

4 Place the CTI at the beginning of the clip, expand the motion effect, click the Position Toggle Animation button to activate keyframing, and move the center of the clip to the upper left corner (position 0,0).

5 Expand the Scale parameter, click the Scale Toggle Animation button, and drag the slider to zero.

That sets the size to zero for the beginning of the clip.

6 Drag the CTI about a third of the way into the clip, and click the Reset button. That creates two keyframes that use Motion's default settings: the clip at full size and centered in the screen.

7 Drag the CTI about two-thirds of the way into the clip, and click the Add/Remove Keyframe button for Position and for Scale.

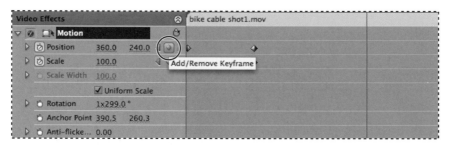

This causes the clip to remain centered and at full screen for the time between the two keyframes (you could also have clicked Reset again to use those default parameters).

8 Move the CTI to the end of the clip (press Page Down, and then the Left Arrow key with the timeline active), and change the Position parameters to 720, 480 (lower right corner).

9 Drag a bounding box corner handle (in the Program Monitor) to shrink the clip all the way down to the center cross hairs. That sets Scale back to zero.

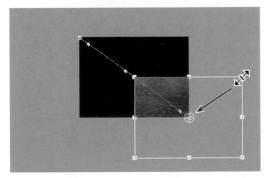

💡 **Changing clip size—like working with text**

As you did in the Titler, you can change clip size by using the bounding box. Deselect Uniform Scale, and then, to scale freely, drag a corner handle; to scale one dimension only, drag a side (not a corner) handle; to scale proportionally, Shift-drag any handle.

10 If you haven't already done so, expand the Position and Scale effects in the Effect Controls panel. It should look like the next figure.

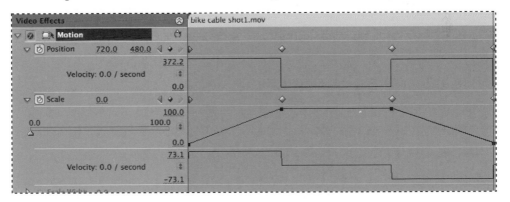

11 Play this clip.

The clip should grow from a tiny dot in the upper left, move to fullscreen in the center, hold there for a while, and then shrink to a dot while moving to the lower right corner.

Adding rotation and changing the anchor point

1 Move the CTI to the beginning of the clip (press Page Up or Home with the timeline active), and click the Rotation Toggle Animation button.

That sets a keyframe for Rotation with 0.0 degrees as the starting point.

2 Move the CTI to the second keyframe (click the Go To Next Keyframe button next to either Position or Scale).

3 Hover the pointer just outside a handle of the bounding box in the Program Monitor until it becomes a curved double-arrow pointer (↰), and then drag the bounding box clockwise two full circles (see the next figure).

Note: You can fine-tune this move in the Effect Controls panel by setting Rotation to 2x0.0 degrees.

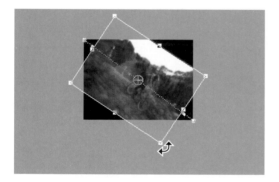

4 Move the CTI to the third keyframe, and click the Rotation Add/Remove Keyframe button. That adds a keyframe with the same value as the preceding keyframe.

5 Move the CTI to the end of the clip.

6 Drag the Rotation circle (click the Rotation disclosure triangle to expand the parameter) counterclockwise twice (you can't use the Program Monitor bounding box because the clip has been shrunk to a point).

That returns Rotation to its default setting of 0.0 degrees. Your settings look like the next figure. If you can't see the keyframe graphs, expand the Scale and Rotation parameters.

Play this clip. It will rotate clockwise twice, hold, and then rotate counterclockwise.

7   Return the CTI to the beginning of the clip.

8   Click the Anchor Point Toggle Animation button, and set the numeric values to 0,0.

Note: This will make the clip spin around its upper left vertex. The Anchor Point location uses the same coordinates as the Position parameter: 0, 0 is the upper left corner of the screen and 720, 480 is the lower right corner. These Anchor Point coordinates are independent of the clip Scale. You can set anchor points outside the clip to have the clip rotate around a point. For example, try –360 and 240.

9   Move to the second keyframe, and change the Anchor Point values to 360, 240 (putting the clip's rotation vertex in the center of the clip—its default location).

Note: You can adjust the Anchor Point values only in the Effect Controls panel. There is no cross hair for the Anchor Point in the Program Monitor. Transform, the clip-based effect upon which Motion is based, displays one cross hair for the clip center and another for the anchor point in the Program Monitor.

10   Go to the third keyframe, and click the Anchor Point Add/Remove Keyframe button to add a keyframe there that uses the previous keyframe's values.

11 Move to the fourth keyframe and change the Anchor Point coordinates to 720, 480 (setting the clip's rotation vertex to the lower right corner of the screen). Your Anchor Point Velocity graph should look like the next figure.

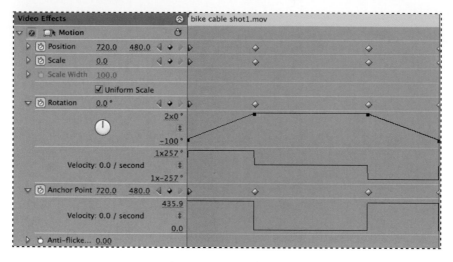

12 Play this effect. It should look very similar to the effect in the Finished sequence. If you like the effect, you can save it as a preset. Right-click (Windows) or Control-click (Mac OS) the Motion effect, and choose Save Preset.

Note: When you save a preset, you can choose for the preset to scale the length of any clip, or anchor to a specific In or Out point. In many cases, setting the effect to scale to the length of the clip is most effective.

Working with keyframe interpolation

The Motion effect moves clips around the screen over a period of time. Adobe Premiere Pro offers keyframe interpolation methods that suit both aspects of that motion: spatial and temporal.

Spatial interpolation refers to the motion path—where the clip appears onscreen. Temporal interpolation refers to changes in velocity.

When you worked with nonmotion effects—Gaussian Blur, Wave Warp, and Replicate, for example—you worked with temporal interpolation in the Velocity and Value graphs in the Effect Controls timeline.

The focus for this lesson is the Motion Position parameter. It has a spatial interpolation option that you are likely to use time and again. You won't find it in the Effect Controls panel. It's in the Program Monitor.

1   Open the Lesson 10-3 project.

2   Choose Fit—the default—from the View Zoom Level menu in the Program Monitor, and expand the Program Monitor's frame to get a better look at the keyframes. Click on the image in the Program Monitor to reveal its keyframes and the Video Effects in the Effect Controls panel.

3   Drag any keyframe handle in the Program Monitor. That changes the Motion curve—the spatial interpolation—but will not convert the keyframes in the Effect Controls timeline into Bezier curves (their icons remain diamonds).

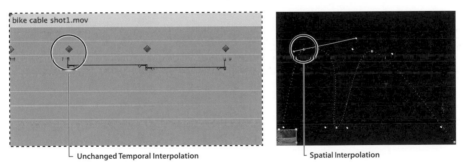

Unchanged Temporal Interpolation   Spatial Interpolation

4   Right-click (Windows) or Control-click (Mac OS) any Position keyframe in the Effect Controls panel, and choose Spatial Interpolation > Linear.

That changes the Motion curve at that keyframe into straight lines and sharp angles (they'll start curving as they approach a keyframe with Bezier spatial interpolation).

bike cable shot1.mov

> Undo
>
> Cut
> Copy
> Paste
> Clear
>
> Select All
>
> Temporal Interpolation ▶
> **Spatial Interpolation** ▶   Linear
>   Bezier
>   Auto Bezier
>   ✓ Continuous Bezier

5   Right-click (Windows) or Control-click (Mac OS) any keyframe in the Program Monitor, and choose Temporal Interpolation > Auto Bezier (or any other Bezier interpolation method).

That changes the temporal interpolation keyframe in the Effect Controls panel into a Bezier curve.

Note: The keyframe in the Program Monitor does not switch to a temporal interpolation keyframe. It remains spatial. To change the temporal characteristics of the keyframe selected in the Program Monitor, you need to drag its handles in the Effect Controls Velocity graph.

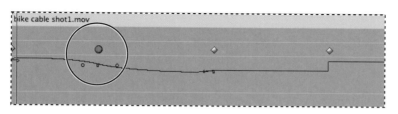

Creating pictures in a picture

The picture-in-picture—PiP—technique is one of the top uses of the Motion effect. It's also one of the easiest ways to see how you can *composite*, or layer, clips. You will begin formal work on compositing later in the book. This mini-lesson will give you a taste.

To simplify things, you'll start with a sequence that has three layered clips in it, all ready to go. You will create Picture in Pictures (PiPs), and add drop shadows and beveled edges to the PiPs.

1   Open the Lesson 10-4 project, and open the Finished sequence by double-clicking it in the Project panel, if it is not already displayed. Render and play that sequence to get an idea of what you can do. It's five PiPs, each with a drop shadow and beveled edge.

2   Open the Start sequence by double-clicking it in the Project panel.

If you play this, you will see only the clip on the top track. It covers all the clips below it in the sequence.

3   In the Effects panel, expand Presets so you can see Effects > Presets > PiPs > 25% PiPs > 25% UL.

Note the following:

• All the PiP presets display clips at 1/16th their normal area (reminder: 25 percent refers to clip perimeter, not area).

• LL, LR, UL, and UR refer to screen locations: Lower Left, Lower Right, Upper Left, and Upper Right.

• Each PiP set offers different types of PiP moves.

• Typically, you select a style and then adapt it to your needs. For example, you might change the preset start or end locations or the size.

Note: There is no 25% Center preset. You use one of the presets to create one. Simply change the start and end Position keyframes to 360, 240.

4   Drag PiP 25% UL Slide In Right from the 25% UL bin to the clip in the Video 3 track.

Look at the Effect Controls timeline, and play the sequence. It slides in from off the right edge of the screen and appears in the upper left corner of the screen.

5   Drag PiP 25% LR Spin In from the 25% LR bin to the clip in the Video 2 track.

Look at the Effect Controls timeline, and play the sequence. It spins in from infinity and appears in the lower right corner of the screen.

The clip in the Video 1 track will remain as is; we want to use it as a background.

6   You can add the other three video clips (that are not used yet) to the sequence and apply PiP presets to them.

The fourth and fifth clips will go in the Video 4 and Video 5 tracks. Dragging a clip to the gray area above the last video track will create a new track for the clip you are dragging.

• Clip in the Video 2 track: Apply Preset PiP 25% LR Spin In.

• Clip in the Video 3 track: Apply Preset PiP 25% UL Slide In Right.

- Clip in the Video 4 track: Apply Preset PiP 25% UR Spin In.

- Clip in the Video 5 track: Apply Preset PiP 25% LL Scale In.

- Clip in the Video 6 track: Apply Preset PiP 25% LL Spin In, but we need to customize this motion so that this PiP shows up in the center rather than the lower left corner.

7   Select the video clip in Track 6, and expand the motion settings in the Effect Controls panel.

8   Change the Position parameters to 360, 240. This centers the clip.

9   Play the clip to see the five PiPs you have added on top of a video background. If you had trouble with any of the steps, open the 5 PiP sequence to see how it should look.

Note: For the video clips that are too short, use the Rate Stretch Tool to lengthen them to match the length of the other stretched clips. If a clip is too long, trim it to match the first three clips in length. It's important that all the clips be the same length for this exercise.

Enhancing motion with shadows and beveled edges

PiPs have a much more realistic feel when their shrunken clips have drop shadows, beveled edges, or some other kind of border.

1   Open the sequence called 5 PiP.

It has six layered clips (you might need to use the Timeline scroll bar to see them all). The top five all have 25% motion presets applied. The clip on the bottom of the sequence in the Video 1 track will serve as the PiP background.

2   Drag the CTI past the one-second point to display the five PiPs.

3   Drag Bevel Edges Thin (Presets > Bevel Edges) to the top clip in the sequence.

4 Zoom the Program Monitor view in to 100 percent to get a better look at this effect. It'll show up in the center of the Program Monitor. The next figure shows how it'll look after you adjust the Bevel Edges parameters.

5 Click the Bevel Edges disclosure triangles in the Effect Controls panel, and change its parameters as follows (use the next figure as a guide):

• Increase Edge Thickness slightly.

• Change Light Angle to about 140 degrees to illuminate the dark beveled edge at the bottom of the clip.

• Increase Light Intensity to about .4 to emphasize the beveled edges.

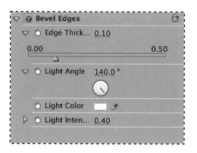

6 Click Bevel Edges in the Effect Controls panel to select the effect so you can create a preset with the parameters you just applied.

7 Open the Effect Controls panel menu, choose Save Preset, type *Lesson 10 Bevel Edges*, give it a description if you want to, and click OK. This new preset shows up immediately in the Presets folder.

Note: If you had used keyframes with this effect, selecting one of the three Types as you're saving the preset—Scale, Anchor To In Point, or Anchor To Out Point—would have been of some value.

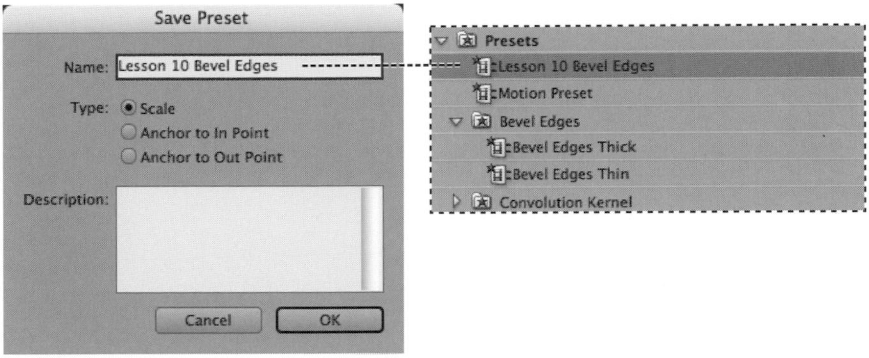

Saving presets for other projects

If you want to use this preset in other projects, export it. To do that, select the preset in the Effects > Presets folder, open the Effects panel menu, choose Export Preset, navigate to an appropriate file folder, give your preset a name (it doesn't have to be the same as its name in the Presets folder), and click Save.

8   Drag Lesson 10 Bevel Edges from the Presets bin to each clip in video tracks 2-5 (not to the clip in Video 1—that's the fullscreen video you'll use as a background for the PiP).

9   Play this sequence (return the Program Monitor View Zoom Level to Fit). All five PiPs have the same beveled-edge look.

Adding a drop shadow

1   Drag Drop Shadow (Video Effects > Perspective) onto the top clip.

2   Change Drop Shadow parameters in the Effect Controls panel as follows (use the next figure as a guide):

• Change Direction to about 320° or -40°.

Note: You want the shadow to fall away from any perceived light source. In this mini-lesson, you set the light direction for Bevel Edges to about 140 degrees. To make shadows fall away from a light source, add or subtract 180 degrees from the light source direction to get the correct direction for the shadow to fall.

• Increase Distance so you can see the shadow (you might need to adjust the View Zoom Level of the Program Monitor to see how this works).

• Change Opacity to 80 percent to darken the shadow (since the background clip is rather dark).

• Give your shadow some Softness to make it more realistic. Generally, the greater the Distance parameter, the more Softness you should apply.

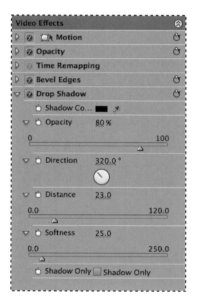

3   Apply these same values to the other four PiPs by using Copy and Paste. Right-click (Windows) or Control-click (Mac OS) the Drop Shadow effect in the Effect Controls panel, and choose Copy.

4   Select the clip in the Video 5 track. Right-click (Windows) or Control-click (Mac OS) in the Effect Controls panel, and then choose Paste. Repeat with the clips in video tracks 2, 3, and 4.

5   Render and play this sequence. It should look like the Finished sequence.

Other motion effects: Transform and Basic 3D

If you use the Motion effect to apply rotation to your shadow and clip, the shadow will rotate with the clip as a single unit. That's unrealistic. It should always fall away from the rotating clip in the same direction. To get a realistic drop shadow with rotation applied to a clip, you can use the Transform or Basic 3D effect to perform rotation.

To *skew* your clips—tilt them to give them a 3D look—use Basic 3D.

1   Open Lesson 10-5, and open the Practice sequence.

2   Drag Gray Matte from the Project panel to the Video 1 track directly below the clip in the Video 2 track.

The matte will let you see the clip's shadow.

3   Click the bike cable shot1 clip to select it, and view the effects already applied in the Effect Controls panel—Drop Shadow and Transform. The Transform filter has many of the same capabilities as the Motion fixed effect, except that the Transform effect can be moved to a lower position in the order of effects applied. You will soon see why this is important. In this case, the Transform effect is scaling the clip to a PiP, moving it left to right and rotating.

4   Play the sequence, and observe the relationship of the shadow to the PiP as it rotates. The shadow rotates with the PiP, which is unrealistic. It is behaving like that because the effects are applied from top to bottom. The shadow is being applied before the transform effect.

5   In the Effect Controls panel, drag the Drop Shadow effect below the Transform effect. Play the sequence again.

Note: *The shadow now remains on the same side while the PiP rotates, for a more realistic effect.*

Get a glint with Basic 3D

Basic 3D can swivel and tilt your clip to give the impression it's moving through 3D space. What makes it even more fun is its specular highlight—a glint on the surface of the image that moves as you animate the clip.

1 Delete Transform, or click its Toggle The Effect On Or Off button (⏻) to switch it off.

2 Drag Basic 3D (Perspective folder) to the Effect Controls panel *above* Drop Shadow.

3 Expand the Basic 3D effect in the Effect Controls panel, and select the Show Specular Highlight option.

4 Adjust Swivel and Tilt until you see the highlight moving across the clip.

As you move the clip around, the shadow follows suit. But the farther out of kilter you go, the more likely the shadow will stop looking realistic.

Note: The highlight gets very bright when centered on the clip. When using Basic 3D, it's best to swivel and tilt the clip such that the specular highlight moves along the edge of the clip.

Review

▶ ## Review questions

1   What Motion Position coordinates would you use to position a clip so it's centered and just off the right edge of the screen?

2   You start Rotation at its default setting, move the CTI and add a Rotation keyframe with a value of 2x, and then give a value of –2x to the next keyframe. Describe what will happen.

3   You want a clip to appear fullscreen for a few seconds and then spin away. How do you make the Motion effect's Rotation feature start within a clip rather than at the beginning?

4   How do you select the spatial interpolation type for the Position parameter of the Motion effects, and how do you change it?

5   If you want to add a drop shadow to a spinning clip, why do you need to use some other motion effect besides the Motion fixed effect?

6   One way to apply the same customized effect to multiple clips is to use a preset. How do you make one?

▶ ## Review answers

1   1080, 240. Here's why: 1080 = 720 (full clip width) + 360 (half the width to put the clip's left edge on the right edge of the screen). The vertical center point is 240.

2   It will spin clockwise twice as it approaches the first keyframe. Then it will spin counterclockwise *four times* as it moves to the next keyframe. The number of spins equals the difference between two keyframe rotation values. Set the Rotation value back to 0 (zero) to have it spin counterclockwise twice.

3   Position the CTI where you want the Rotation to begin, and click the Add/Remove Keyframe button. Then move to where you want the spinning to end and change the Rotation parameter; another keyframe will appear.

4   Remember that spatial interpolation refers to a clip's location onscreen. You set spatial interpolation in the Program Monitor screen by right-clicking (Windows) or Control-clicking (Mac OS) the Position keyframe, choosing Spatial Interpolation, and then selecting the interpolation method. You adjust spatial interpolation in the Program Monitor by dragging the keyframe's Bezier handles.

5   The Motion fixed effect is the last effect applied to a clip. Motion takes whatever effects you apply before it (including Drop Shadow) and spins the entire assemblage as a single unit. To create a realistic drop shadow on a spinning object, use Transform or Basic 3D, and then place Drop Shadow below one of those effects in the Effect Controls panel.

6   Adjust the effect parameters to your liking, click the effect name in the Effect Controls panel to select it, open the Effect Controls panel menu, choose Save Preset, give the preset a name, select one of the three parameters, and click OK.

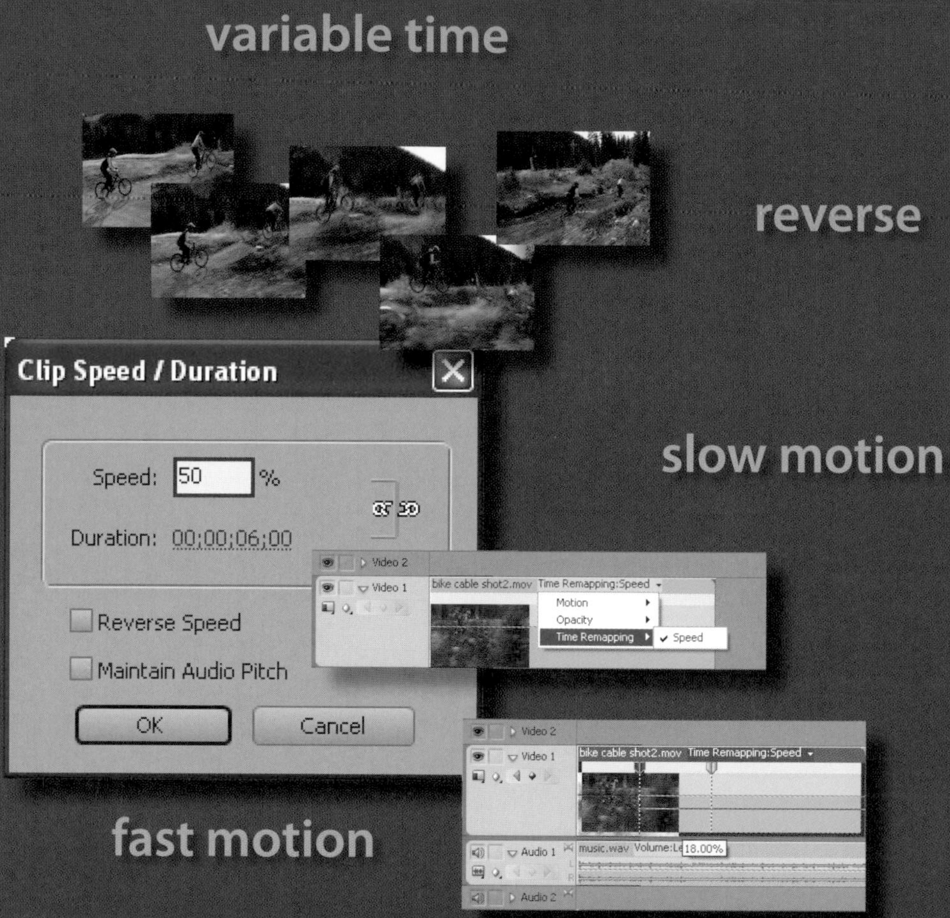

variable time

reverse

Clip Speed / Duration

Speed: 50 %

Duration: 00;00;06;00

☐ Reverse Speed

☐ Maintain Audio Pitch

OK   Cancel

slow motion

Video 2
Video 1   bike cable shot2.mov Time Remapping:Speed ▾
          Motion   ▶
          Opacity   ▶
          Time Remapping ▶ ✓ Speed

Video 2
Video 1   bike cable shot2.mov Time Remapping:Speed ▾

Audio 1   music.wav Volume:Le 18.00%

Audio 2

fast motion

How often we wish we could control time
in real life. Well, in Adobe Premiere Pro
CS3, time control has been significantly
enhanced. Slow-motion quality has been
improved with better in-between frames,
and now the new Time Remapping effect
can vary the speed of a clip with precise
keyframes, including ease in and ease out
options. Time is in your hands.

11 | Changing Time

Topics covered in this lesson:

- Slow motion and reverse motion
- Variable time change with time remapping
- Time remapping with speed transitions
- Time remapping with reverse

Getting started

Slow motion is one of the most often-used effects in video production. A simple slow-motion effect applied to a bride walking down the aisle or to an exciting sports clip can create a very dramatic look. In this lesson, we will review the static speed changes that have always been available in Adobe Premiere Pro, as well as the Time Remapping effect that is new to Adobe Premiere Pro CS3.

If you have used slow motion in Adobe Premiere Pro in the past, you will be excited to see the improved quality in the new version. The variable speed control in the Time Remapping effect is easy to use, yet powerful. Even the static speed changes have received a significant quality improvement.

Let's take time to have a look.

Slow motion and reverse motion

We will start by making a static speed change to a clip. You can speed up or slow down the speed of any clip on the timeline.

1   Open the Lesson 11-1 project.

2   Notice that the bike cable shot 2.mov clip on the timeline is six seconds long. It is important to remember that changing the speed of a clip will change its duration.

3   Right-click (Windows) or Control-click (Mac OS) the bike cable shot2.mov clip, and choose Speed/Duration from the context menu.

4   Change Speed to 50%, and then click OK.

5   Play the clip in the timeline. Render the clip by pressing Enter or Return to see smooth playback.

Notice the clip is now twelve seconds long. This is because we slowed the clip to 50%, making it twice the original length.

6   Press Ctrl+Z (Windows) or Command+Z (Mac OS) to undo the speed change.

There are times when you want to change the speed of the clip without changing the duration. This is impossible without trimming the clip as it is slowed down. Adobe Premiere Pro provides a tool to make this very easy.

7   Once again, right-click (Windows) or Control-click (Mac OS) on the bike cable shot2.mov clip, and choose Speed/Duration from the context menu.

8 Click the link button (highlighted in the next figure) that indicates that Speed and Duration are linked, so that now the settings are unlinked. Then, change Speed to 50%. Notice that with the speed and duration unlinked, the duration remains six seconds.

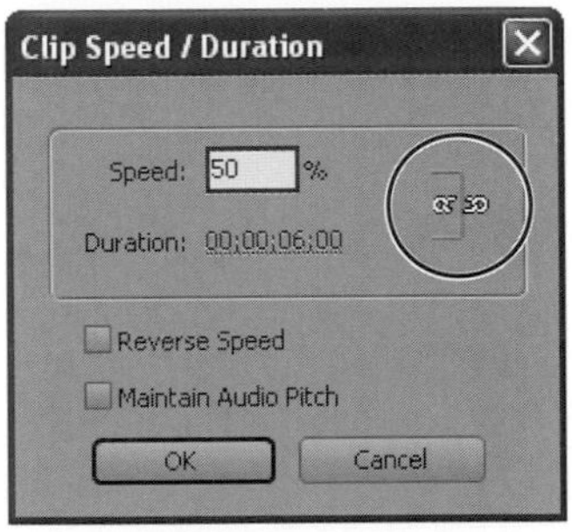

9 Click OK, and then play the clip.

Notice the clip plays at 50% speed, but the last six seconds have automatically been trimmed to keep the clip at its original duration.

Note: The Clip Speed/Duration dialog box also has an option called Maintain Audio Pitch. Selecting this option keeps audio at the original pitch regardless of the speed at which the clip is running. This can be helpful when making small speed adjustments to clips where you want to maintain the pitch in the audio.

Occasionally you will need to reverse time. You can do this in the same Clip Speed/Duration dialog box.

10 Right-click (Windows) or Control-click (Mac OS) the bike cable shot2.mov clip, and choose Speed/Duration from the context menu.

11 Leave Speed at 50%, but this time, also select the Reverse Speed option, and then click OK.

12 Play the clip. Notice it plays in reverse at 50% slow motion.

Speeding up a clip

While slow motion is the most commonly used time change, speeding up clips is a useful effect as well.

1 Undo your changes until you have the clip at its original 100% speed at six seconds. (If you get confused, just reopen the Lesson 11-1 project.)

2   Right-click (Windows) or Control-click (Mac OS) the bike cable shot2.mov clip, and choose Speed/Duration from the context menu.

3   Type *300%* for Speed, click the lock button so speed and duration are linked, and then click OK.

4   Play the clip. Notice its new length is two seconds. This is because the speed is set to 300%—or three times its normal speed.

Changing speed with the Rate Stretch tool

There will be times when you need to find a clip that's just the right length to fill a gap in your timeline. Sometimes you might be able to find the perfect clip—exactly the right length. Other times you will find the perfect clip, but it is just a little too short or a little too long. This is where the Rate Stretch tool comes in very handy.

1   Open the Lesson 11-2 project.

The situation we have in this section is fairly common. The timeline is synchronized to music and the clips contain the content we want, but one of them is just too short. We could guess or "hunt and peck" to change the speed until we get it right, or we can use the Rate Stretch tool.

2   Select the Rate Stretch tool in the Tools panel.

3   Move the Rate Stretch tool over the right edge of the center clip, and drag it until it meets the third clip.

Notice the speed of the center clip changes to fill the space you stretched it to.

4   Play the timeline to view the speed change made by the Rate Stretch tool.

Variable time change with time remapping

Time remapping allows you to vary the speed of a clip by using keyframes. This means that one portion of the same clip could be in slow motion while another portion of the clip could be in fast motion. In addition to this flexibility, you can also alter speed changes from fast to slow or from forward motion to reverse motion. Hang on—this is really fun.

1 Open Lesson 11-3.prproj.

2 Open the sequence named *working*. As we add time adjustments to the clip, it will change length.

3 Adjust the height of the Video 1 track by positioning the Selection tool over the Video 1 label and dragging the edge of the track up. Increasing the track height makes adjusting keyframes on the clip much easier.

4 Right-click (Windows) or Control-click (Mac OS) the movie clip, and choose Show Clip Keyframes > Time Remapping > Speed. With this option selected, the yellow line across the clip represents the speed.

5 Scrub the timeline to the point where the first bike leaves the ground on the first jump (about 00;00;01;05).

6 Ctrl-click (Windows) or Command-click (Mac OS) the yellow line to add a speed keyframe at this point. We are not yet changing the speed, just adding control keyframes.

7 Add another speed keyframe at 00;00;02;13, just as the second bike hits the ground. Notice that by adding two speed keyframes, the clip is now in three "speed sections." We will now set different speeds between keyframes.

8 Leave the first section, between the beginning of the clip and the first keyframe, set as is (100% speed). Position the Selection tool over the yellow line between the first and second keyframes, and drag it down to 18%. Notice the clip has stretched in length to accommodate the speed change of this section.

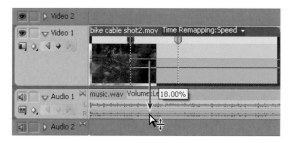

9 Play the clip. Notice the speed changes from 100% to 18% and back to 100% at the end. Render the clip for the smoothest playback.

Note: If you have problems setting the speed keyframes, open the sequence named complete *to see the completed process.*

Time remapping with speed transitions

Setting variable speed changes on a clip can be a very dramatic effect. In the previous section, we changed from one speed to another, instantly. To create a more subtle speed change, it is possible to transition from one speed to another smoothly by using speed keyframe transitions.

1   Open Lesson 11-4.prproj.

2   Select the sequence named *working*. As we add time adjustments to the clip, it will change length.

3   Right-click (Windows) or Control-click (Mac OS) the movie clip, and choose Show Clip Keyframes > Time Remapping > Speed.

4   Scrub the timeline to about 00;00;00;22 and add a speed keyframe. Add another speed keyframe at 00;00;01;14. The clip now has three segments in which you can adjust speed.

5   Drag the yellow line of the first segment to 200%, the second segment to 30%, and the last segment to 200%. This creates a dramatic change from fast motion to slow motion and then back to fast motion. Play the clip to see the effect.

To make the speed changes more subtle, we will smooth out the transition from 200% down to 30% and back, to make it less sudden.

Note: The speed keyframes are actually two icons next to each other. You can drag these two icons apart to create a speed transition.

6   Drag the right half of the first speed keyframe to the right to create a speed transition. Notice the yellow line now ramps down, rather than making a sudden change from 200% to 30%.

7   Repeat step 6 on the second speed keyframe to create a transition there also.

8   Render and play the clip to see the effect.

Note: If you have problems creating these speed keyframe transitions, open the sequence named complete *to see the completed project.*

Time remapping with reverse

Reversing a clip can add comedy or drama to a sequence. Time remapping allows you to easily adjust variable speed and do reverse motion in the same clip.

1   Open Lesson 11-5.prproj.

2   Select the sequence named *working*. As we add time adjustments to the clip, it will change length.

3   Right-click (Windows) or Control-click (Mac OS) the movie clip, and choose Show Clip Keyframes > Time Remapping > Speed.

4   Scrub the timeline to about 00;00;01;13, and add a speed keyframe.

5   Ctrl-drag (Windows) or Command-drag (Mac OS) the right half of the speed keyframe to the right until you reach timecode 00;00;00;00 (see timecode in the Program Monitor). Notice the keyboard modifier creates a reverse speed keyframe; that is, when you drag to the right, you are dragging backwards in time.

Note: *After the reverse motion keyframe is created, Adobe Premiere Pro adds an additional keyframe to the right, at the point in the clip where you started the reverse motion.*

6   Play the clip to see the effect.

7   To make the reverse portion of the clip move in slow motion, drag the yellow line to -50% for that section of the clip. (-50% represents 50% slow motion in reverse.)

8   Drag the right half of the first keyframe to the right to make the transition from forward motion to reverse motion gradual.

9   Drag the clip in Audio 1 to match the duration of the video, and play the clip.

Time remapping is a great new feature in Adobe Premiere Pro CS3. The quality of the slow motion is also very good. Experiment with slowing down and speeding up time, but always try to make the effect match the mood of your project or the story you are telling.

Review

▶ **Review questions**

1   Changing the speed of a clip to 50% has what effect on the length of the clip?

2   What tool is useful in stretching a clip in time to fill a gap?

3   Where is the Time Remapping filter located?

4   Can you make time remapping changes directly on the timeline?

5   How do you create a smooth ramp-up from slow motion to normal speed?

6   How do you create reverse motion in the Time Remapping effect?

▶ **Review answers**

1   Slowing a clip speed causes the clip to become longer, unless the Speed and Duration parameters have been unlinked in the Clip Speed/Duration dialog box, or the clip is bound by another clip.

2   The Rate Stretch tool is very useful for the common situation of needing to fill a small amount of time.

3   The Time Remapping effect is not found in the Effects folders. It is a common effect available on all clips by default.

4   Time remapping is best done on the timeline; because it affects time it is best (and most easily) used and seen within the timeline sequence.

5   Add a speed keyframe, and split it by dragging away half of the keyframe to create a transition between speeds.

6   Add a speed keyframe, and then Ctrl-drag (Windows) or Command-drag (Mac OS) half of the keyframe to create reverse motion.

mics

waveform

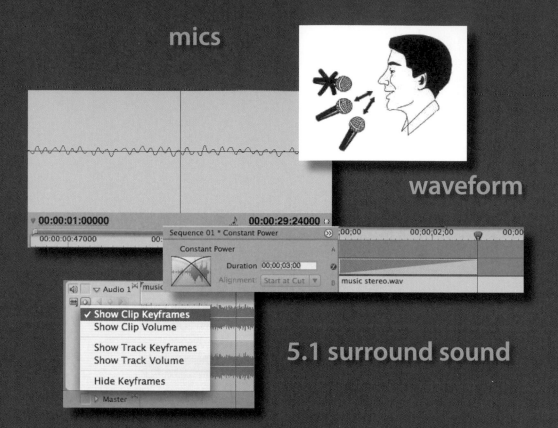

Sequence 01 * Constant Power

Constant Power

Duration 00;00;03;00
Alignment: Start at Cut

▼ Audio 1 music

✓ Show Clip Keyframes
Show Clip Volume

Show Track Keyframes
Show Track Volume

Hide Keyframes

▷ Master

00;00   00;00;02;00   00;00

music stereo.wav

5.1 surround sound

J-cut

Audio is critical to your video production, and Adobe Premiere Pro has the right complement of tools to take your audio editing to a higher level. It features industry-standard plug-ins, audio conforming, sample-specific editing, and multiple track types. To ensure the highest audio quality, select the right microphones for the job, turn to wireless audio if your budget allows, and use professional voice-over techniques.

12 | Acquiring and Editing Audio

Topics covered in this lesson:

- Connecting microphones to your computer
- Setting up a basic voice-recording area
- Voicing professional narrations
- Adobe Premiere Pro audio features
- Examining audio characteristics
- Adjusting audio volume
- Adding J- and L-cuts

Getting started

Audio typically takes a back seat to video, but it is crucial to your projects. The best images lose their impact if their audio is mediocre. Your first goal is to acquire high-quality audio at the get go, both in the field and when recording a narration.

Adobe Premiere Pro gives video producers and audiophiles all they need to add top-notch aural quality to their productions. The program has a built-in Audio Mixer that rivals hardware found in production studios. The Audio Mixer lets you edit in mono, stereo, or 5.1 surround sound, has a built-in instrument and vocal recording feature, and offers several ways to mix selected tracks.

You can perform industry-standard edits such as J- and L-cuts on the Timeline, as well as adjust audio volume levels, keyframes, and interpolation.

In addition, Adobe Premiere Pro is in compliance with two audio industry standards: ASIO (Audio Stream In/Out) and VST (Virtual Studio Technology), ensuring that it works smoothly with a wide range of audio cards and dozens of audio effect plug-ins.

Making the connection

Adobe Premiere Pro lets you record a narration directly to your project by using a microphone connected to your computer's sound card. Most sound cards have only a 1/8″ (3.5 mm) stereo minijack outlet. Mics built specifically for PCs typically cost less than $25. When you visit your local electronics store, you'll have two basic options:

- **Dynamic mics**—Headsets or long-necked versions that sit on your desk.
- **Condenser mics**—Typically lavalieres, these offer slightly better voice-over quality, and require a battery.

Plug the mic into the correct sound-card outlet (usually marked Mic or with a mic icon), and not the Line-in jack used with amplified devices such as CD players and sound mixers.

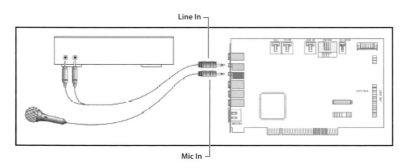

Whichever mic you choose, make sure that you also get a good headset—one that covers your ears to block extraneous sound. Use that headset both when shooting your video and voicing a narration. It's important to hear how the mic hears you.

Setting up a basic voice-recording area

To create your voice-over narration, you'll need a quiet, sound-absorbing location. The easiest solution is to build a temporary recording area simply by hanging some thick blankets or fiberglass insulation on two adjoining walls. If you can create something like a four-sided, blanketed cubicle, so much the better.

Note: It is an old audio myth that egg cartons, carpeting, and foam rubber work well. Avoid them.

If you drape the blankets in a single corner, point the mic *toward* that corner, place yourself between the mic and the corner, and speak *away* from the blankets. It seems counterintuitive, but the mic is sort of like a camera. It "sees" what's in front of it. In this case, it *sees* your face and the hanging, sound-absorbing blankets.

Voicing professional narrations

Review this checklist before recording your voice-over:

- **Practice reading your copy out loud**—Listen to your words. They should sound comfortable, conversational, even informal.

- **Avoid technical jargon**—That demands extra effort from your listeners, and you might lose them.

- **Short sentences work best**—If you find yourself stumbling over certain phrases, rewrite them.

- **Stress important words and phrases**—As you review your copy, underline important words. When you record your voice-over, you'll want to give those words extra emphasis—more volume and punch.

- **Mark pauses**—Mark logical breaks in narration with short parallel lines.

- **Avoid overly smooth and constant pacing**—That's characteristic of a scripted delivery. You don't want to remind viewers that this is TV. It's real life. It's conversational.

- **Punch up your voice**—Do not slip into a dull, monotone voice. Add some zest and enthusiasm to your narration.

- **Practice**—Record a couple of narrations and listen to them. Most first-time narrators mumble or swallow words. Have you made yourself clear?

- **Don't pop your Ps and Ts**—As you say P- and T-words, you project a small blast of wind. Avoid speaking directly into the mic.

- **Wear a headset**—Hearing yourself helps you avoid popping Ps or speaking with too much sibilance (an overemphasis on the S sound). It also helps minimize room noise and other extraneous sounds.

Adobe Premiere Pro—A high-quality aural experience

Adobe Premiere Pro offers professional-quality audio editing tools that rival many stand-alone audio mixing and editing products. For example, it includes the following:

• **Sample-specific edits**—Video typically has between 24 and 30 frames per second. Edits fall between frames at intervals of roughly 1/30 second. Audio typically has thousands of samples per second. CD audio is 44,100 samples per second (44.1kHz). Adobe Premiere Pro lets you edit between audio samples.

• **Three types of audio tracks**—Mono, stereo, and 5.1 (six-channel surround). You can have any or all of these track types in a sequence.

• **Submix tracks**—You can assign selected audio tracks to a submix track. That lets you apply one instance of audio and effect settings to several tracks at once.

• **Channel editing**—You can split out individual audio channels from stereo and 5.1 surround sound files and apply effects only to them. For example, you can select the two rear channels in a 5.1 track and add reverb to them.

• **Recording studio**—you can record any instrument or mic you can connect to an ASIO-compliant sound card. Record directly to a track on an existing sequence or to a new sequence.

• **Audio conforming**—Adobe Premiere Pro upconverts audio to match your project's audio settings. It also converts so-called fixed-point (integer) data to 32-bit floating-point data. Floating-point data allows for much more realistic audio effects and transitions.

Note: Floating-point data has no fixed number of digits before and after the decimal point; that is, the decimal point can float. This leads to more accurate calculations.

Camcorder kHz and bit-rate settings

Many DV camcorders give you two audio quality options: 16-bit audio recorded at 48kHz (16 bits of data per sample at 48,000 samples per second) or lower quality 12-bit audio recorded at 32kHz. The latter option lays down two stereo tracks on your DV cassette: one with audio recorded by the on-camera mic and the other giving you an option to insert a narration or some other audio. If you recorded at 32kHz and set your project to 48kHz, that is not a problem. Adobe Premiere Pro will simply take a little longer to upconvert your audio during the conforming process.

Examining audio characteristics

Audio editing is similar to video editing. It uses most of the same tools and you apply transitions and effects in much the same way.

But audio has some characteristics that are different from video and affect the way you approach editing. In this lesson, you will be introduced to the basics of audio editing. More advanced audio-editing topics will be covered in Lesson 13.

1   Start Adobe Premiere Pro, and open the Lesson 12-1 project.

It has three music clips—mono, stereo and 5.1 surround sound—as well as three movie clips.

2   Double-click Mono.wav to open it in the Source Monitor.

That displays a waveform. The peaks and valleys indicate volume levels.

Note: As highlighted in the next figure, the Toggle Take Audio And Video button automatically switches to Audio-only when you add an audio-only clip to the Source Monitor.

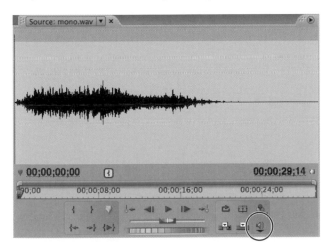

3   Open the Source Monitor panel menu, and choose Show Audio Time Units.

That switches the time ruler from the standard video-oriented time increments (seconds; frames) to audio samples.

4   Drag the left handle of the viewing area bar to the right to zoom in on the Source Monitor timeline until the difference between numbered markers is 1,000 samples (use the following figure for a reference).

5   Type *1:0* in the current time display, and press Enter or Return.

6   Press the Left Arrow key once, and note that the sample that precedes 1:0 is 0:47999.

There are 48,000 audio samples per second in this clip (48kHz). Switching to audio units enables you to make sample-specific edits down to (in the case of this project's settings) 1/48,000 of a second. This might seem like splitting hairs, but there are times when cutting audio with this precision will come in handy.

Note: Audio units display with colons (:) versus semi-colons (;) for Video frame timecode.

7   Drag the center of the viewing area bar to the left and right to take a closer look at the audio peaks and valleys.

Note: You can drag the right or left handle of the viewing area bar to change the zoom level.

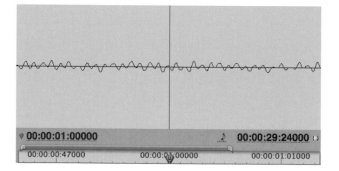

8   Double-click Music Stereo.wav, and take a look at it in the Source Monitor.

This is how a stereo signal looks. The layout follows the industry standard: left channel on top, right on the bottom.

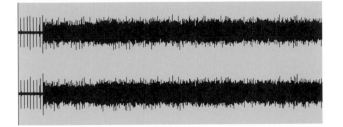

9   Choose Edit > Preferences > Audio (Windows) or Premiere Pro > Preferences > Audio (Mac OS), and make sure the 5.1 Mixdown Type is set to Front + Rear + LFE. You need to use that setting to hear all six channels of the 5.1 clip in the next step.

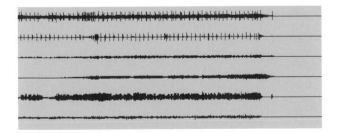

10   Double-click Music 11 5.1.wav, and take a look at it in the Source Monitor.

This is a 5.1 surround sound clip. It has six channels: right, left, center, right-surround (rear), left-surround (rear), and LFE (low-frequency effects—the subwoofer channel).

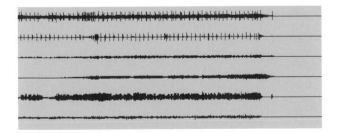

11   Click Music 11 5.1 in the Project panel to select it, and then choose Clip > Audio Options > Breakout To Mono.

That creates six links, one for each channel (it does not create six new audio files). Using Breakout To Mono lets you edit individual channels of a stereo or 5.1 clip. For example, you might want to give the LFE channel a bass boost. That does not change the original 5.1 clip. You can link this edited channel to the other 5.1 mono channels and create another 5.1 clip.

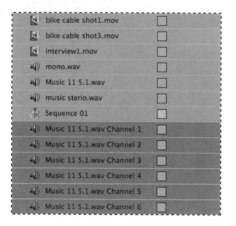

> ### 💡 Waveforms are immutable
>
> *Adding an effect to a clip in Adobe Premiere Pro will not affect the original audio or video clip or the visible audio waveform. If you change a clip's volume or apply audio effects to it, the waveform will always display the clip's original volume levels.*

12 Drag Music 11 5.1 to the Timeline, and notice that Adobe Premiere Pro will not let you drop it in the Audio 1 track.

Audio 1 is a stereo track. When you drag an audio clip to a sequence that does not have a track that matches the clip's type, Adobe Premiere Pro automatically creates a new track to suit that clip type. Even though Adobe Premiere Pro appears to move the new clip below the Master audio track, the new track will appear above the Master audio track once you release the mouse button.

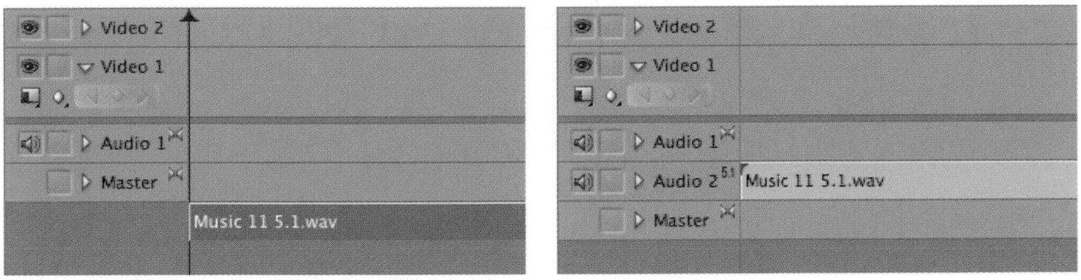

13 Expand the view of the newly-added Audio 2 track by clicking its Collapse/Expand Track triangle (highlighted in the next figure) to open its waveform view. Drag the boundary between Video 1 and Audio 1 up the screen, and then drag the bottom of Audio 2 down.

Your sequence should look like the next figure. Note the labels for each of the six channels in this 5.1 surround sound clip.

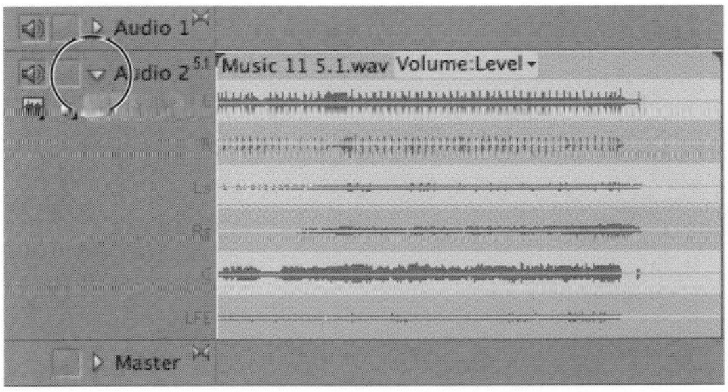

14 Click the menu of open clips in the Source Monitor (highlighted in the next figure), and select Mono.wav.

15 Move the Timeline CTI to the beginning of the sequence.

16 Click the Audio 1 track header.

Note: You need to target an audio track for the Source Monitor Insert or Overlay feature to place an audio clip in the Timeline—even if, as is true in this case, the track is for stereo clips only and the clip is mono. In this case, Adobe Premiere Pro will automatically add the correct type of track. Were there no targeted audio track, clicking Insert or Overlay would have no effect.

17 Click the Overlay button in the Source Monitor, and note that because there was no mono audio track in the sequence, Adobe Premiere Pro adds a mono audio track below the 5.1 track and inserts that clip there.

Note: You can tell the audio track type by its icon: Mono is a single speaker, Stereo is a double speaker, and 5.1 says 5.1. The Master audio track is stereo by default. You can change that by choosing Project > Project Settings > Default Sequence.

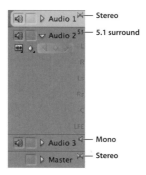

Adjusting audio volume

You might want to decrease or increase the volume of an entire clip or parts of a clip. For example, you might want to bring the natural sound on a video clip down by half while you narrate, gradually fade up the audio at the start or end of a clip, or fade up an interview just as the narrator completes a segment. The latter is part of a J- or L-cut. These will be explained later in the lesson.

1 Choose Window > Workspace > Reset Current Workspace to get your workspace back in order.

2   Delete the audio clips in the Timeline by marquee-selecting them and pressing Delete.

3   Delete all the added audio tracks by right-clicking (Windows) or Control-clicking (Mac OS) an audio track header, selecting Delete Tracks, selecting the Delete Audio Tracks option in the Delete Tracks dialog box (shown in the next figure), and then clicking OK.

Your sequence now has only two audio tracks: Audio 1 and Master (both are stereo).

4   Drag Music Stereo.wav from the Project panel to the Audio 1 track.

5   Expand the track view by clicking the Collapse/Expand Track triangle.

6   Click the Show Keyframes button (◔), and select Show Clip Keyframes, to ensure you are looking at clip keyframes.

This lets you edit a clip's volume in the Timeline rather than using the Volume effect in the Effect Controls panel.

7 Hover your pointer over the volume level graph—the thin, horizontal yellow line between the left and right channels—until it turns into the Vertical Adjustment tool (⬍) pointer, and then drag that yellow line up and down.

Note: *A dB (decibel) level readout gives you feedback on the volume change (0dB is the default starting point no matter the actual volume of the original clip). It's not easy to move to an exact setting. You use the Effect Controls panel Volume effect to do that.*

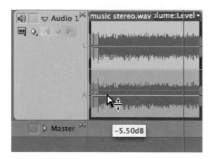

8 Ctrl-click (Windows) or Command-click (Mac OS) the volume level graph in four places, evenly spaced along the yellow line.

That adds four keyframes on the volume line.

9 Drag the first and last keyframes all the way to the left and right, respectively, to place those keyframes on the first and last frames of the clip.

10 Drag the second and third keyframes left and right, respectively, to about two seconds from the beginning and two seconds from the end.

11 Drag the start and end keyframes all the way to the bottom of the clip view to create a fade up and a fade out.

12 Play the beginning and end of the clip to see how this works.

Note: As you slide keyframes around in the clip, you will invariably change their volume settings. Adjusting keyframes on the Timeline is quick and easy. You'll want to use the Volume effect in the Effect Controls panel to fine-tune those keyframe parameters.

13 Right-click (Windows) or Control-click (Mac OS) the second and third keyframes, and choose Ease In and Ease Out, respectively.

Note: As you can see, you can apply keyframe interpolation in the Timeline. However, selecting one of the Bezier curve options would create a more pronounced curve in the middle. So stick with Ease In and Ease Out for most audio keyframes.

Adjusting audio in the Effect Controls panel

The Audio fixed effect works like any other effect in that you can use keyframes to change audio over time. You can also apply an audio transition (which changes audio volume levels over time) and adjust its settings in the Effect Controls panel.

1 Make sure the Music Stereo clip is selected on the Audio 1 track, and open the Effect Controls panel. Click the Volume disclosure triangles to display the parameters, and widen the Effect Controls panel so you can see its timeline.

If the timeline is not open, click the Show/Hide Timeline View button. Make note of a few things:

- **Bypass**—This is something you haven't seen up to this point because only audio effects have this option. For the Volume effect, turning on Bypass at any point in the clip (Bypass is keyframeable) switches back to the clip's original volume level. You can use Bypass to switch any audio effect off and on any number of times within a clip.

- **Level**—This is the only adjustable parameter.

- **Keyframes**—All the keyframes and keyframe interpolation methods (hourglass icons) you applied to the clip in the Timeline show up in the Effect Controls timeline.

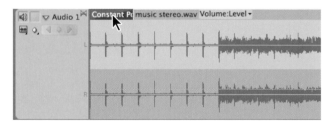

2 Add several keyframes, and change the volume level on each one. Play the clip to hear the level adjustments. Click the box next to Bypass, and notice the level adjustments you made are not used.

3 Marquee-select all the keyframes in the Effect Controls timeline, and press Delete.

4 Drag the Constant Power audio transition (Audio Transitions > Crossfade) to the beginning of the clip on the Timeline.

5 Click the transition rectangle on the clip to select it, and view its parameters in the Effect Controls panel.

6 Change the duration to three seconds.

That gives you a nice fade-in.

7   Drag the Constant Power transition to the end of the clip, and you have a fade-out.

8   Drag the interview1.mov clip to the timeline just after the Music Stereo clip.

9   Trim the end Music Stereo.wav back one second. Then, trim the beginning of interview1.mov to about 00;00;04;12. This gives them both tails for a smooth transition.

10   Drag Constant Power to that edit point, and listen to how that works.

11   Replace Constant Power with Constant Gain, and listen to it.

Note: Open the Lesson 12-2 project if you get confused or want to see the completed lesson to this point.

💡 Favor Constant Power

Constant Gain changes audio at a constant rate in and out as it transitions between clips. This can sometimes sound abrupt. Constant Power creates a smooth, gradual transition, like a video cross-dissolve. It decreases audio for the first clip slowly at first, and then quickly falls off at the end of the transition. For the second clip, this audio crossfade increases audio quickly at first and then more slowly as it reaches the end of the transition. Constant Power is the default audio transition. Rely on it for most transitions. But your ears are the best judge.

Adding J-cuts and L-cuts

Frequently you'll want to start a video clip by having its sound play under the previous video clip and then transition to its associated video. This is a great way to let your audience know that someone is about to say something or that a transition is coming. This is called a J-cut, so named because it looks vaguely like a 'J' on the sequence.

Conversely, another slick editing technique is to let audio tail off under the next video clip. This is an L-cut.

To do either of these cuts requires that you unlink the audio and video portions of a linked A/V clip so you can edit them separately. After they've been unlinked, you can move that audio segment to another audio track, and then extend or shorten the audio portion to make the J- or L-cut. There are two unlinking methods—a context menu and a keyboard modifier.

1   Open and play the Lesson 12-3 Complete sequence.

This is how your J- and L-cuts will look and sound by the end of this mini-lesson. It has the sound bite and cutaway clips used in Lesson 8.

Note: In this case, the cutaway clips aren't being used as cutaways. They're B-roll—basic video used to piece together a project.

The cutaway *video* plays over the first few words of the sound-bite *audio,* and then the cutaway *video* dissolves to the interview clip while the cutaway *audio* fades out—a J-cut. That process is reversed for the end of the sound bite—an L-cut.

2   Open the Lesson 12-3 Working sequence.

3   Right-click (Windows) or Control-click (Mac OS) the second clip, and then choose Unlink.

4   Complete the unlinking process by clicking outside that clip in the Timeline to deselect it.

Now when you click either the audio or video portion of that clip, only that portion is selected. You'll relink these clips, and then use a keyboard modifier to temporarily unlink them.

5   Shift-click both of those unlinked clips to select them (if one is already highlighted, there's no need to Shift-click it).

6   Right-click (Windows) or Control-click (Mac OS) one of them, and choose Link.

Now you'll use the keyboard modifier unlinking method.

7   Alt-click (Windows) or Option-click (Mac OS) the audio portion of the second clip. That unlinks it and selects it.

8   Drag that unlinked audio portion of the second clip straight down to the Audio 2 track and deselect it.

Note: As you move the audio portions of your clips in the sequence, take care that you don't slide them left or right when you drag them, otherwise the audio and video will get out of sync. Adobe Premiere Pro gives you a visual cue to help you line up your clips: If you see a black line with a triangle, your clips are properly lined up. If that black line disappears, you have moved out of sync. In that case, move the clip around a bit until the black line reappears.

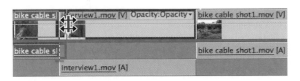

9   Use the Rolling Edit tool (N) to move to the right about one second the edit that is between the first and second video clips (not the audio clips).

Use the Program Monitor and the Timeline pop-up timecode displays to help make the edit.

10   Apply a fade-out using the Constant Power transition (you used this transition in the previous mini-lesson) on the first audio clip to fade the bike sound out gradually as the subject starts to speak.

11   Play that J-cut. The bike sound should fade as the interviewer begins speaking.

Adding an L-cut

Now that you've unlinked the center clip, adding an L-cut at the end of this segment will take only a few steps.

1   Trim the third clip by dragging the left end of the bike cable shot1 clip to the right about one second. This will shorten it a bit and give it head frames for a transition.

2   Drag the entire third clip (video and audio) to the left about one second so it overlaps the audio from clip 2. This is creating a L-cut.

3   Create a fade-in of the third audio clip to gradually fade in the bike audio over the end of the interview from the second clip.

4   Add a video Cross Dissolve between the video portions of these two clips.

5   Play that L-cut.

The closing biker's natural sound should fade up quietly beneath the interviewer's closing comment.

Review

▶ **Review questions**

1   When you set up a voice recording space in the corner of a room, which way do you face to voice the narration and why?

2   When I videotape indoors, my audio has a "tin-can" quality. What's going on?

3   Explain three ways to start your piece by fading up your audio.

4   Why use a J-cut or an L-cut?

5   You have a quiet video clip, but in the middle someone honks a car horn. How could you remove that sound and replace it with the original quiet background of the original clip?

▶ **Review answers**

1   As counterintuitive as it seems, you face away from the sound-absorbing material. The mic picks up sound from the direction it's facing. The absorbing material minimizes the reflections the mic picks up.

2   The mic is probably too far from your subject, and you're in a room with reflective surfaces such as flat walls and an uncarpeted floor.

3   Drag an Audio Crossfade transition (Constant Power or Constant Gain) to the beginning of the clip. Or, use the Volume graph in the Timeline clip display with two keyframes, dragging the first keyframe to the first frame and dragging that keyframe to the bottom of the clip. Or, use the Volume audio effect and two keyframes to fade up the audio. Use interpolation controls to smooth what would otherwise be a straight-line fade-in.

4   You use these cuts either to ease into a clip such as a sound bite, or to let it fade out. A J-cut starts audio under the preceding video (which also has associated audio or a narration) and then fades up as you transition or cut to the video portion of that clip. An L-cut fades audio under the next clip as a way to ease out of that audio/video clip.

5   Use keyframes to silence that portion of the audio. Then add part of the original audio to another audio track, and fade that up to fill the audio gap you created in the original clip.

voice-over

Reverb

Loopology

20.00 dE   1.00
Threshold   Ratio

Master
Read

0

-6

-12

-18

-30

-∞

0.0

Audio 1 | Music 13 - Sonoma-Left.wav
Audio 2 | Music 13 - Sonoma-Right.wav
Audio 3 | Music 13 - Sonoma-Clarinet.wav
Audio 4 | Music 13 - Sonoma-Flute.wav
Audio 5 | Music 13 - Sonoma-Bass.wav
Audio 6 | Music 13 - Sonoma-Left.wav
Audio 7 | Music 13 - Sonoma-Right.wav

Audio Mixer

Audio effects in Adobe Premiere Pro can dramatically change the feel of your project. Some are specialized effects from a family of audio plug-ins that use Virtual Studio Technology. The Audio Mixer— with its submix track option, track- level audio effects, live narration, and instrumental recording—brings additional flexibility to your audio management. To take your audio talents to a higher level, leverage the integration and power of the new Adobe Soundbooth CS3.

13 | Sweetening Your Sound and Mixing Audio

Topics covered in this lesson:

- Sweetening sound with audio effects
- Trying out stereo and 5.1 surround sound effects
- Working with the Audio Mixer
- Outputting tracks to submixes
- Recording voice-overs
- Creating a 5.1 surround sound mix
- Fixing, sweetening, and creating soundtracks in Soundbooth

Getting started

Adobe Premiere Pro contains more than 20 audio effects that can change pitch, create echoes, add reverb, and remove tape hiss. As you did with video effects, you can set keyframeable audio effect parameters to adjust effects over time.

The Audio Mixer lets you blend and adjust the sounds from all the audio tracks in your project. Using the Audio Mixer, you can combine tracks into single submixes and apply effects, panning, or volume changes to those groups as well as to individual tracks.

Adobe Soundbooth is a new audio application that is designed for video and Flash editors. Soundbooth provides the tools video editors need to sweeten and repair typical audio challenges. Don't let the easy interface mislead you—Soundbooth is a powerful tool.

Sweetening sound with audio effects

For most projects, you will probably be happy to use audio in its original, unaltered state, but at some point you might want to start applying effects. If you use music from old cassette tapes, you can use the DeNoiser audio effect to detect and remove tape hiss automatically. If you record musicians or singers in a studio, you can make it sound like they were in an auditorium or a cathedral by adding Reverb. You can also use Delay to add an echo, DeEsser to remove sibilance, or Bass to deepen an announcer's voice.

You'll try a few audio effects in this mini-lesson, but you can expand your knowledge by going beyond that. Experiment. Listen to the possibilities. Test some effects not covered here. Each effect is non-destructive—that is, it does not change the original audio clip. You can add any number of effects to a single clip, change parameters, and then delete those effects and start over.

1 Start Adobe Premiere Pro, and open the Lesson 13-1 project.

2 Drag Ad Cliches 13 Mono.wav from the Project panel to the Audio 1 track (it's a mono track) of the Practice sequence.

Feel free to play this little ditty.

3 Open the Audio Effects > Mono folder in the Effects panel.

Note: All the mono effects have the mono single-speaker icon (◀). If you open the Stereo folder, you'll see a double speaker icon (◀), and you'll also recognize 5.1 (◀).

4   Drag Bass to the Ad Cliches clip, and then open the Effect Controls panel and click its two disclosure triangles to expand the parameters.

5   Play the clip, and move the Bass Boost slider left and right. This increases or decreases bass.

6   Delete Bass from the Effect Controls panel, and add Delay. Try out its three parameters:

- **Delay**—Time before the echo plays (0 to 2 seconds).
- **Feedback**—Percentage of echo added back to audio to create echoes of echoes.
- **Mix**—Relative loudness of echo.

Note: Listing all the attributes of all the audio effects is beyond the scope of this book. To learn more about audio effect parameters, choose Help > Adobe Premiere Pro Help, and then click the Audio section under Contents.

7   Play the clip, and move the sliders to experiment with the effect.

Lower values are more palatable, even with this over-the-top audio clip.

8   Delete Delay, and add PitchShifter to the Effect Controls panel.

This has three nifty items: knobs, presets, and a Reset button. You can tell an audio effect has presets by the tiny triangle next to what would normally be the Reset button (🕐.) and the addition of a rectangular Reset button (both highlighted in the next figure).

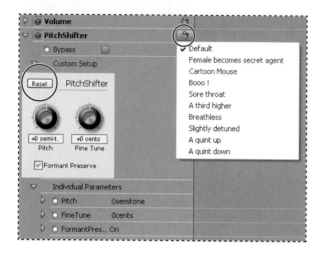

9   Try some of the presets, and note their values below the knobs in the Effect Controls panel.

10   Use the Individual Parameters sliders, and add keyframes at the beginning and end of a few phrases.

Use wildly different Pitch settings from –12 to + 12 semitone steps (2 steps equals a second in musical parlance—from C to D, for example) and switch Formant Preserve on and off.

Note: "Formant Preserve" is not a misprint. Formant is the character, resonance, and phonetic quality of a particular voice. Formant Preserve attempts to retain those elements even with severe pitch changes. Unlike Bypass, which uses a checkbox connected to its keyframe feature, Formant Preserve's checkbox keyframe is connected to a slider. That can lead to an inaccurate placement of the moment when you switch Formant Preserve on or off. To help remedy that, move the slider only far enough to go from on to off or vice versa, rather than using the checkbox.

11 Delete Ad Cliches from the sequence, and replace it with Music 13 Mono (you can do that by dragging Music 13 Mono to the beginning of the sequence, on top of Ad Cliches, to do an overlay edit).

12 Drag Treble to that clip, and increase its parameter.

This guitar clip lends itself to a treble boost.

Note: Treble is not simply Bass in reverse. Treble increases or decreases higher frequencies (4,000 Hz and above) while Bass changes low frequencies (200 Hz and less). The human audible frequency range is roughly 20 Hz to 20,000 Hz. Apply both Bass and Treble to a clip, and switch between them by clicking their Toggle Effect On Or Off buttons ( ).

13 Delete Treble, drag Reverb to the Effect Controls panel, and open Reverb's Custom Setup.

14 Play the clip, and drag the three white handles in the display to change the character of the reverb.

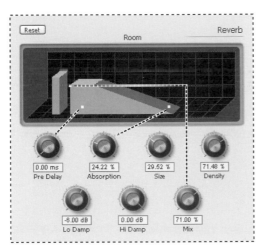

This is a fun effect that can give some real life to audio recorded in a "dead" room—a room like a recording studio with minimal reflective surfaces. As shown in the figure above, each of the three handles in the graphic control corresponds to a knob below it:

• **Pre Delay**—The apparent distance the sound travels to the reflecting walls and back.

• **Absorption**—How much of the sound is absorbed (not reflected).

• **Mix**—The amount of reverb.

Additional controls:

- **Size**—The apparent relative size of the room.

- **Density**—The density of the reverb "tail." The higher the Size value, the greater the Density range (from 0 to 100%).

- **Lo Damp**—Dampens low frequencies to prevent the reverb from rumbling or sounding muddy.

- **Hi Damp**—Dampens high frequencies. A low Hi Damp setting makes the reverb sound softer.

> ### A treasure trove of VST plug-ins
>
> *Reverb's rack of control knobs is a signal that this is a VST (Virtual Studio Technology) plug-in. These are custom-designed audio effects that adhere to a standard set by Steinberg audio. Invariably, those who create VST audio effect plug-ins want them to have a unique look and offer some very specialized audio effects. A wide variety of VST plug-ins is available on the Internet.*

Trying out stereo and 5.1 surround sound effects

The mono audio effects collection is a subset of the stereo and 5.1 effects. Those multi-channel effect groups have additional effects that relate to their extra channels. You'll see here how they work:

1　Open the Lesson13-2 project.

2　Drag Music 13 Stereo from the Project panel to the Audio 1 track in the sequence. In this project, the Audio 1 track is set up as a stereo track.

3　Attempt to drag any mono audio effect to the Music 13 Stereo clip.

You'll get a universal "No" symbol (⊘)—you can't apply a mono effect to a stereo clip.

4   Drag Balance from Effects > Audio Effects > Stereo to the Music 12 Stereo clip.

5   Drag the Balance slider in the Effect Controls panel left and right while you play this clip.

This clip was mixed with the guitar panned all the way left and the honky-tonk piano panned hard right. If you move the slider all the way to either end, you will hear only one instrument.

6   Add two keyframes, and have the audio pan from left to right. (Using keyframes for audio effects is similar to using them for video effects, which you learned in Lesson 9.)

7   Add two Bypass keyframes somewhere toward the middle of the clip.

The first one should have the Bypass option selected, and the second should not. (Your Effect Controls panel timeline should look like the next figure.)

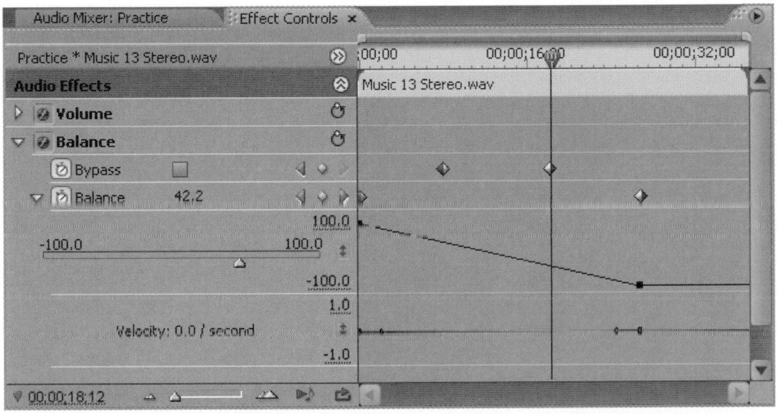

8   Play the clip.

The sound begins to move from the left to the right, jumps to the center at the first Bypass keyframe, holds there until the next Bypass keyframe, and then jumps toward the right and finishes its move to the right channel. Bypass tells Adobe Premiere Pro to ignore any effect settings.

9   Delete Balance, and apply Fill Right.

The Fill effects duplicate the selected channel, place it in the other channel, and discard that other channel's original audio. So Fill Right will play the honky-tonk piano in both left and right channels and will discard the guitar (the track in the left channel).

💡 **Use the same effect more than once**

You've probably seen an equalizer. Many car and home stereos have them. They enable you to punch up or cut a number of preset frequency ranges. The EQ effect in Adobe Premiere Pro fits that bill, but offers only five frequency ranges. If you want more possibilities, you can use Parametric EQ, which lets you select only one frequency range, but you can use it multiple times and select multiple frequencies. In effect, you can build a full graphic equalizer within the Effect Controls panel.

10 Drag Music 13 5.1 to the sequence, and Adobe Premiere Pro adds a 5.1 audio track to accommodate this new audio clip type.

11 Mute the Audio track containing the Music 13 Stereo clip by clicking the speaker button on the left side of the track label.

12 Drag Channel Volume from the Audio Effects > 5.1 folder to the Music 13 5.1 clip. Channel Volume lets you control the volume level for each of the six channels in a 5.1 surround sound clip and both channels of a stereo clip. The default setting for each channel is 0 dB, meaning no change from the original volume.

13 Play the clip, and drag the sliders for each channel to experiment with this effect.

Note: If you don't hear all six channels, it's because you need to change the 5.1 Mixdown setting. Choose Edit > Preferences > Audio (Windows) or Premiere Pro > Preferences > Audio (Mac OS), and change 5.1 Mixdown Type to Front + Rear + LFE.

A look at one more VST plug-in

Let's check out one more audio effect. This one is guaranteed to make your head spin. Drag MultibandCompressor to the Music 13 5.1 clip. As the next figure shows, you'll need to dramatically expand the Effect Controls panel to see its parameters (it might help to put the Effect Controls panel in a floating window).

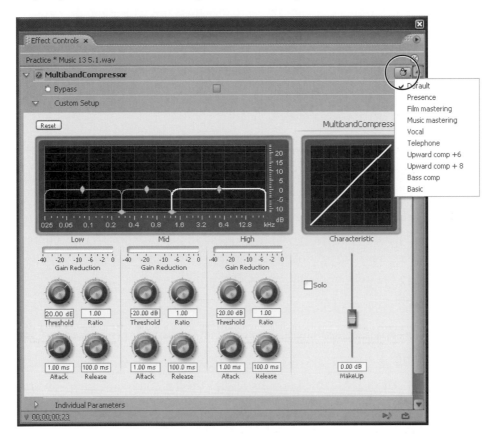

The MultibandCompressor's purpose is to narrow the dynamic range for up to three sets of frequency ranges. Explaining its parameters could take a full lesson (refer to Adobe Premiere Pro Help for parameter details). Instead, note that it offers a collection of presets accessed by clicking the button highlighted in the previous figure.

Editing keyframes by using the clip effect menu

You might have noticed that tucked away along the top edge of all clips—audio and video—is a pop-up menu of all the effects applied to a selected clip. You can find it just to the right of the clip name.

You might not be able to see the clip effect menu in all instances. The audio or video track needs to be in its expanded view. To do that, click the disclosure triangle to the left of the track name. If that does not reveal it, the clip is not wide enough. Zoom in on the Timeline to expand the width of the clip and reveal the clip effect menu.

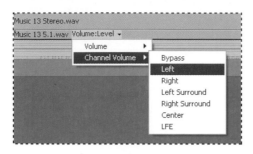

For audio clips, the header is always Volume: Level. For Video clips, it's Opacity: Opacity (despite Motion residing on the top of that pop-up menu). Every time you add an effect—video or audio—Adobe Premiere Pro adds that effect (along with a list of its parameters) to the bottom of that clip's effect menu.

1   Delete the MultibandCompressor effect.

2   Open the clip effect menu by clicking Channel Volume (shown in the previous figure).

3   Select Left.

4   Drag the yellow line, which now represents the left channel volume, up or down to change the left channel's volume.

5   Click the Show Keyframes button (🌑) on the left side of the audio track, and then set it to show Clip Volume. This will cause the track to display the clip's volume, rather than the track's volume.

6   Ctrl-click (Windows) or Command-click (Mac OS) the yellow line to add a couple of keyframes, and adjust them by dragging them left or right along the graph line or dragging them up or down.

The advantages of clip-based effect and keyframe editing are that you can get a better overall view of the entire clip, and if you want to change only one or two parameters, you can easily access them. Some disadvantages are that you can't change the parameters while the clip is playing, setting an exact parameter value is challenging, and changing more than a couple of parameters in the Timeline View gets tedious.

Working with the Audio Mixer

There is a big difference in how Adobe Premiere Pro handles layered audio tracks and layered video tracks.

Clips in higher-numbered video tracks cover what's below them on the Timeline. You need to do something to those higher video track clips—adjust opacity, create PiPs, or use specialized keying effects—to let clips below them show through.

Clips in audio tracks all play together. If you have ten layered audio tracks loaded up with a variety of audio clips and do nothing to them in terms of adjusting volume levels and stereo panning, they'll all play as one grand symphony (or cacophonous mess).

While you can adjust volume levels by using each clip's volume graph in the Timeline or Volume effect in the Effect Controls panel, it's much easier to use the Audio Mixer to adjust volume levels and other characteristics for multiple audio tracks.

Using a panel that looks a lot like production studio mixing hardware, you move track sliders to change volume, turn knobs to set left/right panning, add effects to entire tracks, and create submixes. Submixes let you direct multiple audio tracks to a single track so you can apply the same effects, volume, and panning to a group of tracks without having to change each of the tracks individually.

In this mini-lesson, you will mix a song recorded by a choir in a studio.

1 Double-click Music 13 - Sonoma Stereo Mix, and play it in the Source Monitor. This is how your final mix should sound.

2 Open the Lesson 13-3 project.

3 Play the Practice sequence, and note that the instruments are way too loud compared to the choir.

4 Choose Window > Workspace > Audio, and adjust the Audio Mixer so you can see all five tracks plus the Master track.

5   Change the track names along the top row of the Audio Mixer by selecting each one in turn and typing a new name: *Left, Right, Clarinet, Flute*, and *Bass* (see next figure). Those name changes also appear in the audio track headers in the Timeline.

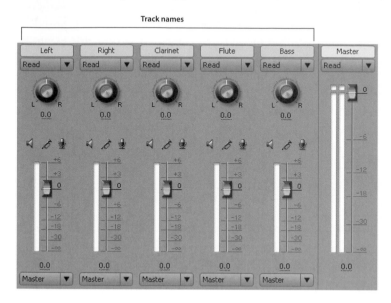

6   Play the sequence, and adjust the sliders in the Audio Mixer to create a mix that you think works well. (A good place to start is setting Left to 4, Right to 2, and dropping the Clarinet, Flute and Bass to -12, -10, and -12, respectively.)

7   Watch the Master track VU (volume unit) meter as you make your adjustments. Little hash marks (highlighted in the next figure) indicate the loudest passages. They remain for a couple of seconds and then move as the music volume changes. These hash marks provide a good way to see how balanced your left and right channels are. You want them to approximately line up most of the time.

Note: You want to avoid setting the volume too high (the VU meter line will turn red). That leads to distortion.

8 Adjust each channel's Left/Right Pan by using the knobs at the top of each track (when completed, your parameters should match those in the next figure):

- **Left**—all the way left (-100)
- **Right**—all the way right (+100)
- **Clarinet**—left-center (-20)
- **Flute**—right-center (+20)
- **Bass**—centered (0)

Note: It's best to pan a choir recorded with left and right mics all the way to the left and right, respectively, to fill both channels, but there's no need to spread the instruments out that much. They should sound like an ensemble. Furthermore, in general a bass should be centered because listeners do not perceive low frequencies as directional.

9 Click the Show/Hide Effects And Sends button (highlighted in the next figure).

This opens a set of empty panels where you can add effects to entire tracks and assign tracks to submixes.

10 Click the Effect Selection button for the Left track, and choose Reverb from the pop-up menu.

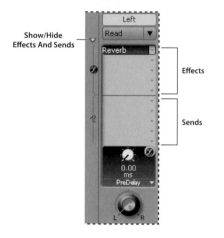

11 Isolate that track by clicking its Solo button (that mutes the rest of the channels).

You can click Solo buttons on more than one track to listen to a group of tracks. You can also click the Mute button to switch off audio playback for one or more tracks. You'll use the Enable Track For Recording button in the next mini-lesson.

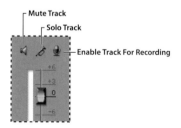

💡 **Keep tabs on Mute and Solo settings**

After working in the Audio Mixer for a while and then returning to the Timeline, you might not hear anything. Audio Mixer Mute and Solo settings do not show up in the Timeline, but are still in effect when you play a clip in the Timeline, even if the Audio Mixer is closed. So check those Mutes and Solos before shutting down the Audio Mixer.

12 Click the Reverb effect pop-up menu, and make changes to each parameter. Play the clip to listen to your changes as you make them.

Note: It's easier to apply effect parameters in the Effect Controls panel, but you can edit only clips there—not audio or video tracks. In this case, you could apply this effect to the clip instead of the track because there is only one clip on the track, but it's good to see how track-based effects work.

13 Undo your settings by removing the Reverb effect. To do that, click the Effect Selection button, and select None.

Automating changes in audio tracks

In this section, we set volume and panning values for entire tracks while listening to the audio. Adobe Premiere Pro also lets you apply volume and panning values that change over time, and you can apply them as you play your sequence.

To do that, use Automation Modes, accessed via pop-up menus at the top of each track in the Audio Mixer. Using one of the automation modes creates a series of track (as opposed to clip) keyframes for volume and panning, saving you from adding them one at a time.

Briefly, here's what each setting means (you can read more about this in Adobe Premiere Pro Help):

• **Off**—Ignores any changes you apply. Lets you test some adjustments without recording them.

• **Read**—Adjusting a track option (such as volume) affects the entire track uniformly. This is the default setting you used when setting the mix volume in step 6.

- **Write**—Records adjustments you make as you listen to a sequence.

- **Latch**—Works like Write but won't apply changes until you move the volume slider or panning knob. The initial property settings are from the previous adjustment.

- **Touch**—Works like Latch except when you stop adjusting a property, its option settings return to their previous state before the current automated changes were recorded.

Outputting tracks to submixes

You place your audio clips into audio tracks on the Timeline. You can apply effects and set volume and panning on a clip-by-clip basis. Or you can use the Audio Mixer to apply volume, panning, and effects to entire tracks. In either case, by default Adobe Premiere Pro sends audio from those clips and tracks to the Master track.

But sometimes you might want to route tracks to submix tracks before sending them on to the Master track.

The purpose of submix tracks is to save you steps and ensure some consistency in how you apply effects, volume, and panning. In the case of the Sonoma recording, you can apply Reverb with one set of parameters to the two choir tracks, and Reverb with different parameters to the three instruments. The submix can then send the processed signal to the Master track, or it can route the signal to another submix.

1 Open the Lesson 13-4 project. This project picks up where we left off with the Sonoma Choir.

2 Right-click (Windows) or Control-click (Mac OS) an audio track header in the Timeline and, using the next figure as a guide, choose Add Tracks. Set the Add values for Video Tracks and Audio Tracks to 0, the Add value for Audio Submix Tracks to 2, and the Track Type for Audio Submix Tracks to Stereo, and then click OK.

That adds two submix tracks to the Timeline, two tracks to the Audio Mixer (they have a darker hue), and adds those submix track names (Submix 1 and Submix 2) to the pop-up menus at the bottom of the Audio Mixer.

3   Click the Left track's Track Output Assignment pop-up menu (at the bottom of the Audio Mixer), and select Submix 1.

4   Do the same for the Right track.

Now both the Left and Right tracks have been sent to Submix 1. Their individual characteristics—panning and volume—will not change.

5   Send the three instrument tracks to Submix 2.

6   Apply Reverb to the Submix 1 track by clicking the Show/Hide Effects triangle and adding Reverb as an effect. Click its Solo button, play the audio, and adjust the Reverb parameters to make it sound like the choir is singing in a large auditorium (setting Size to about 60 is a good place to start).

7   Apply Reverb to the Submix 2 track, click its Solo button, switch off the Submix 1 Solo button (remember you can solo more than one track, but in this case you want to solo only Submix 2), play its audio, and set its parameters to create a sound a bit less dramatic than the voices.

8   Click the Solo button on Submix 1, and listen to these two submixes as a single mix to see how they sound.

Feel free to tweak the Volume and Reverb settings.

Recording voice-overs

The Adobe Premiere Pro Audio Mixer is also a basic recording studio. It can record anything you can connect to your sound card. In this case, you'll use your computer's microphone to do a voice recording.

1   Remove any audio files from the timeline, and set your CTI at the beginning.

2   Make sure that your computer's mic is plugged in to the Mic input on your sound card and your audio setup is set to recognize and record from the mic, and that it is not muted. Check your computer's documentation if you are not sure how to set up a microphone to record.

3   Choose Edit > Preferences > Audio Hardware (Windows) or Premiere Pro > Preferences > Audio Hardware (Mac OS), and ensure that your Default Device is the hardware you have connected your mic to.

Note: Generally, selecting Default will cover most circumstances. However, if you have a higher-end audio card, you should select it, refer to its product manual, and make any needed changes to its ASIO settings.

4   In the Audio Mixer, click the Enable Track For Recording button (the microphone) at the top of the audio track to which you wish to record.

You can enable as many tracks as you like, but you can't record to the Master track or a submix track.

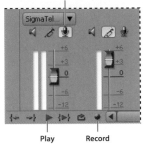

Enable Track For Recording

Play Record

5   Click the red Record button at the bottom of the Audio Mixer. It'll start blinking.

6   Move the CTI to where you want this narration to begin (it'll cover up any audio on the selected track at that location).

7   Click the Play button in the Audio Mixer, and start your narration.

Note: If you chose to locate the CTI in the music, you'll hear the music as you record your voice. Being able to hear your sequence's audio as you narrate can be a big help. Laying down video clips and then recording a narration is a workflow some editors follow.

8   When you finish recording, click the Stop button.

An audio clip appears on the selected audio track and in the Project panel. Adobe Premiere Pro automatically names that clip based on the Audio track number or name, and adds that audio file to the project file folder on your hard drive.

💡 What about feedback?

If you record audio and you have not taken steps to mute the output, you might get feedback—that lovely screeching noise that happens when a mic gets too close to a loudspeaker. There are several ways to deal with that: You can click the Mute button for the track, turn down your speakers (use headphones to listen to yourself), or choose Edit > Preferences > Audio (Windows) or Premiere Pro > Preferences > Audio (Mac OS), and then select Mute Input During Timeline Recording.

Creating a 5.1 surround sound mix

Adobe Premiere Pro lets you create a full, digital, 5.1 surround sound mix. You can use 5.1 surround sound in two places: audio on a DVD or an audio file for playback on a computer with 5.1 surround sound speakers.

5.1 digital audio has six discrete channels: left front, front center, right front, right rear or surround, left rear or surround, and the LFE (Low Frequency Effects) channel designated for a subwoofer.

If you have a 5.1 surround sound setup on your computer, this section will be a lot of fun and lead to much experimenting. If you don't have a six-speaker setup, this will give you at least a feel for how to add 5.1 surround to a DVD.

Here are the basic steps to follow:

1   Open the Lesson 13-5 project, and create a new sequence (File > New > Sequence) with seven mono tracks and a 5.1 audio Master track.

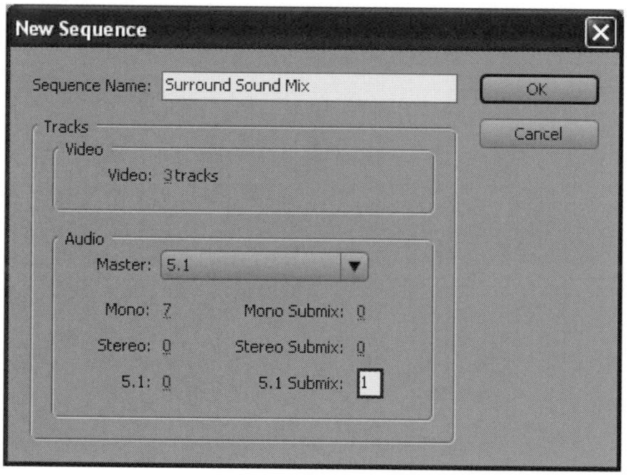

2   Drag the music clips to the timeline as shown below. Note that Sonoma-Left and Sonoma-Right appear on the timeline twice.

3   In the Audio Mixer, drag each track's 5.1 Panner puck to the proper location (use the next figure as a reference).

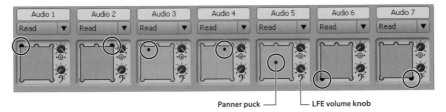

Panner puck ——   —— LFE volume knob

4   Set volume levels for tracks 1-5 that are similar to those you set for the stereo mix. For Audio 5, the bass, adjust the volume of the bass using the LFE volume knob, and place its puck in the center. Set volume levels for tracks 6 and 7 (left-rear and right-rear) to 0 and −2, respectively.

Now you have some options:

• You can move the clips on Audio 6 and Audio 7 about a tenth of a second (3 frames) into the timeline (causing them to play a little after the rest of the clips) to make it sound like they're coming from the back of the room. To do that, select each clip in turn, press the plus sign (+) on the numeric keypad, type 3 on the numeric keypad, and press Enter.

• You can add a Reverb with a Size parameter a bit higher than what you choose to set for the front channels. You might find that you don't need to have as much reverb for the front channels when you work in 5.1 surround sound.

Fixing, sweetening, and creating soundtracks in Soundbooth

Adobe Soundbooth is a brand new application designed especially for video and Flash editors. Soundbooth can be run as a standalone audio tool, or it can be invoked from Adobe Premiere Pro. While many audio tools are built into Adobe Premiere Pro, Soundbooth is designed to deal with specific audio challenges that video editors face every day. You will find Soundbooth easy to use, yet very powerful.

Rather than give you a series of full-blown lessons on Soundbooth, we will review the most common uses you will run into: adding effects, cleaning up noisy audio, and creating a royalty-free soundtrack.

Cleaning up noisy audio

Of course it's always best to record perfect audio at the source. However, there are times when you cannot control the origin of the audio, and it's impossible to re-record it, so you are stuck needing to repair a bad audio clip. To that end, the sample we will work on is a real-world nightmare—a voice-over style narration with a horrible 60hz hum and a cell phone ringing in the background—but don't pull your hair out, because Soundbooth is up to the task.

1   Open the Lesson 13-6 project.

2   Double-click audio problems.wav to open it in the Source Monitor. Play the clip, and notice the 60hz hum throughout and the cell phone ringing near the end.

Note: A 60hz or 50hz hum can be caused by many electrical problems, cable problems, or equipment noise.

3   Open the audio problems fixed.wav in the Source Monitor, and listen to it. Soundbooth was used to remove the hum and the cell phone without noticeably affecting the voice.

4   Drag audio problems.wav to the Audio 2 track on the timeline.

5   Right-click (Windows) or Control-click (Mac OS) the audio problems clip on the timeline, and choose Edit In Adobe Soundbooth > Render And Replace from the context menu. Adobe Soundbooth starts, and displays the clip.

Note: You can also choose to edit the source file, if you don't need to keep the original file. The Render And Replace command does not affect the original file. Rather, it renders a new copy of the file and replaces it automatically on the timeline, so the original file is not changed.

6   By default, Soundbooth displays two views of your audio file: the common waveform view showing audio amplitudes near the top of the screen, and a colorful spectral display view showing audio frequencies near the bottom of the screen. If you can't see both views, drag the horizontal divider between the panels up or down so they are both visible. Give the frequency display more room.

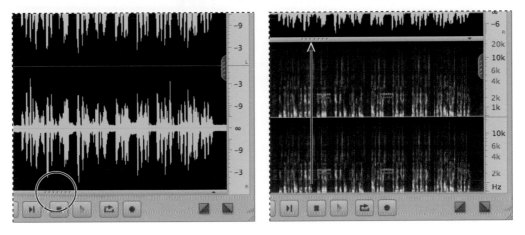

Note: The spectral display shows frequencies over time rather than amplitudes over time. In this display, colors represent amplitude—dark blue for low amplitude and bright yellow for high amplitude.

7   Play the file to hear the problems again, the hum and the cell phone ringing. You can drag the CTI, similar to the way you would in Adobe Premiere Pro, and use the playback controls at the bottom of the screen.

8 To remove the 60hz hum, click on the Effects tab in the left-center panel. Click the Stereo Rack Preset pop-up menu, and choose Fix:Remove 60 Cycle Hum.

9 Play the file again, and hear the amazing difference.

10 The effect is not permanently applied to the file yet. To permanently apply this change, click the Apply To File button at the bottom of the Effects Rack.

11 To remove the cell phone, we need to use the spectral display. The ringing cell phone is not visible as a change in amplitude, so it is not useful to use the waveform display for this problem. However, if you zoom out so the whole file is visible, the cell phone rings are quite obvious in the spectral display as short horizontal dashes between 2Khz and 3Khz.

12 Position the CTI over the first cell phone ring, and zoom in by pressing the equal sign key (=) on the keyboard or the plus sign (+) on the numeric keypad.

13 Select the Rectangular Marquee tool, and then select the cell phone ring. Make the marquee selection just slightly bigger than the visible ring. Be as precise as possible. When you are finished, the selection appears as an opaque box around the cell phone ring with a dB adjustment tool floating above it.

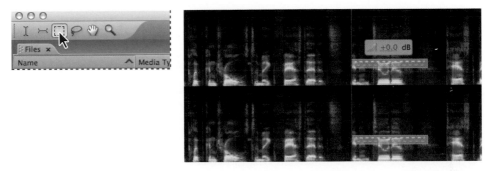

14 Adjust the selection to -34dB. This reduces the frequencies you selected with the Marquee tool by negative 34dB.

Note: A common mistake is to reduce noise selections to the maximum (-96dB) to remove them completely. However, this creates a complete void in that frequency spectrum for your selection, which is often noticeable. Most noises are soft enough that -34db is enough to eliminate them without removing the frequency space completely. Experiment by removing the least amount possible to keep your audio sounding natural.

15 Zoom out, and play the clip. Even though it appears that some of the ring tone is still there, notice it is dark blue, which means very low volume.

16 Save the changes to the clip by choosing File > Save. Switch back to Adobe Premiere Pro, and notice that the audio file on the timeline has been updated with the changes.

Adding audio effects in Soundbooth

1 We will use the same audio file to add a few effects in Adobe Soundbooth. Either continue where you left off, or open the audio problems fixed.wav in Soundbooth.

2 Choose Vocal Enhancer from the Effects menu. In the Effects panel, choose Male as the Effect Preset for the Vocal Enhancer effect.

3   Remove this Vocal Enhancer effect by selecting it and then clicking the trash can icon in the lower right of the Effects panel.

4   Another way to add an effect to the Effects panel is to click the Add An Effect To The Rack icon (⊘) in the lower right corner of the panel. Choose Analog Delay, and experiment with the many presets available.

5   Remove the Analog Delay effect.

You can add multiple effects to the Effect Rack at the same time. When you get a combination of effects you like, you can save them as a Rack preset. There are many pre-loaded Rack presets you can choose from and experiment with.

6   Try one of the Rack presets: Choose Voice: Old Time Radio, and play the effect.

7   If you want to get more advanced and tweak some of the settings yourself, click the Settings link to the right of each effect name. This gives you access to the detailed settings of each effect.

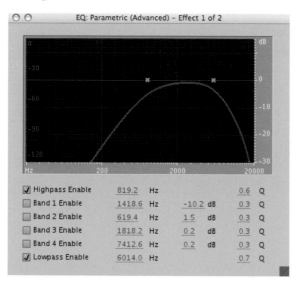

Creating a soundtrack in Soundbooth

Adobe Soundbooth CS3 has the ability to create custom soundtracks based on themes or scores provided with the program.

1   Choose Tasks > Auto Compose Score.

2   Click Browse Scores in the Tasks panel to use Adobe Bridge to browse the included Soundbooth scores.

Note: Bridge should automatically open in the Soundbooth Scores content directory and display several folders of scores. If this does not happen, please review the installation of Soundbooth to ensure you have installed all functional content.

3   Open the Rock-Pop folder and double-click Lost Highway to open that composition in Soundbooth.

Notice that the composition is made up of different segments, such as part1, part2, and so on. Soundbooth automatically assembles these parts to achieve the length and style audio you require.

4   Change the duration by using the Duration box at the top of the Tasks panel. Notice that Soundbooth recomposes the sections to accommodate the length you specify.

5   Change the Editing mode from Basic to Keyframing. (You may need to expand the Tasks panel to see these options.) Move the CTI to the center of the composition, and then click the keyframe icon next to the Guitar segment to add a guitar keyframe. Adjust the Guitar setting to 0% at this keyframe.

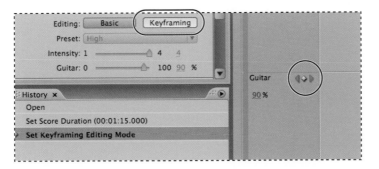

6 Move the CTI several seconds to the right of this keyframe, and adjust Guitar to 100%. Notice that Soundbooth added a new keyframe at this point. Play the composition and listen to how the amount of solo guitar changes over the keyframe area.

7 Click Export Score to export the composition to an audio file. (You may need to expand the Tasks panel to see this button.) Several audio formats are available in the export options.

There are endless combinations of changes you can make to the composition to customize it for your project. Experiment with all the options, and consult Soundbooth Help for information about additional features.

Review

▶ Review questions

1 There are at least four ways to make audio move from the right channel to the left and back. What are they?

2 You are playing a 5.1 surround sound clip but can't hear all the channels. What's a possible cause?

3 What's the difference between Delay and Reverb?

4 Can you record a voice-over while other audio is playing on the timeline?

5 How do you apply the same audio effect with the same parameters to three audio tracks?

6 Describe the difference between the Edit Source File and Render And Replace commands when editing a file from Adobe Premiere Pro in Soundbooth.

▶ Review answers

1 Balance adjusts the overall balance, left or right. Channel Volume enables you to adjust the volume of each channel individually. You can also use the Audio Mixer's Left/Right Pan knob, or use clip or track keyframes on the Timeline.

2 Check the Audio preferences, and make sure the 5.1 Mixdown setting includes all channels.

3 Delay creates a distinct, single echo that can repeat and gradually fade. Reverb creates a mix of echoes to simulate a room. It has multiple parameters that take the hard edge off the echo that you hear in the Delay effect.

4 Yes. When you start recording the voice-over, any other audio tracks on the timeline will be heard as you record.

5 The easiest way is to create a submix track, assign those three tracks to that submix track, and apply the effect to the submix.

6 Edit Source File changes the original source audio file. Render And Replace creates a new copy of the audio file, and changes the copy rather than the original.

compositing

alpha channel

keying

Opacity

One important feature of Adobe Premiere Pro is its ability to composite (or layer) any number of video clips, graphics, and still images. You've already done some compositing: placing text over videos and creating PiPs. Other compositing techniques involve changing opacity, using chroma keys, working with mattes, or applying Adobe Premiere Pro keying effects that combine multiple clips. Compositing will become a significant part of your video productions.

14 | Compositing Techniques

Topics covered in this lesson:

- Making compositing part of your projects
- Working with the Opacity effect
- Two multiple-track video effects: Blend and Texturize
- Working with alpha-channel transparencies
- Applying chroma, color, and luminance keying effects
- Blurring a moving face with a track matte

Getting started

Adobe Premiere Pro and other nonlinear editors have a general operating practice: Clips in video tracks above Video 1 trump clips in tracks below them on the timeline. In other words, whatever appears on a track covers up whatever is below it.

However, the object isn't to use clips in tracks above Video 1 to obliterate what's beneath them. It's to use compositing to enhance what's down there. Adobe Premiere Pro gives you many ways to layer videos, graphics, and images for best effect.

You use compositing techniques on clips so the clips below them on the timeline can show through. There are four basic compositing methods:

- Reducing the opacity of an entire clip
- Alpha-channel transparencies in clips and effects
- Chroma, color, and luminance keying effects
- Matte keying effects

In the upcoming mini-lessons, you will try all of these compositing methods, and use different techniques with a few you've already tried. Once you see all the possibilities, you'll start to plan and shoot your projects with layered videos, graphics, and images in mind.

Making compositing part of your projects

You see compositing when you watch a TV meteorologist standing in front of a map or some other graphic background. As shown in the following photos, most times they're standing in front of a green or blue wall. The technical director uses a keying effect to make that wall transparent, and then inserts a weather graphic. You can do the same thing in your video projects by using an Adobe Premiere Pro video keying effect.

Matt Zaffino, Chief Meteorologist—KGW-TV, Portland, Oregon

Many movies, as well as most computer games with live actors, use compositing. "Green screen" studios enable game developers and film directors to place actors in science-fiction and other settings created with 3D computer graphics. Such sets make it possible for actors to work in relative safety while the finished product shows them dangling from a skyscraper, hundreds of feet in the air.

Shooting videos with compositing in mind

Making keying effects work well takes some extra effort. Proper backdrop colors, lighting, and keying techniques all come into play. You need to consider which keying effect will work best for your circumstances.

Some keys use textures or graphics, so there is not a whole lot of planning you need to do, but most keying effects take some extra thought and work:

- High-contrast scenes lend themselves to making either the dark or light portions transparent. The same holds true for shooting light objects against a dark background or vice versa.

- Solid-color backgrounds are fairly easy to make transparent. Take care that the subjects you *don't* want to key out aren't wearing clothing with colors that match the background.

- For most keying shots, you need to use a tripod and lock down your camera. Bouncing keyed objects creates viewer disconnects. There are exceptions to this rule. Typically, if you're keying in wild, animated backgrounds, then camera movement will not be a problem.

- Most times you want your background (or the other images you'll insert in the transparent areas you create with keying effects) to match those keyed shots. If you're working with outdoor scenes, try to shoot the keyed shots outside or use lights balanced for daylight.

Examples of composited clips

Before you get started on this lesson, take a look at some composited clips created for the upcoming mini-lessons. This will give you an idea of some of the compositing techniques you'll be working on.

1   Start Adobe Premiere Pro, and open the Lesson 14 project. The Project panel appears with a wide range of goodies: graphics, videos, still images, and mattes.

Note: The Mac OS version of Adobe Premiere Pro does not currently support the Chroma Key filter. Mac users will get the following error when loading the Lesson 14 project file: "Video Filter missing: AE.ADBE Legacy Key Chroma." Mac users please skip the sections pertaining to the Chroma Key filter.

2   Open the Lesson 14 Finish sequence, and look at the collection of composited clips there:

- Three views of the Duomo, the main cathedral in Sienna, Italy: superimposed over a sunset, with an added stained-glass window, and with both a sunset and stained glass.

- A model, shot in front of a green screen, with an animated background inserted behind her.

- Leaves floating over a sunset, created with the Luma key effect.

- A cat's eyes revealed in the sky, using a garbage matte key.

- An image revealed in another image, using the Track Matte Key effect and a blur effect.

- A traveling matte that blurs the face of a bike rider.

Working with the Opacity effect

One easy way to see compositing at work is to place a video or graphic on a superimposing track, and then make it partially transparent—turn down its opacity—to let videos on lower tracks show through. You can accomplish this using the Opacity effect. Though it can be very useful, you'll discover in this mini-lesson that Opacity's blanket approach to compositing is not always effective. In certain circumstances, you might want to use some other similar Adobe Premiere Pro tools.

In this lesson, you'll reduce opacity on several items. Later, you'll learn ways to achieve more effective results using some of the same clips.

1   Open the Lesson 14 Practice sequence.

2   Drag Photo 14b from the Project panel to the Video 1 track.

3   Drag Orange Matte to the Video 2 track directly above Photo 14b.

The matte completely covers the photo.

4   Select the Orange Matte clip, and expand Opacity in the Effect Controls panel.

Opacity has only one parameter: percent.

5   Use keyframes to set an Opacity of 100% (opaque) at the beginning of the clip and an opacity of 0% (completely transparent) at the end.

6   Play the clip. The orange gradually becomes less opaque and more like a tint. Finally it disappears altogether.

7   Right-click (Windows) or Control-click (Mac OS) the Orange Matte clip, and then choose Copy.

You'll paste the Opacity parameters on another clip to save a few steps.

8   Drag Gradient 14 on top of the Orange Matte clip in Video 2 to do an overlay edit.

9   Right-click (Windows) or Control-click (Mac OS) the Gradient 14 clip, and choose Paste Attributes.

That applies the Opacity parameters with the keyframes you set for the Orange Matte clip to the Gradient clip.

> ### 💡 Copy a clip and paste its attributes
>
> *This is a tremendously useful tool. You can copy a clip and paste it somewhere else in any sequence. Or, you can merely paste its attributes—any effects applied to it along with their parameters and keyframes—onto another clip. That latter feature is a great way to achieve consistent results. If you do PiPs, you can set a clip size, and then apply that to all the clips in the PiP, changing only their screen locations.*

10   Play the composited clips.

This gradient was set up using the Titler. It's simply a rectangle with a four-color gradient fill applied. You can double-click Gradient 14 in the Project panel to open the Titler and change the characteristics of the gradient.

11   Drag Texture 14.psd on top of Gradient 14 in the Video 2 track to do an overlay edit.

12 Right-click (Windows) or Control-click (Mac OS), and choose Paste Attributes.

Since you have not done any other copying, the previous Copy remains in effect, and the texture clip acquires the Opacity parameters and keyframes.

This texture graphic was made using a simple preset in Photoshop CS3.

13 Play this composited clip, and note how the texture shows up in the clip.

You'll use a much more effective means to add texture later in the lesson.

14 Replace Texture 14 with Photo 14a, apply the Paste Attributes command to it as before, and then play it.

It adds a nice sunset glow to the clip. Later you'll see a *much* better way to composite the sunset with the cathedral.

Note: If you place the sunset photo on the lower track and the building above it, and apply a reduced opacity to the building, the effect will look the same.

It is relatively effective to use Opacity to composite a scene with another clip that has a bright object with a dark background. But sometimes shots composited using Opacity have a washed-out look, and later you'll see ways to avoid that undesirable effect.

Two multiple-track video effects: Blend and Texturize

Two video effects combine clips on two tracks:

- **Blend**—Works something like Opacity but gives you extra options that can have some surprisingly colorful results.

- **Texturize**—Enables you to give a clip something akin to an embossed feel using a clip below it on the sequence.

1   Marquee-select the clips in the Lesson 14 Practice sequence, and press Delete.

2   Drag Photo 14b back to the Video 1 track.

3   Drag Photo 14a to the Video 2 track, directly above Photo 14b.

Note: To see this effect, you need to switch off the display of the clip in Video 2. You could turn off the entire Video 2 track by clicking its Toggle Track Output eyeball, but then nothing on that entire track would be visible. Adobe Premiere Pro gives you the option of switching off an individual clip.

4   Right-click (Windows) or Control-click (Mac OS) the clip in the Video 2 track, and then deselect Enable.

That switches off that clip's display and changes the clip color in the sequence to light blue.

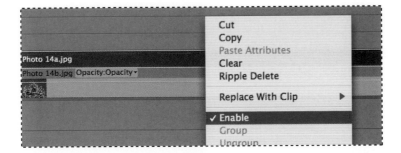

5   Apply the Blend video effect (Video Effects > Channel) to the clip in the Video 1 track.

6 Select Video 2 from the Blend With Layer menu.

That menu includes every video track in your sequence.

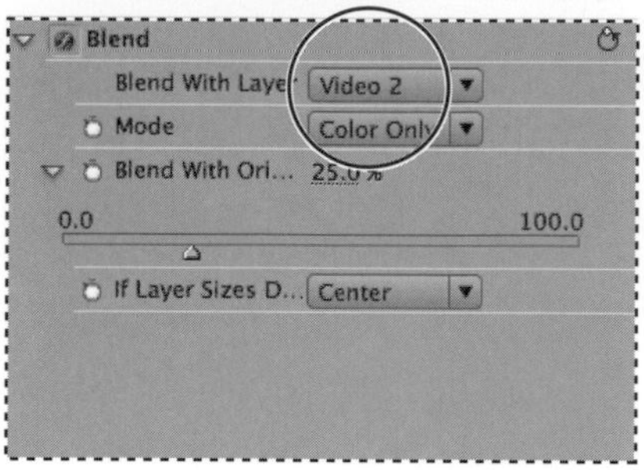

7 Work your way through the Blend modes, and move the Blend With Original slider to see how this effect works.

Crossfade duplicates the Opacity effect. Color Only is the most colorful. The Mode parameter is keyframeable, so you can switch from mode to mode within a single clip.

8 Delete Blend from the Effect Controls panel and replace it with Texturize (Video Effects > Stylize).

9 Choose Video 2 from the Texture Layer menu.

Note: As with Blend, you need to disable the Texture Layer clip to see this effect. Since you've already done it by deselecting the Enable command in step 4, there's no need to duplicate that step here.

10 Set Texture Contrast to its highest value (2), and then adjust Light Direction for greatest impact.

Even in something as untextured as a sunset, you get an embossed feel (see the image on the left in the next figure).

11 Drag Texture 14.psd on top of Photo 14a in the Video 2 track to do an overlay edit.

12 Right-click (Windows) or Control-click (Mac OS) the new clip, and deselect Enable.

It should look like the image on the right in the next figure (you might need to move the Texturize Contrast slider slightly to see that).

Note: You might need to adjust a parameter in the Texturize effect to see it switch from the old sunset texture to the new clip's texture.

Two examples of the Texturize effect

13 Replace Texture 14.psd on the sequence with Stained Glass 14a.psd, right-click (Windows) or Control-click (Mac OS) the new clip, and then deselect Enable.

This is a 200x200 pixel graphic. Texturize can use clips that have a small frame size like this to create a repeated texture pattern. Because DV is 720x480, there will be slightly more than three across and more than two down.

14 Set Texture Placement to Tile Texture. That distributes several instances of this circular graphic around the scene.

Note: Because you disables the Texture Layer clip, you can't apply Motion or any other effect to it, but all is not lost. You can use a nested sequence to accomplish that. Such a sequence has been set up for the next step.

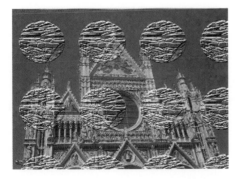

15 Drag Lesson 14 Nested Sequence 1 (it's a logo with Motion applied to it) on top of Stained Glass 14a.psd in the Video 2 track. This is a spinning logo.

16 Right-click (Windows) or Control-click (Mac OS) the clip, and deselect Enable.

17 Play the clip. The spinning logo moves through the image, even though the nested sequence's clip is disabled.

Working with alpha-channel transparencies

Many graphics and some of the Adobe Premiere Pro transitions have what are called alpha channels—portions of the clips or gaps in the transitions that can be made transparent, revealing what's below those clips and transitions on a sequence. You'll work with both in this mini-lesson.

1 Drag Photo 14e to Video 1, past the clips you worked on previously.

2 Place Logo 14 in Video 2 above that clip.

This is a Photoshop CS3 graphic with an alpha channel. By default, Adobe Premiere Pro makes the graphic opaque and its alpha channel transparent, allowing whatever is below the alpha channel on the sequence to show through. You can use the Alpha Adjust effect to see the alpha channel.

3 Apply Alpha Adjust (Video Effects > Keying) to Logo 14.

Alpha Adjust is the clip-based version of the Opacity fixed effect. As with the Transform effect's connection to Motion, you can use Alpha Adjust to apply Opacity at some other point in the effect chain, instead of second-to-last, where it would occur if you were to use the Opacity fixed effect. Alpha Adjust has a few extra parameters in addition to Opacity:

- **Ignore Alpha**—Makes the alpha channel opaque, covering up the clip below it.
- **Invert Alpha**—Makes the graphic transparent and the alpha channel opaque.
- **Mask Only**—Converts the graphic to a white silhouette.

4   Select both Invert Alpha and Mask Only to create something like a spiral porthole.

5   Select Alpha Adjust in the Effect Controls panel, and press Delete.

Video effects that work with graphic-file alpha channels

Four video effects work well with graphic-file alpha channels: Alpha Glow, Bevel Alpha, Channel Blur, and Drop Shadow. You've already seen Drop Shadow, so here we'll look at the other three:

1   Apply Alpha Glow (Video Effects > Stylize) to the graphic in Video 2, open its Settings dialog box, and experiment with its settings.

The Start Color and End Color parameters set the colors of the glow.

2   Delete Alpha Glow from the Effect Controls panel, and drag Bevel Alpha (Video Effects > Perspective) in its place.

Give this graphic a 3D beveled feel by adjusting the effect's parameters.

3   Add Channel Blur (Video Effects > Blur & Sharpen) below Bevel Alpha in the Effect Controls panel.

This shifts individual color values—red/green/blue—as well as blurring the graphic into its alpha channel. As you adjust Channel Blur parameters, consider that these color and blurring changes are all keyframeable—all these cool color shifts can happen over time.

Applying chroma, color, and luminance keying effects

Using Opacity to combine two or more clips works well for some images, but it's an inexact science. You can get more precise compositing results by using keying effects.

Keying effects use various methods to make portions of a clip transparent. To get a quick overview, open Video Effects > Keying in the Effects panel. There are many effects. With the exception of Alpha Adjust (the clip-based Opacity video effect), they fall into three basic camps:

- **Color/Chroma**—Blue Screen (Windows only), Chroma (Windows only), Color, Non-Red, and RGB Difference (Windows only).
- **Luminance**—Luma, Multiply (Windows only), and Screen (Windows only).
- **Matte**—Difference, Garbage, Image, Remove, and Track.

You'll work with Color/Chroma and Luminance keys in this mini-lesson, and with Matte keys later on.

Color keys and Chroma keys all work in basically the same way: You select a color for them to make transparent, and apply a few other parameters (basically adjusting the width of that color selection).

Luminance keys look for dark or light areas in a clip, and make them transparent (or opaque). In this mini-lesson we'll see the Chroma, Color, and Luma keying effects.

Mattes typically do the equivalent of cutting a hole in a clip using a graphic or some other user-defined region.

Using the chroma key effect (Windows only)

1   Drag Photo 14a to Video 1 and Photo 14b to Video 2 (place them after the clips you worked on earlier).

You will *key out* the blue sky (make it transparent) to display the sunset clip below it in the sequence.

2   Apply Chroma Key (Video Effects > Keying) to the clip in Video 2.

Take a look at its parameters in the Effect Controls panel:

- **Similarity**—The range of the target color that will be made transparent.
- **Blend**—How much of the clip that you are keying out blends with the underlying clip.
- **Threshold**—Shadow amounts of objects not keyed out that are retained in the keyed-out color.
- **Cutoff**—Darkens or lightens shadows. Dragging too far to the right (beyond the Threshold slider) effectively switches off the Chroma Key effect.
- **Smoothing**—The amount of anti-aliasing (edge softening) applied to the boundary between transparent and opaque regions.

- **Mask Only**—Displays a white silhouette of the opaque areas in the keyed clip. Use this to fine-tune the parameters to avoid creating transparent holes in areas you don't want to key out.

3 Drag the eyedropper from the Color parameter into the clip in the Program Monitor, and click somewhere in the sky to select its blue color.

💡 **Get an average color value to improve keying**

The eyedropper selects a color from a single pixel. Frequently that single pixel does not represent the average color of the region you want to key out, leading to keying results that are less than satisfactory. When using the eyedropper to get a color sample for a key, Ctrl-click (Windows) or Command-click (Mac OS) to get a subsample—a 5x5-pixel area.

4 Adjust the Similarity slider until all the blue disappears and some of the sunset starts showing through sections of the cathedral—to about 25%.

If you have not seen a chroma key at work before, that little parameter change is sure to get your attention, but you've keyed out too wide a selection of color. You'll fine-tune that in the next steps.

5 Click Mask Only.

Your keyed shot should look like the image on the left in the next figure.

6 Adjust the Similarity slider until there are no more holes in the silhouette—to about 13%.

💡 **Zoom in to adjust parameters**

Use the View Zoom Level pop-up menu in the Program Monitor to zoom in on the image and get a closer look at the boundary between the silhouette and the sunset. That will help you fine-tune Similarity and other parameters. You'll notice that it's hard to get rid of all the artifacts near the edges without cutting some small holes in the building. You will need to find a reasonable compromise such that, at regular magnification, your viewers won't notice.

7 Deselect Mask Only.

Your keyed shot should look like the image on the right in the next figure. Because the sky is so uniformly blue (that's why this was a good shot for this exercise), there's no real need for you to adjust the other parameters.

8　Delete the sunset clip in Video 1, move the clip in Video 2 to Video 3, and place Stained Glass 14 in Video 4, above the cathedral photo in Video 3.

You placed the stained glass image above the cathedral clip to help position it (you'll move it to Video 2 in a moment), and you moved the cathedral clip up because you're going to put another instance of it below the original on the timeline.

9　Drag and slightly expand the stained glass clip in the Program Monitor so it completely covers the window (see next figure, left image).

10　Drag that stained glass clip from Video 4 to Video 2, below the clip in Video 3.

11　Select the clip in Video 3 to display its parameters in the Effect Controls panel (Chroma Key is still applied to it), drag the eyedropper to the cathedral window, and then Ctrl-click (Windows) or Command-click (Mac OS) there to get a 5x5-pixel subsample or average color value.

12　Use Mask Only, Similarity, and Blend to attempt to key out the window without keying out edges of the cathedral (refer to the next figure, center image).

You will not be able to do it. But because this graphic has a transparent alpha channel, you can put another instance of the cathedral image below it on the sequence to fill the holes left by the chroma key, in effect creating a three-layer image sandwich.

13　Drag another instance of Photo 14b to Video 1.

14　Deselect Mask Only for the clip in Video 3.

Your image should look like the image on the right in the next figure.

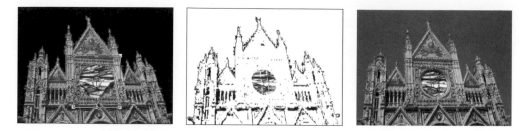

Using a nested sequence to add another chroma key (Windows only)

If you try to add the sunset to this three-clip composite, it won't work. You could drag the cathedral photo to Video 4 and place the sunset image in Video 3, but that would cover the stained glass graphic and the cathedral shot in Video 2 and Video 1. The solution is to create a nested sequence.

1   Drag Photo 14a to Video 1 and Lesson 14 Nested Sequence 2 to Video 2 (place them after the clips already in your sequence).

That nested sequence is the same three-layer image sandwich you just created.

2   Apply Chroma Key to the Nested Sequence clip, select the sky color, and adjust Similarity. Your clip should look like the next figure.

Using the Color Key effect

The Color Key effect is your best bet for accurate, relatively-low-budget-but-professional-looking keying, but shooting video that will key cleanly is not guaranteed. See the following tips for some helpful advice.

Tips for effective chroma key shots

Chroma key video shoots don't always go smoothly. For the key effects to work effectively, you should follow these tips:

• Use flat lighting (two lights at 45° angles to the screen) to avoid creating hot spots. No need to overdo the lighting. Simply make it even.

• The actor's lighting does not have to be flat. Controlled spotlights or lights with "barn doors" work well.

• If you're going to key in an outdoor background, use daylight-balanced blue gels over your lights to re-create outdoor lighting (or shoot your chroma key shots outdoors). If you're working with live actors, use a fan to blow their hair around to enhance the illusion.

• Avoid chroma key spill—keep actors at least four feet away from the backdrop to avoid picking up its reflected color. A backlight on the actors minimizes spill.

• The tighter the shot, the more realistic the finished look will be.

• Fast-paced action is harder to key right to the edges of your subjects.

• Use a wide-open iris on your camcorder to limit the depth of field and to throw the blue or green screen a bit out of focus, making it easier to key out.

• Chroma key fabric and paper cost about $8 a square yard, and paint about $60 a gallon. You can find many dealers online.

• Which color to use? With chroma key green, you have a reasonable assurance that no one will have clothing that matches it and therefore will key out. Chroma key blue works well because it's complementary to skin tones.

• Consumer and prosumer camcorders do not key as well as professional camcorders because they record less color information. However, because they give more weight to green colors to correspond to the color sensitivity of human eyes, green screens key more cleanly than blue.

1   Drag Gradient 14 to Video 1 and Video 14 to Video 2 (place them after the clips already on the sequence).

2   Use the Rate Stretch tool (X) to drag the end of Video 14 to make it as long as the clip below it (Background 14)—that is, five seconds.

3   Play the sequence, and note a couple things:

•   The production crew used a chroma key green screen.

•   The green screen in this shot is not as brightly lit as most green screen shots. You will use the Brightness & Contrast video effect to add some sparkle to it.

- There is no camera movement, although on some other shots from this production there is movement because the crew knew the editors would use wildly animated backgrounds that lend themselves to that kind of action.

4 Apply the Color Key effect (Video Effects > Keying) to the clip in Video 2.

5 In the Effect Controls panel, expand the Color Key effect to view its parameters.

6 Drag the eyedropper to the green screen to sample the green color. You should see small parts of the gradient background appear.

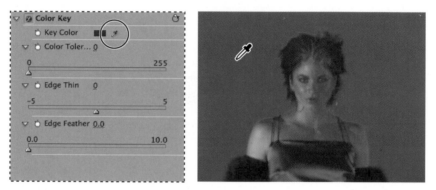

7 Adjust the Color Tolerance slider until the green background is gone. If you slide it too far, the subject will start to become transparent.

8 Move the Edge Thin slider to the right, to reduce the edge of the key. Try setting it to 1.

9 Set the Edge Feather slider to 5. This makes the edge of the key softer.

10 Play the clip to see the effect.

It looks like the model could have a bit more illumination and contrast. You'll add that in the next step.

💡 **Blurring the background can be effective**

Sometimes blurring the background of a keyed shot can give it a realistic look. Typically, you want to make the subject, which you've shot with a key in mind, the focal point of your composited clip. If you use a background that's a bit out of focus, the subject stands out even more. To create that illusion, simply use a blur effect on the background clip.

11 Ensure the clip in Video 2 is selected, and then drag the Brightness & Contrast effect (Video Effects > Color Correction) to the Effect Controls panel *above* the Color Key effect.

12 Make some adjustments to suit your taste. For example, you might try setting Brightness to 25 and setting Contrast to 43.

13 Since the background and model are now brighter, you will need to adjust the Color Key effect. Reset the values on the Color Key effect, and set it up again. You will find the key is much cleaner now, because the scene has more contrast.

Using the Luma Key effect

Luminance keys—Luma, Multiply, and Screen—create transparencies using clip brightness values. Luma Key is the catch-all of this category. Multiply Key (Windows only) creates transparencies in bright areas of the clip; Screen key (Windows only) creates transparencies in dark areas.

1 Drag Photo 14e to Video 1 and Photo 14f to Video 2 (place them after the clips you worked on in previous lessons).

2 Apply the Luma Key (Video Effects > Keying) effect to the clip in Video 2 (the leaf).

3 Adjust its parameters in the Effect Controls panel to remove the dark background.

There is no Mask Only option in this effect, so it's a little more difficult to find a happy medium. A good starting place is Threshold 51 and Cutoff 43.

Extra credit tasks

Take this key a few steps further.

1   Use the Motion effect to move the leaf to the lower left corner.

2   Apply the Drop Shadow effect (Video Effects > Perspective) to it, and adjust those parameters to have the shadow fall down to the right.

3   Drag another instance of Photo 14f from the Project panel to Video 3 above the clips in Video 1 and Video 2.

4   Right-click (Windows) or Control-click (Mac OS) the clip in Video 2, choose Copy, right-click or Control-click the clip in Video 3, and then choose Paste Attributes.

That applies the Luma Key, Motion, and Drop Shadow effects to that clip.

5   Use Motion to move the clip in Video 2 to the upper right, spin it 180 degrees. Change the Drop Shadow direction to have it fall at the correct angle (add 180 to whatever setting you chose for the first clip).

Your composited shot should look like the next figure.

Using matte keys

Matte keys cut "holes" in one clip to allow portions of another to show through, or to create something like cutout figures you can place on top of other clips.

The nomenclature can be confusing. Matte keys are not the same as color mattes, such as the orange matte you used earlier in this lesson. However, matte keys generally use matte graphics that you create to define the areas you want to make transparent or opaque.

There are two basic types of matte keys:

• **Garbage**—Four-, eight-, or sixteen-sided polygons. Named "Garbage" because you typically use them to remove something you don't want in the video. You move their vertices to define the outline of an area you want to display.

• **Graphic**—Shapes that you create for keying out or keying in another graphic or a clip. Includes Difference Matte, Image Matte Key, Remove Matte, and Track Matte Key.

In this mini-lesson, you will work with the Sixteen-Point Garbage Matte Key effect and the Track Matte Key effect. You'll start by trying to use the Luma Key effect. You'll see it has some limitations that a garbage matte can help you overcome.

1   Drag Photo 14e and Photo 14g to Video 1 and Video 2 (place them after the clips you worked on previously).

2   Apply Luma Key to the clip in Video 2, and adjust the parameters to attempt to show only the cat's eyes.

No matter what values you select for the Threshold and Cutoff parameters, the white highlights on the cat's fur show through the sunset.

3   Toggle Luma Key off by clicking the little "f" icon (⊘) next to its name in the Effect Controls panel.

4 Drag Photo 14g from the Project panel to Video 3 above the other two clips. You will use a garbage matte key on the clips in the Video 2 and Video 3 tracks to display only the cat's eyes in the sky.

5 Apply the Sixteen-Point Garbage Matte Key effect to the clip in Video 3.

6 Click the effect's Transform button (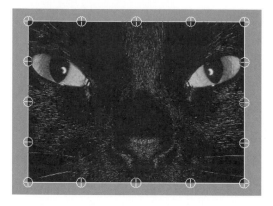) (to the left of the effect name) in the Effect Controls panel to highlight its 16 cross-hair target handles in the Program Monitor.

7 Drag the 16 handles to make a rough outline of the cat's right eye (you'll fine-tune it later).

8 Click the clip in Video 2 to select it, drag the Sixteen-Point Garbage Matte Key effect to it, and follow the same procedure to outline the cat's left eye.

Note: When you select the second clip, the cat looks unchanged. In fact, what you're seeing is the cat's right eye from the clip in Video 3 and the rest of the cat from the clip in

Video 2, revealed when you created the garbage matte cutout in Video 3. The reason you are applying this garbage matte to two instances of the same clip is because you can't apply this effect to the same clip twice. Once you create a cutout, you can't create another one elsewhere in the same clip.

9 Fine-tune the placement of the garbage matte's vertices by using the View Zoom Level menu in the Program Monitor to zoom in on the cat's eyes. Try to remove the black areas around the edges of the eyes.

You've created something that looks too much like you cut holes in the sky! There are several ways to remedy that. Here are four:

• Switch the Luma Key effect back on (giving the eyes an orange cast to match the sky).

• Apply a blur effect to the two cat clips.

• Apply the Tint effect, and use Map Black To to map dark colors to the dark areas of the sky, and Map White To to map light colors to a light orange area of the sky.

• Use the Orange Matte with opacity in a five-layer composite.

That last approach was used for the example in the Lesson 14 Finish sequence. In addition, motion was applied to the cat photos to make the eyes appear in the upper right corner, and the same garbage matte parameters (Copy > Paste Attributes) that were used on the cat photos were used on the Orange Mattes, to have them fit exactly over the cat's eyes so they wouldn't add an extra orange hue to the sky. The whole thing was finished off by applying Cross Dissolves to gradually reveal the cat's eyes.

Create a split-screen effect

You can use garbage mattes to create split-screen effects. The most frequent application is simply to layer two clips, apply the Four-Point Garbage Matte effect to each, and move the vertices to create two side-by-side rectangles. You can also layer more clips and use the Eight- and Sixteen-Point Garbage Matte effects to create all sorts of shapes.

The one little gotcha is that the garbage matte effect reveals part of a clip—it doesn't shrink the clip to fit it in the borders of the garbage matte, as happens when you use Motion to make PiPs. So plan your shots accordingly. If you want to put more of the scene within the garbage matte's borders, use Motion or some other effect to accomplish that.

A cool effect is to lock down your camcorder on a tripod, ensure the lighting, focus, and exposure settings don't change for the duration of the shoot, and have an actor do a scene on one side of a set and then play another role on the other side of the set. You can use a garbage matte on one of the scenes to have the actor appear on both sides of the set at once.

This takes some planning. The actor shouldn't cross the line that divides the set in two (though you can keyframe the garbage matte box edges to accommodate some overlap), and there can't be any movement in the vicinity of the scene's dividing line.

Mattes that use graphics or other clips

There are four Keying effects that fall into this category. You'll work with the Track Matte key, because it's the most useful and works the best. Here's a quick rundown on the others:

- **Difference Matte**—Making this effect work smoothly is very difficult. In theory, you use it to place in a single set multiple actors, animals, or objects that could not all be in a scene at the same time in the same set. You have to create the various shots with exactly the same lighting and camera angle, and you need to work with high-end video to have a chance of making it work. It's best to stick with green/blue screens.

- **Image Matte**—Works like the image mask used in the Gradient Wide transition. You apply it, open a graphic or still image, and the effect makes dark areas transparent and light areas opaque. This is a static effect with limited usability.

- **Remove Matte**—Specifically for graphics that, when used in keyed shots, have something akin to a thin halo around their edges. Apply this effect to remove it.

Using Track Matte Key

Track Matte Key works like Image Matte Key, but has several advantages and one obvious difference. What makes it different is that you place the matte—a still image, graphic, or something you created in the Titler—in a video track (thus its name) rather than applying it directly to the clip.

Track Matte Key uses the clip in a separate track to define areas of transparency in the selected clip and reveal whatever is below it on a sequence. Its huge advantage is that you can animate the matte. For example, you can use Motion's Scale parameter to gradually reveal the matte or move it in the clip to follow some action. The latter application of Track Matte Key is called a traveling matte.

Making a traveling matte

You will use this effect time and time again. It's a great way to follow action or hide an object. In this case, you will use Track Matte Key to blur the moving face of our bike rider. If necessary, refer to the example of this effect in the Lesson 14 Finish sequence.

1   Layer three clips: bike race.mov in Video 1, a copy of bike race.mov directly above it in Video 2, and face matte in Video 3. Stretch the face matte to the same length as the others. If you play this sequence, you will notice the face matte is on the correct location only for the first frame. The biker's face is moving, but the matte is not. So, we need to animate the matte to follow the blue biker's face.

2   Select the face matte clip, and then expand the Motion effect in the Effect Controls panel.

3   Set a Position keyframe at the beginning of the clip by clicking the Toggle Animation button (Ö) to the left of Position.

4   Scrub the timeline to about the halfway point of the clip, and adjust the matte to be over the blue biker's face. Move halfway across the remainder of the clip, and do the same thing again. Continue setting keyframes until you can scrub the clip and have the matte over the face at all times.

Note: Keyframing motion can be a tedious task, but you don't have to set a keyframe at every frame. A good technique is to set a keyframe at the beginning, then the end, then in the middle. The in-between times will be smoothly calculated. If the motion is constant and there is no camera movement, you will not need to set many in-between keyframes. If you need to add more keyframes, keep dividing the space between keyframes in half until the animation is correct.

5   Select the Video 2 clip, and apply the Mosaic (Video Effects > Stylize) effect to it. Set the horizontal and vertical blocks' values to 60. This will make the clip in Video 2 a mosaic. Now we need to use a matte to make the mosaic appear only over the face as it moves.

6   Apply the Track Matte Key effect to the bike race clip in Video 2 (the same clip you applied the mosaic filter to).

7   Set Matte to Video 3 and Composite Using to Matte Alpha.

8   Play the sequence, and notice the mosaic effect is now only on the blue biker's face.

You can also use this technique to highlight, rather than obscure, a person or object in motion. To highlight with a track matte, simply change the effect on the matted clip from mosaic to a tinted color, or brighter color, or even black and white.

Review

▶ Review questions

1 List at least three ways to blend two full-screen clips.

2 How do you create a logo with beveled edges and a glow that grows and then shrinks?

3 You want to create a silhouette of a teapot in a video, and you want to add a logo in that silhouette. Describe a way to do that.

4 In a color/chroma key, what do Similarity, Blend, Threshold, and Cutoff do?

5 What's the value of the Mask Only parameter?

6 What's the difference between Image Matte Key and a Track Matte Key?

▶ Review answers

1 Opacity (or its non-fixed twin, Alpha Adjust) and the Blend and Texturize video effects. You can also use Multiply and Screen. Screen works a lot like Opacity in that it combines both clips. Multiply tends to have more dramatic results.

2 Apply Bevel Alpha and Alpha Glow. Use keyframes on Alpha Glow to animate the size of the glow.

3 There are always multiple means to an end in Adobe Premiere Pro. Here's one approach. Shoot the teapot so that the background contrasts with the pot. Use the Luma Key effect to create the silhouette, and use Motion to position the logo in the silhouette. (A very slick extra effect is to use a white pot, have steaming hot water in it so the steam comes out of the spout, and shoot that over a black background. Then the steam will add some animation to the silhouette.)

4 Similarity and Blend work together to set a width for the color range that will be keyed out of a superimposed clip and to blend the two clips smoothly together. Threshold and Cutoff deal with shadows. Threshold controls the amount of shadows from the superimposed clip that will appear on the lower track's clip. Cutoff controls how dark or light those shadows are.

5 Mask Only is the best way to view your keyed effect critically. Switch it on before you fine-tune parameters such as Similarity, Threshold, and Cutoff.

6 You apply Image Matte Key directly to a clip by clicking that clip's Image Matte Settings box and selecting the Image Matte Key graphic file. Track Matte Key is not as direct. For that, you use a matte graphic that you place on a separate video track. Track Matte Key is much more useful in that you can animate and apply effects to its matte graphic.

Fast Color Corrector

nested sequences

shortcuts

color wheel

Adobe Premiere Pro offers about a dozen video effects to enhance or adjust colors. You will take a few of them for a test drive in this lesson, including a workhorse—the Fast Color Corrector. You will explore some specialized editing techniques, including the new Replace Clip feature, and you'll use nested sequences. You will also learn some keyboard shortcuts to speed up your editing.

15 | Color, Nested Sequences, and Shortcuts

Topics covered in this lesson:

- Overview of color-oriented effects
- Adjusting and enhancing color
- Using nested sequences
- Replacing clips
- Recommended keyboard shortcuts.

Getting started

Most feature films are color-corrected. The purpose is less to fix a shot gone bad and more to give the film a look that matches its mood or genre: from warm reds for landscapes and sepia tones for historic shots to cold blues for hard edged films or a gritty look for urban dramas. Color correction (or color enhancing) is big business, and Adobe Premiere Pro has a full suite of professional color-enhancing effects.

Those color-oriented effects offer more than just color correction. You can select a color and change it, convert a clip to grayscale (with the exception of a single color), or remove all colors outside a specific color range. You'll see samples of some of these in this lesson.

You'll learn about the power of nested sequences as we change the look of a complex effect by changing one nested clip.

As you work with multiple video projects, you will sometimes want to reuse portions of a project with new source media. The new Replace Clip feature makes this very easy to do.

The default keyboard shortcuts in Adobe Premiere Pro are too numerous to use, much less memorize, but there are several you will come to rely on. You'll learn how to customize keyboard commands to suit your editing style.

An overview of color-oriented effects

Adobe Premiere Pro has many video effects that adjust or enhance color. Some have narrow functionality, while others are professional-level tools that take a lot of trial and error to gain some level of expertise. There are entire books on color correction and a good number of video editors who specialize in that field.

Adobe Premiere Pro offers a wide range of "colorful" possibilities—more than enough to spark some ideas for your upcoming video projects.

To see what Adobe Premiere Pro has to offer in the color effect department, click the Effects tab and type *color* in the Contains text box. However, that's just a start; there are several more that have to do with color.

Here, the color-oriented effects have been grouped into four categories and listed within those groups more or less from simplest to most complex. (This taxonomy is one example of why you might want to create and organize some custom effects bins.) Here's a brief overview of the color effects.

Coloring effects

- **Tint**—A simple way to apply an overall color cast to a clip.
- **Change Color**—Like Tint, but with more control, and you can change a wider range of colors.
- **Ramp**—Creates a linear or radial color gradient that blends with the original image colors.
- **4-Color Gradient**—Like the Titler's eponymous feature, but this has more options, and you can keyframe the parameters for some wild results.
- **Paint Bucket**—Paints areas of a scene with a solid color.
- **Brush Strokes**—Applies a painted look to a clip.

- **Channel Blur**—Creates a glow by blurring red, green, or blue channels separately and in user-specified directions.

Color removal or replacement

- **Color Pass**—Converts an entire clip to grayscale, with the exception of one user-specified color. (Windows only)

- **Color Replace**—Changes a user-selected color in a scene to a different user-specified color. (Windows only)

- **Leave Color**—Similar to Color Pass, with much more control.

- **Change To Color**—Like Color Replace, but with more options and control.

Color correction

- **Color Balance, Color Balance (HLS), and Color Balance (RGB)**—Color Balance offers the most control over red, green, and blue values in midtones, shadows, and highlights. HLS controls only overall hue, lightness, and saturation; RGB controls only red, green, and blue color values.

- **Auto Color**—A simple generic color balance.

- **RGB Color Corrector and RGB Curves**—Offers even more control than Color Balance, including controls over the tonal range of shadows and highlights, and controls for midtones values (*gamma*), brightness (*pedestal*), and contrast (*gain*).

- **Luma Color and Luma Curve**—Adjusts brightness and contrast in the highlights, midtones, and shadows of a clip. Also corrects hue, saturation, and luma in a selected color range.

- **Color Match**—A useful but difficult-to-master tool that lets you match up the overall color schemes in scenes with different color lighting. In this way, for example, you can color-match scenes shot under fluorescent lights (blue-green) with scenes shot under tungsten lights (orange). (Windows only)

- **Fast Color Corrector**—Lets you make instant color changes that you can preview in a split-screen view within the Program Monitor. This is a tool you are likely to use frequently.

- **Three-Way Color Corrector**—Gives you the ability to make more subtle corrections by letting you adjust hue, saturation, and luminance for highlights, midtones, and shadows.

Technical color effects

- **Broadcast Colors**—Conforms video to display properly on TV sets. Corrects problems created by overly bright colors and geometric patterns due to some effects or added graphics.

- **Video Limiter**—Like Broadcast Colors, but with much more precise control to preserve the original video quality while conforming to broadcast TV standards.

Adjusting and enhancing color

In this mini-lesson, you will work with five color-oriented effects: Leave Color, Change To Color, Color Balance (RGB), Auto Color, and Fast Color Corrector.

Leave Color

1   Open the Lesson 15-1 project to the Lesson 15 Practice sequence.

2   Drag bike cable shot3.mov to Video 1 track, and position the CTI at about 00;00;00;20 so you can see the yellow jacket of rider 2.

3   Apply the Leave Color effect (Video Effects > Color Correction) to that clip.

4   Expand Leave Color in the Effect Controls panel. Using the eyedropper next to Color To Leave, click the yellow on the rider's yellow sleeve to select the color to retain.

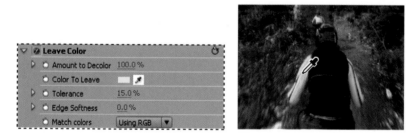

5   Set the Amount To Decolor to 100%. This turns everything but the selected color to grayscale.

6   Set the Tolerance to about 38%. You might need to adjust this a little to get the effect you want.

7   Play the clip to see that only the yellow sleeves are in color.

Change To Color

1 Drag start race countdown.mov to the Video 1 track after the clip you just worked on, and apply the Change To Color effect to that clip.

2 Expand the Change To Color effect in the Effect Controls panel.

3 Move the CTI over the clip so you can see the lake clearly in the Program Monitor.

4 Use the eyedropper next to From to sample the green color from the lake.

5 Click on the To color swatch and choose a medium blue.

The lake should change from a green hue to a blue hue. The color you select will retain the shadows, midtones, and highlights of the scene it's replacing, so if that scene is generally dark, the color in the scene will look darker than the color you select.

Color correction

Depending on how you define *color correction*, there are several color-correction effects. They run the gamut from basic color balance (like an auto white balance on a camcorder) to the richly detailed and complex Three-Way Color Corrector effect. The next mini-lesson will focus on the middle ground: Fast Color Corrector.

The Fast Color Corrector and the Three-Way Color Corrector effects offer what are called Hue Balance and Angle color wheels. You use them to balance the red, green, and blue colors to produce the desired white and neutral grays in the image.

Note: The Three-Way Color Corrector effect lets you make separate adjustments, using individual wheels, to adjust tonal ranges for shadows, midtones, and highlights.

Depending on the desired effect, you might not want the color balance in a clip to be completely neutral. That's where color enhancement comes in. For example, you can give your videos a warm orange color or a cool blue color.

Before tackling the Fast Color Corrector, we'll look briefly at two other color correction effects.

Color Balance (RGB)

1 Delete Change to Color from the start race countdown.mov, and replace it with the Color Balance (RGB) effect.

This is probably the most intuitive color-correction effect. It has a settings window where you can manually adjust the red, green, and blue levels. The starting point for all clips is 100 no matter what the actual color levels in the clip are.

2 Change the RGB settings to give this scene a cooler appearance (more blue). Try Red—98%, Green—104%, and Blue—116%.

Auto Color

1   Delete Color Balance (RGB) from the start race countdown.mov clip, and replace it with the Auto Color effect.

This effect analyzes frames based on your settings of the parameters.

2   Try out some parameters.

Temporal Smoothing looks at several frames at once and averages their values to smooth any color-balance differences. Higher Black and White Clip values increase contrast.

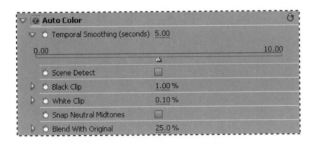

Fast Color Corrector

Fast Color Corrector is the workhorse of color correction filters in Adobe Premiere Pro. It is extremely useful when correcting the color or lighting of a clip.

1   Drag interview_blue.mov to the Practice sequence to the right of the previous clips.

2   Apply the Fast Color Corrector filter.

This very detailed effect signals a tidal shift in editing possibilities. It is loaded with options, including a color wheel—an intuitive means to adjust hue and saturation.

3   Click the White Balance eyedropper (highlighted in the next figure), and use it to sample an area that has a neutral color in the Program Monitor (on the wall to the right of the subject is a good spot).

You don't have to have a white area to do a white balance. A neutral, medium gray area will work well. Setting a new white balance is only a supporting role for the Fast Color Corrector. The purpose here is to change the look of the clip.

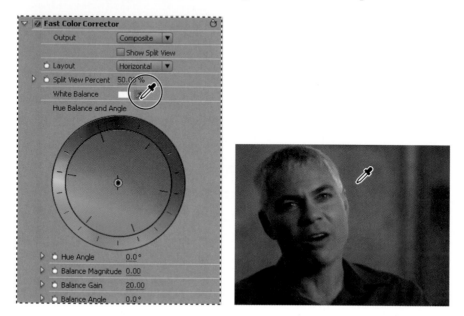

4   Notice how the blue cast to the clip is now gone. Select the Show Split View option (under the Output parameter) to see the difference.

5   Adjust the amount of color correction by increasing Balance Magnitude to about 27. This shifts the tone a little more toward red. Notice the circle near the center of the color wheel moves farther from the center as you adjust this parameter.

Take a look at the color wheel. Here are its parameters (refer to the next figure):

•   **Hue Angle**—Shift the overall color toward red (by moving the outer ring clockwise) or green (counterclockwise).

•   **Balance Magnitude**—Increase the magnitude (intensity) of the color introduced into the video (by moving the circle out from the center).

•   **Balance Angle**—Shift the video color towards a target color.

- **Balance Gain**—Set the relative coarseness or fineness of the Balance Magnitude and Balance Angle adjustments. Moving the handle towards the outer ring makes the adjustment very obvious. Keeping the perpendicular handle of this control close to the center of the wheel makes the adjustment very subtle.

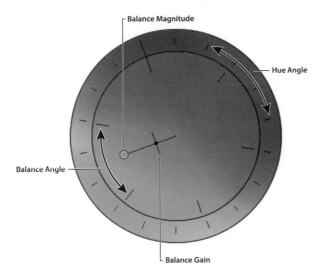

6 Make some adjustments to the color wheel (you can use the sliders below it as well).

- Drag Balance Gain (the small perpendicular line) to about 15. That will let you fine-tune your adjustments.

- Change Balance Angle to about 260 to shift the color to orange.

- Change the Saturation parameter (below the color wheel) to about 108 to make the colors a bit more intense.

7 Slide the black input level to about 10 to increase the amount of blacks.

8 Deselect the Show Split View option, and play the clip.

9 Choose Window > Workspace > Color Correction.

Note that you have a new video panel: a Reference Monitor.

10 Click the Reference Monitor panel menu, and choose All Scopes.

These are three Waveform monitors and a Vectorscope (in the upper right corner). For decades, broadcast TV engineers have used these to ensure that TV signals meet standards (that is, they don't get too bright or have too much contrast).

As you ramp up your color-enhancing skills, you might want to use them for that reason as well as to adjust color. To learn more about them, choose Help > Adobe Premiere Pro Help, and then open Applying Effects > Vectorscope And Waveform Monitors.

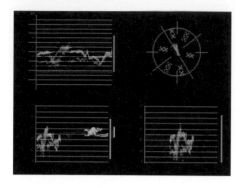

Using nested sequences

A nested sequence is a sequence-in-a-sequence. You can break your project up into more manageable chunks by creating a project segment in one sequence and dragging that sequence—with all its clips, graphics, layers, multiple audio/video tracks and effects—into another sequence. There it will look and behave like a single audio/video clip.

One great way to take advantage of a nested sequence is to apply color correction to a long sequence with multiple edits. Instead of applying that effect to each clip in turn, you simply place—nest—that sequence in another sequence, and apply a single instance of that effect to it. If you want to change the effect parameters, you can then do it on one nested sequence clip, rather than changing each individual clip within that original sequence.

Multiple uses for nested sequences

Nested sequences have many other uses:

- Apply an effect or effects to a group of layered clips. That saves having to apply effects to each layer, one at a time.

- Simplify editing by creating complex sequences separately. This helps you avoid running into conflicts and inadvertently shifting clips on a track that is far from your current work area.

- Reuse sequences, or use the same sequence but give it a different look each time.

- Organize your work, in the same way you might create subfolders in the Project panel or in Windows Explorer. It avoids confusion and shortens editing time.

- Apply more than one transition between clips.

- Build multiple picture-in-picture effects.

Nesting a video inside a newspaper

In this mini-lesson, you will learn to create the classic newspaper spinning onto the screen—except we will use a nested sequence to add a motion video as a "picture" on this spinning newspaper. Using nested sequences will make it very easy.

1   Open the final sequence (yes, that is its name), and play it to see the effect you will create. The spinning newspaper is the last set of clips in the sequence.

2   Open the nested practice sequence. Initially, it is empty.

3   Drag start race.mov to the Video 1 track of the nested practice sequence.

4   Drag newspaper.psd to the Video 2 track, directly above the start race.mov clip. Adjust the length of the newspaper clip to match the movie clip. Notice the newspaper has a square transparent area where the movie clip underneath shows through.

5   Select the start race clip and, using the Scale and Position parameters of the Motion effect, adjust the video to fit in the window of the newspaper. The settings Scale=53 and Position= 306, 300 will probably work well.

6   Delete the audio of the start race clip by Alt-clicking (Windows) or Option-clicking (Mac OS) the audio and pressing Delete.

That's all we need to do with the nested sequence. We will animate the newspaper and video together by animating the sequence, not the individual clips.

7 Click the Practice sequence to make it active.

8 Drag interview_blue.mov to the Video 1 track of the Practice sequence to the right of the last clips you added.

9 Drag the nested practice sequence to the Video 2 track, directly above the interview clip.

10 With the nested practice sequence clip selected, add a Scale keyframe in the Motion effect at about the halfway point on the clip. Set its value to 80. Set another Scale keyframe at the beginning of the clip, and set its value to 0.

11 Set a keyframe for the Rotation parameter in the Motion effect at the beginning of the clip. Set its value to -4x0.0. Set another Rotation keyframe at the halfway point on the clip, and set its value to 0.0.

12 As a nice touch, you can right-click (Windows) or Control-click (Mac OS) the last rotation keyframe you set, and set it to Ease In. This will make it gradually stop rotating, rather than stop suddenly.

13 Play the clip.

The power of nesting allows you to apply effects to multiple clips at once by nesting clips inside a sequence. You can also nest sequences inside sequences.

Replacing clips

The replace-clip feature is new to Adobe Premiere Pro CS3, and a welcome addition. This feature can save a lot of time in trying different clips in different positions, or in creating a template-style, prototypical project where you replace certain clips to create new projects.

This feature not only replaces one clip with another, but automatically preserves the attributes and filters of the replaced clip. We will use this feature to replace the video inside our rotating newspaper without having to reset the Scale and Position parameters.

1 Select the nested practice sequence. You'll remember we had to set specific values for Scale and Position to the start race.mov clip to make it show through the newspaper correctly. If you had problems doing this, switch to the nested final sequence to see the completed one.

Now, you want to replace the start race clip that plays inside the newspaper with the start race countdown clip.

2 Drag the start race countdown.mov clip down, and allow it to hover over the start race.mov clip, as if you are doing an overlay edit, but don't drop it yet. Notice the new clip is too long and has audio attached.

3 Before dropping the clip, hold down the Alt (Windows) or Option (Mac OS) key. This tells Adobe Premiere Pro to do a replace-clip edit rather than an overlay edit. Notice the clip becomes the correct length and the audio disappears, because the original clip has no audio. Drop the clip while still holding down Alt or Option. You have performed a replace-clip edit.

4 Play the sequence. Notice the new clip is the correct length and took on the Scale and Position values of the original.

Recommended keyboard shortcuts

Adobe Premiere Pro has more than 100 keyboard shortcuts. You won't use all of them, but there are about 25 that should become a part of your repertoire. You can customize them and create additional ones to suit your needs.

To get an idea of just how vast the shortcut opportunities are, choose Edit > Keyboard Customization. Not surprisingly, that opens the Keyboard Customization dialog box, shown in the next figure.

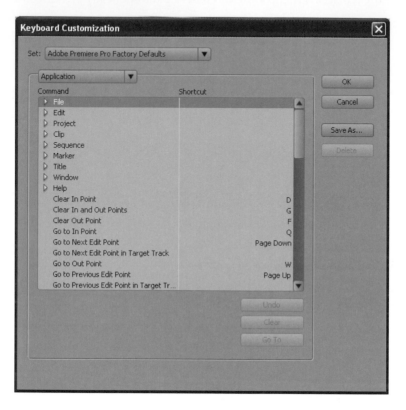

Note that the Adobe Premiere Pro Factory Defaults list includes the main menu headings: File, Edit, Project, and so on. You can open each of those lists and find commands that match virtually everything available in the menus.

Many mimic standard system-level shortcuts:

Function	Windows	Mac OS
Save	Ctrl+S	Command+S
Copy	Ctrl+C	Command+C
Undo	Ctrl+Z	Command+Z

Adobe Premiere Pro has three sets of keyboard shortcuts: Factory Default, and sets for two competing products, Avid Xpress DV 3.5 and Final Cut Pro 4.0. The latter two are to facilitate migration from those products to Adobe Premiere Pro.

Changing a shortcut

You can create a fourth, custom set of shortcuts. The more you work with Adobe Premiere Pro the more you'll want to do that. Here's how:

1 Choose Edit > Keyboard Customization.

2 Open the Edit list, and click Redo.

You'll see that the keyboard shortcut to redo something you've undone is Ctrl+Shift+Z (Windows) or Command+Shift+Z (Mac OS). That shortcut is valid in various Adobe products. Your experience with other products might be to use Ctrl+Y or Command+Y.

3 Click the Redo shortcut (the shortcut, not the word Redo), and then press Ctrl+Y or Command+Y.

That puts *[Custom]* in the Set pop-up menu. You'll name and save this as a custom set in a moment, but first, check out what happens when you try to change a keyboard shortcut to one that's already in use.

Set: [Custom]

Application

Command	Shortcut
▷ File	
▽ Edit	
Undo	Ctrl+Z
Redo	Ctrl+Y
Cut	Ctrl+X
Copy	Ctrl+C
Paste	Ctrl+V
Paste Insert	Ctrl+Shift+V

4 Click Copy to highlight it in the list, and then click its shortcut—Ctrl+C (Windows) or Command+C (Mac OS)—to clear that entry.

5 Press Ctrl+Y (Windows) or Command+Y (Mac OS).

That pops up a little warning (shown in the next figure) that notes you are about to redefine an existing shortcut. If you click just about anywhere in the dialog box, you will make that change.

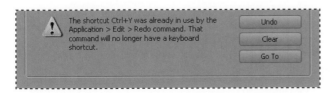

The shortcut Ctrl+Y was already in use by the Application > Edit > Redo command. That command will no longer have a keyboard shortcut.

Undo

Clear

Go To

6   Click Clear to undo that change.

If you were to click OK, you would close the dialog box, and the [Custom] set would have the new shortcut for Redo and would be the currently selected set of keyboard shortcuts. If you click Save As instead, you can give that [Custom] collection a more descriptive name.

7   Click Save As, give your customized keyboard shortcut collection a name, and then click Save.

Most frequently used shortcuts

There are about 25 shortcuts that seem to be the most frequently used (including system-level "imitations" such as Ctrl+C/Command+C). In no time at all, the following shortcuts will become second nature to you:

• **Tools**—Each tool has a single-letter keyboard shortcut. To remind yourself of those shortcuts, open Keyboard Customization, click the Application pop-up menu, and select Tools.

You'll use these frequently. At the very least, Selection (V), Ripple Edit (B), Rolling Edit (N), and Razor (C) should be ingrained in your brain. In case you need reinforcement, roll your pointer over each icon in the Tools panel to see a tool tip with the tool's keyboard shortcut.

- **Backslash** (\)—Resize the Timeline to display your entire project. It's a great way to get a handle on where you are in the workflow.

- **J** and **L**—Playback controls. J is reverse, L is forward. Press two or three times to increase speed incrementally.

- **K**—Multi-function, playback modifier key. Press K to stop playback. Hold down K while either pressing or holding down the J or L key to change playback speeds.

  - Hold down K while pressing J: Play in reverse one frame at a time.

  - Hold down K while pressing L: Play forward one frame at a time.

  - Hold down K and J simultaneously: Play in reverse slowly (8 fps).

  - Hold down K and L simultaneously: Play forward slowly (8 fps).

- **Plus sign (+)** or **minus sign (-) and a number**—Move a clip by a specified number of frames. Select the clip, and then type + or - on the numeric keypad (not Shift+= or the hyphen key), followed by the number of frames (you also need to use the numeric keypad). Press Enter to move the clip.

Note: When viewing the Timeline panel in audio units, the clip will move by the specified number of audio samples.

- **Home** and **End**—Move to the beginning or end of a sequence if the Timeline is active or the first or last clip in the Project panel if it's active.

- **Page Up** and **Page Down**—Move to the beginning or end of the selected clip or next edit point in the Timeline or to the top or bottom clip currently displayed in the Project panel.

- **Asterisk** (*)—Add marker. The asterisk key on the numeric keypad (not Shift+8) adds a marker to the timeline. (Markers will be covered in more detail in the final lesson.)

- **S**—Snap. Pressing S turns on or turns off the snap feature (the little two-pronged icon in the upper left corner of the Timeline window). You can toggle snap on or off even while dragging or trimming a clip.

Note: The CTI does not snap to items—items snap to it. If the CTI did snap to edit points, moving the CTI through the sequence would become a jumpy mess.

- **Alt/Option**—Temporarily unlink audio and video. Press the Alt (Windows) or Option (Mac OS) key as you click the video or audio portion of a linked A/V clip to unlink that portion, enabling you to trim or move that portion of the clip without affecting the other portion.

• **Alt+[/ Option+[** and **Alt+] / Option+]**—Set work area bar end points (shown in next figure). If you want to render or export a part of your project, you need to set the beginning and end of that section. Pressing Alt+[/ Option+[sets the beginning to wherever the CTI edit line is. Alt+] / Option+] sets the end. You can simply drag the ends of the bar to those points as well. The work area bar end points will snap to clip edit points.

Note: Double-clicking the center of the work area bar sets the bar ends to the visible area of the sequence or to the full length of the sequence if it's visible in its entirety in the Timeline.

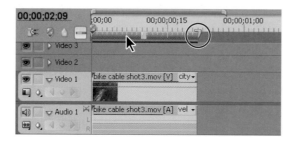

• **F1**—Opens Adobe Premiere Pro Help.

• **Ctrl+T** (Windows) or **Command+T** (Mac OS)—Opens the Titler.

• **Marquee select**—Drag a marquee to select a group of clips in the Timeline or Project panel. This should be a routine part of your workflow. Marquee-selecting clips in the Timeline lets you move a whole group of clips, and marquee-selecting clips in the Project panel lets you add all of those clips at once to a sequence.

• **Import folders**—Instead of importing a file or collection of files, you can import an entire folder. Select Import and click the Import Folder button in the lower right corner of the Import dialog box. That creates a bin in the Project panel with the exact folder name, and imports the associated files.

Review

► Review questions

1 What's the difference between the Color Pass and the Color Replace effects?

2 What's the basic workflow order for Color Match?

3 What is the purpose of the split-screen option in the Fast Color Corrector?

4 What are the basic settings you apply with the color wheel in the Fast Color Corrector?

5 How is a replace-clip edit different from an overlay edit?

6 What keyboard shortcuts enable you to rewind, stop, and play your project?

► Review answers

1 Color Pass turns everything in a scene gray with the exception of objects that have a user-selected color. Color Replace replaces a user-specified color with another color.

2 Apply the effect to the clip you want to change. Select a Target color/luminance in the Source clip (the one with the color you prefer) and apply that to a sample area in the clip you're changing.

3 The split-screen function allows you to instantly preview the effect of your color corrections and compare it to the original.

4 Balance Angle (the color added to the clip) and Balance Gain (the intensity of that color). You also can adjust the overall Hue Angle to move all colors in a clip toward a selected color.

5 An overlay edit replaces the original clip with the new clip, with the new clip having no attributes. A replace-clip edit allows the new clip to take on the attributes of the original clip. You can even replace a video clip with a still image and have the new still image take on the attributes of the video clip.

6 J, K, and L. Pressing J or L more than once speeds up the reverse and forward speeds. K stops playback.

Clip Notes

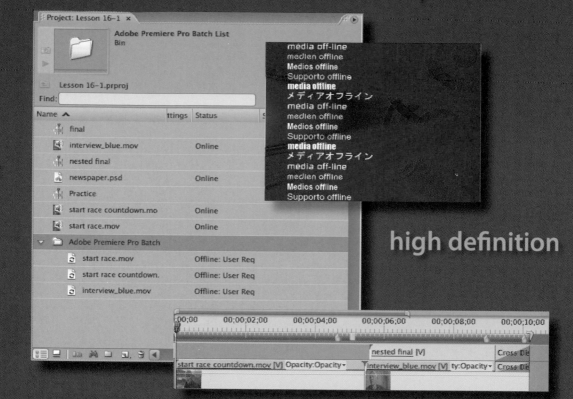

AAF

high definition

Project Manager

In the professional video production world, managing assets and tracking client comments are critically important. Adobe Premiere Pro features two tools to facilitate these efforts. Clip Notes lets you embed a project into a PDF file so a client can make written comments tied directly to timecodes. Project Manager lets you easily consolidate a project to the essential assets. Video production companies are turning more frequently to high-definition video. Adobe Premiere Pro fosters that migration.

16 | Project Management

Topics covered in this lesson:

- Project menu overview
- Using the Project Manager
- Conducting a Clip Notes review
- High-definition video features

Getting started

If you are a one-man band, tracking projects is probably a snap for you. However, once you start bringing others into the production mix, you need to find ways to manage your assets. Adobe Premiere Pro has a slick project-management tool that reduces a project's storage size and consolidates the files associated with a project.

Adobe Premiere Pro Clip Notes streamlines a collaborative workflow by facilitating feedback from clients and colleagues. You can embed a rendered sequence either as a video file within a PDF file or store it on a server and put a link to that file in the PDF file. In either case, a reviewer can open the PDF file, play the movie, and enter comments directly into the PDF file. Later you can read those comments from within the Timeline.

Adobe Premiere Pro lets you capture, edit, and output full-resolution, high-definition (HD) video. If you are venturing into this growing medium, Adobe Premiere Pro offers you a number of solutions.

Project menu overview

Project management starts in the Project menu. It presents several options that let you track projects or reuse assets. In particular, it offers three ways to export your project:

• **Batch list**—A text file of audio/video asset names and timecodes. It contains no information about your project such as edits, transitions, or graphics.

• **AAF (Advanced Authoring Format)**—A widely recognized file exchange standard for video editing that includes clip, sequence, and editing data. It has some strict limitations. The Adobe Premiere Pro implementation has been tested only with the Avid Xpress family of products (see Adobe Premiere Pro Help for more information). Note that AAF export is available only for the Windows version of Adobe Premiere Pro CS3.

• **Project Manager**—Creates a trimmed version of your project by saving only the portions of the assets you used in your sequences, or consolidates the project by storing all its assets in a single file folder. If you choose to create a trimmed project, you can use only offline file names that you later recapture. Whether you trim or consolidate your project, the Project Manager also stores a copy of your original Adobe Premiere Pro project file with all its information on edits, transitions, effects, and Titler-created text and graphics.

We will briefly run through the Project menu commands, and then focus on its most important feature—project management.

1   Start Adobe Premiere Pro, and open the Lesson 16-1 project.

2   Click in the Project panel to select it, but don't select any of the clips (otherwise several options in the Project menu will be unavailable).

Note: If you select a clip, that will be the sole entry in the batch list you will make in step 5.

3   Open the Project menu in the menu bar.

You'll see the following options:

• **Project Settings**—You worked with these in Lesson 4.

• **Link Media**—Use this to link offline filenames to their actual files or videotapes.

- **Make Offline**—Convert an online file to offline.

- **Automate To Sequence**—Move selected files to a sequence. You worked on this in Lesson 5.

- **Import/Export Batch List**—Create or import a list of filenames.

- **Project Manager**—You'll work with this in the next mini-lesson.

- **Remove Unused**—A quick and easy way to clean up your project. Choose it to remove any assets from the Project panel that you are not using in your project.

- **Export Project As AAF** (Windows only)—Exchange media and metadata between platforms and other applications.

4   Choose Export Batch List, accept the default name and location (the current project folder), and click Save.

That creates a comma-delimited (CSV) file that you can read with most text editors. The contents are simply the filenames, timecodes, and original source tape names (if any). The batch list stores only audio and video filenames, not graphics or images.

5   Choose Import Batch List from the Project menu, and double-click on Adobe Premiere Pro Batch List.csv (the file you just created in step 4).

That adds a bin to the Project panel.

6   Open the Adobe Premiere Pro Batch List bin.

Note that the Status of each clip is Offline. You might need to scroll the Project panel to the right to see the Status column.

7 Click start race.mov in the Adobe Premiere Pro Batch List bin.

8 Choose Project > Link Media.

Note: The Import Batch List feature has a limitation in functionality. It can link to only A/V files. If you attempt to link to audio-only or video-only files, you will get an error message.

9 In the Link Media dialog box, navigate to the Lesson 16 folder, and then double-click start race.mov.

Note: If you select more than one offline file, the Link Media dialog box appears in turn for each file you select. Pay attention to the offline filename in the title bar of the dialog box so that you relink the correct source file to each offline file.

Making a clip offline

It is possible to purposely make clips offline and still work with them on the timeline. This can be useful to save disk space while working in the early stages of a project, or to relink to a clip that is being re-shot.

1   Delete the Adobe Premiere Pro Batch List folder you just imported.

2   Click the start race.mov clip in the Project panel to select it.

3   Choose Project > Make Offline.

4   In the Make Offline dialog box, select Media Files Remain On Disk, and click OK.

In that way, the file will be offline in the project but remain on the hard drive. Selecting Media Files Are Deleted will take the file offline and remove it from the hard drive. If you select that option and you want to use that file in a project, you'll need to recapture it (or, in this case, copy it from the DVD).

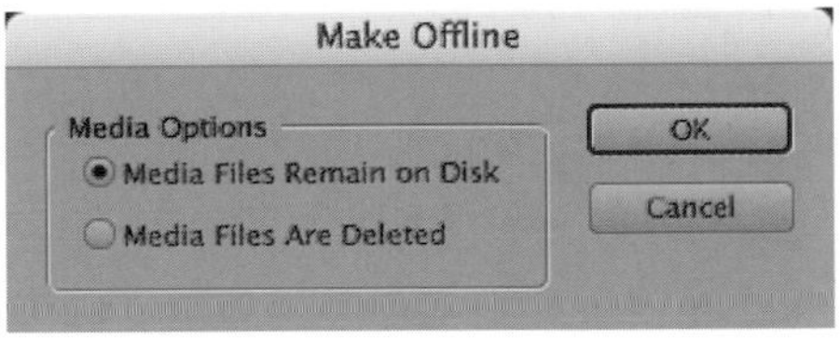

5   Move the CTI over the second set of clips in the Timeline, and note two things:

•   The clip remains in the project with all its effects applied. (The start race.mov clip is the clip playing inside the newspaper.)

•   The Program Monitor displays a *Media Offline* placeholder graphic for that clip.

This is useful if you work with massive files and want to speed up editing. The drawback is that you can't see the video if you want to make frame-specific edits.

Note: If you're using the clip in another project, it will still be online there.

Exporting a project to AAF (Windows only)

1   Choose Project > Export Project As AAF, give the file a name and location, and click Save.

2   The AAF Export Setting dialog allows you to choose the type of export settings. Choose Save As Legacy AAF, and then click OK.

An AAF Export Log information window appears letting you know what elements of the project were not included in the AAF file.

Note: Adobe Premiere Pro has one other text-based export option: Edit Decision List (EDL). It's used primarily to take a sequence created in Adobe Premiere Pro and perform final editing on production studio, high-end hardware. You access it by choosing File > Export > Export To EDL. EDLs are covered in Lesson 18.

Using the Project Manager

Typically, the Project Manager comes into play after you complete a project.

You can use it to create a separate file folder that consolidates into one spot all the assets used in your sequences. This is a great way to archive a project and make it easier to access later. Once consolidated, you can remove all the original assets if you choose.

You can conserve hard-drive space by saving only those assets you used in the project, trimming them to the portions you used in your sequences, and then saving them (or offline references to them) in a single file folder.

If you originally captured your footage at a low resolution to save hard-drive space, you can use the trimmed project, in conjunction with batch capture, to recapture only the footage that you need at the highest possible quality.

To see your options, choose Project > Project Manager.

You have two basic choices, each with its own set of options:

- Create New Trimmed Project

- Collect Files And Copy To New Location

Trimmed project

In the trimmed project, the resulting files (or offline file references) refer only to the portions of the clips you used in the project sequences. You have some options:

- **Exclude Unused Clips**—This almost goes without saying when you are making a trimmed version of your project.

- **Make Offline**—Instead of storing the clips as files, create a list of file data so that you can capture them from videotape.

Note: If you select Make Offline, Project Manager checks all the video files to see if they have source tape names associated with them. If not, because they can't be recaptured, it will copy those files into the newly created project rather than just list them as offline.

- **Include Handles**—This works the same as video capture in that you retain some extra head and tail frames to allow for smooth transitions or slight editing changes later.

- **Rename Media Files To Match Clip Names**—If you changed the clip names to make them more descriptive, you can use the new names in the trimmed project.

Collect Files And Copy To New Location

This option will store all the media assets from the current project to a single location. You might use it to prepare a project for sharing or archiving. This feature is very useful if you have media assets stored in many different folders or many different drives. It will organize all your files into one location.

This selection shares two options with the trimmed project selection: Exclude Unused Clips and Rename Media Files To Match Clip Names. In addition, it has two others:

- **Include Preview Files**—These are files created when you render effects. It saves you time later but takes up more disk space.

- **Include Audio Conform Files**—This is only a minor time-saver. Audio conforming goes on in the background when you import files with audio into a project. There is generally no need to include audio conform files.

Final project management steps

Click Calculate (at the bottom of the Project Manager dialog box), and Adobe Premiere Pro will determine the size of the files in the current project and the resulting trimmed project's estimated size. You can use this to check what difference it'll make to select Make Offline or to include preview files, audio conform files, or handles.

Finally, select (or create) a file folder for the trimmed or consolidated project, and click OK.

Note: Because the video files in all of the lessons in this book do not have source tape names associated with them, clicking Calculate with Make Offline selected or unselected will yield the same results. By default, even if you select Make Offline, Project Manager copies all video files that don't have source tape names associated with them to the new project to ensure you don't delete them accidentally.

Conducting a Clip Notes review

Anyone who has sought feedback on a project from a client will embrace Clip Notes. This feature resolves the headaches and miscommunications common to collaboration.

You use Adobe Premiere Pro Clip Notes to create an Adobe PDF (portable document format) file. PDF files have become the de facto standard in multi-platform document exchange. A Clip Notes PDF contains either a video of your selected sequence or a link to a video on a server.

A reviewer opens the PDF, plays the video, and enters comments into the PDF, which automatically tags the comments directly to the timecode. You import those comments into Adobe Premiere Pro, and they appear as markers in the Timeline.

You don't need Adobe Acrobat to create a Clip Notes PDF, because the engine is built into Adobe Premiere Pro CS3. To make comments, you do need Adobe Acrobat 8 Standard, Adobe Acrobat 8 Professional, or Adobe Reader (the latter is available as a free download at *http://www.adobe.com/reader*).

1   Check that the Lesson 16 Practice sequence is open and selected.

2   Choose File > Export > Adobe Clip Notes.

You have three main options for Export Settings:

- **Format**—Windows Media or QuickTime.

- **Range**—Entire Sequence or Work Area.

- **Preset**—Presets for high- and low-quality bitrates for NTSC, PAL, and Widescreen formats.

On the right side of the dialog box are five tabs for various detailed settings:

- **Filters**—You can enable the Video Noise Reduction filter to reduce noise introduced in the encoding process. Setting this value too high will make the video blurry. As a rule of thumb, use the least amount of noise reduction you can for a clean picture. Test your export with this option turned off, and then increase it by small amounts, if needed.

- **Video**—The recommended settings for video frame size and bit rate are determined by the preset you choose, but you can customize these settings and save them as your own customized preset.

- **Audio**—As with the video tab, the audio setting is determined by the preset you choose, but is customizable to many other audio encoding options.

- **Clip Notes**—Embed Video or Stream Video. Embedding the video means a larger PDF file size, but ensures that all reviewers will be able to play the movie regardless of their network connection. Streaming the video means a smaller PDF file size, but reviewers must have access to the server you're using to post the video file. If you choose to stream the video, enter the URL where the file is located.

  - PDF Password: You have the option to enter a password which would be required for opening the PDF file, as well as PDF instructions.

  - Return Comments To: You have the option to add an e-mail address to which comments will be returned.

- **Others**—If you choose the Stream video option in the Clip Notes tab, you can have the video automatically uploaded to your FTP server. Add the FTP server information in the boxes on this tab, as specified by your FTP server host.

3   Click OK to accept the default settings: Windows Media (QuickTime on Mac OS), Entire Sequence, NTSC Source to 512Kbps preset, and Embed Video. (Note that the Embed Video field is on the Clip Notes tab.)

4   Navigate to an appropriate file folder, give this Clip Notes PDF file a name, and then click Save.

Adobe Premiere Pro displays a Rendering information window that shows its progress as it converts the clips and effects into a Windows Media file.

Review your Clip Notes PDF file

You can e-mail the PDF file to a client or circulate it in-house. In either case, anyone with access to the file can view its associated rendered sequence and make comments.

1   Minimize Adobe Premiere Pro.

2   Navigate to the newly created PDF file, and open it by double-clicking.

Note: There is a sample PDF file for your use and reference, if needed, in the Lesson 16 folder. It's called Lesson 16 clip notes.pdf.

3   Make a selection that suits you in the Manage Trust For Multimedia Content dialog box.

4   Read the instructions (you can access them at any time by clicking the View Instructions button in the reviewing area), and click OK.

5   Type your name in the Reviewer Name text box.

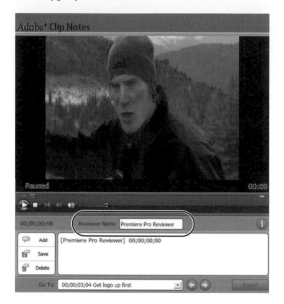

6   Click the Play button in the movie viewer.

7   Click Pause when you want to enter a comment (clicking Stop will put the CTI back to the beginning of the video).

Adobe Premiere Pro automatically enters a timestamp in the comment box.

8   Type your comment.

9   Click Play to continue reviewing the movie and adding more comments.

10   Click the Go To pop-up menu to jump to any of your comments.

11 When you finish entering comments, click the Export button (in the lower right corner below the screen), give your comments a name (the default is [*original PDF file name*]_data) and file folder location, and click Save.

That creates an XFDF (eXtensible Markup Language forms data format) file.

View the Clip Notes Comments in Adobe Premiere Pro

1 Quit Acrobat and return to Adobe Premiere Pro.

2 Make sure the sequence you sent out for review is open in the Timeline panel.

3 Choose File > Import Clip Notes Comments, navigate to that file, and click Open. Comments appear as markers in your sequence.

Note: There is a sample clip notes comments (XFDF) file for your use, if needed. It's in the Lesson 16 folder.

4 Double-click a marker to view the comments.

Alternatively, choose Marker > Go To Sequence Marker to move from one marker to another.

Notice that the comments the reviewer makes are accurate in time on the timeline. This is an extremely helpful tool for reviewing draft videos with customers or clients.

High-definition video and film features

Adobe Premiere Pro CS3 lets you work with any high-definition (HD) format, including HDV (JVC and other companies), HDCAM (Sony), DVCPRO HD (Panasonic), and D5-HD (Panasonic). Adobe Premiere Pro supports these formats at any resolution (including 720p, 1080i, 1080p) and frame rate (including 24, 23.98, 30, 60fps).

You can choose from a wide range of capture cards and other hardware to best fit your needs and budget. Adobe Premiere Pro CS3 support extends from low-cost FireWire for DV and HDV editing up to high-performance workstations capturing uncompressed 10-bit 4:4:4 HD. Standard-definition (SD) and HD hardware from vendors including AJA, Blackmagic Design, BlueFish444, and Matrox let you handle any video and film format.

To learn more about these various formats, resolutions, and products, read "Understanding and Using High-Definition Video" at *www.adobe.com/products/premiere/pdfs/hdprimer.pdf*. Adobe Premiere Pro Help has a short explanation under "About high definition (HD) video." For now, here's a brief overview.

HDV editing

HDV is a compressed high-definition format created by JVC, Canon, Sharp, and Sony. It compresses the video signal, using MPEG-2, and stores it on standard DV cassettes. Adobe Premiere Pro can handle HDV natively—that is, with no additional hardware or software. In addition, editing is done on the video in its original MPEG-2 form, with no additional compression. To use it, select one of the HDV presets from the New Project dialog box.

HD production with third-party cards

Adobe designed Adobe Premiere Pro to handle most types of video you can throw at it. The only limitation is your hardware's ability to handle the significantly higher data rates inherent with HD and an appropriately installed codec.

Several hardware firms have created video cards that can take on the video data processing, freeing up your computer's central processing unit for other functions.

These cards come with plug-ins for Adobe Premiere Pro to handle video capture and export as well as some editing functionality.

Third-party cards allow you to capture analog or digital uncompressed HD or compressed HDV video. The minimum system to handle the throughput necessary to work with HD is substantially more powerful than the standard minimum platform for Adobe Premiere Pro. You'll need a computer with at least two processors, 2GB of RAM, a high-end video processing card, and a RAID (redundant array of independent/inexpensive disks) hard drive system.

Film projects

This is a realm few beginning and intermediate video producers will venture into. If you do want to pursue producing film projects on Adobe Premiere Pro, you might consider working with video cameras that record in 24P (progressive) and 24PA (advanced) frames per second—the same rate as film. Entry-level 24P camcorders are priced at less than $5,000. When you set up your project, use one of the DV-24P presets.

The jump from 24P to film is substantial and goes beyond the scope of this book. At the very least, you'll probably need to work with a production studio that specializes in transferring film to video and back. For a brief overview of how to produce projects for output to film, search Adobe Premiere Pro Help for "Creating motion-picture film" and "24P footage."

Review

▶ **Review questions**

1 What are the basic differences between Export Batch List, AAF, and Project Manager trimmed projects?

2 Explain the two principal uses of the Project Manager.

3 Why does selecting Make Offline in the Project Manager have no effect for clips with no source tape name associated with them?

4 How do you access Clip Notes comments from within Adobe Premiere Pro?

5 How is HDV different from HD?

▶ **Review answers**

1 Batch lists are simply text files consisting of audio/video filenames, timecodes, and their source tape names. AAF adds information about edits and some effects and transitions. Project Manager trimmed projects have full project information, plus the trimmed original clips or offline filename references.

2 You use the Project Manager either to create a trimmed version of your project or to consolidate the original, untrimmed project files in one folder. In either case you can store all your assets in one, easily accessible spot to simplify collaboration or archiving.

3 Adobe Premiere Pro has a built-in failsafe mechanism. If it sees that a video clip has no source tape associated with it, it won't allow the Project Manager to make that an offline clip, since you might not be able to recapture it.

4 Open your project to the sequence you created the Clip Notes for, choose File > Import Clip Notes Comments, and double-click any of the markers that appear along the sequence time ruler.

5 HDV is a compressed HD format. It displays at the same screen dimensions as HD but has a much smaller file size because it's stored as an MPEG video.

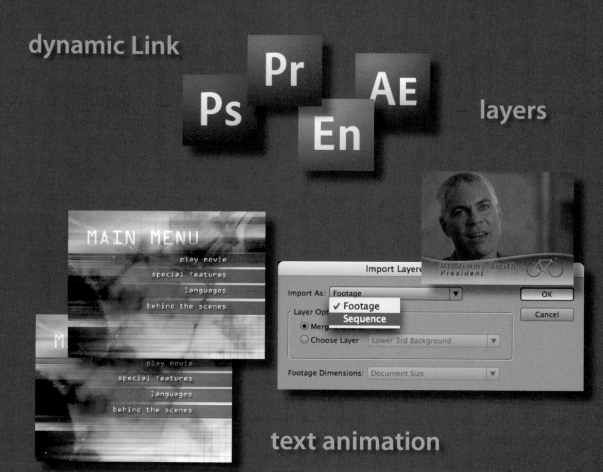

dynamic Link

layers

text animation

menu customization

Adobe Photoshop CS3 and Adobe After Effects CS3 can play valuable roles in your video production workflow. You can animate Photoshop CS3 layered graphics in Adobe Premiere Pro. You can customize or create new menu designs for use in Adobe Encore CS3. After Effects CS3 can dynamically link text and graphic animations with Adobe Premiere Pro CS3.

17 | Using Photoshop and After Effects to Enhance Your Video Projects

Topics covered in this lesson:

- Adobe® Creative Suite® 3 Production Premium
- Importing Photoshop CS3 files as sequences
- Editing Encore CS3 menus in Photoshop CS3
- Dynamic link with After Effects CS3

Getting started

Adobe Premiere Pro CS3 is a powerful tool on its own, but it is also part of Adobe Creative Suite 3 Production Premium. You can purchase Adobe Premiere Pro CS3 by itself and use all its built-in features, or you can purchase it as part of Creative Suite, where it becomes one piece of a powerful combination of integrated components.

Anyone who does anything with print graphics and photo retouching has probably used Photoshop. It is the workhorse of the graphic design industry. Photoshop is a powerful tool with great depth and versatility, and is becoming an increasingly important part of the video production world. We will explore how to use the integration features between Photoshop CS3, Adobe Premiere Pro CS3, and Encore CS3.

Encore CS3 is now included with the purchase of Adobe Premiere Pro as a full-featured DVD authoring tool. In this lesson, we will explore how to edit Encore menus directly in Photoshop CS3.

After Effects CS3 is the de facto standard in the video production industry as a text animation and motion graphics tool. We will explore the unique integration between Adobe Premiere Pro CS3 and After Effects CS3 for powerful and timesaving techniques.

Adobe Creative Suite 3 Production Premium

Adobe® Creative Suite® 3 Production Premium is not just a collection of software bundled together in a box. This suite of components is designed to work together through common interface elements and tight integration to provide you with the tools you need to move from vision to output on virtually any platform.

Adobe Premiere Pro CS3 by itself is a powerful tool for acquiring, editing, and outputting video projects. As part of Creative Suite Production, however, it becomes even stronger. If you have purchased Adobe Premiere Pro by itself, you may not be able to follow along with all the mini-lessons in this chapter, but please read through them to understand how Adobe Premiere Pro fits into the larger picture of this suite of products. If you have purchased Adobe Premiere Pro as part of Creative Suite Production Premium, hang on and experience the impressive integration and timesaving techniques engineered into the product.

Included in Adobe Creative Suite 3 Production Premium

Adobe® Creative Suite® 3 Production Premium software combines Adobe Bridge CS3, Adobe Dynamic Link, Adobe Device Central CS3, and Adobe Acrobat® Connect™ with:

- Adobe Premiere® Pro CS3
- Adobe After Effects® CS3 Professional
- Adobe Photoshop® CS3 Extended
- Adobe Flash® CS3 Professional
- Adobe Illustrator® CS3
- Adobe Soundbooth™ CS3
- Adobe Encore® CS3
- Adobe OnLocation™ CS3 (Windows only)
- Adobe Ultra® CS3 (Windows only)

We have already had a look at Adobe OnLocation, importing Photoshop CS3 and Illustrator CS3 files, and Soundbooth. In Lesson 19, we'll take a closer look at exporting to Encore. In this lesson, we'll focus on the integration between Adobe Premiere Pro, After Effects, Encore, and Photoshop CS3.

For more information on any of these products, please visit http://www.adobe.com/products.

Importing Photoshop CS3 files as sequences

Note: This mini-lesson uses a Photoshop CS3 PSD file to be animated in Adobe Premiere Pro. The PSD file is provided on the DVD, so it is not necessary to have Photoshop CS3 to complete this mini-lesson.

Making the move to Photoshop CS3 means joining forces with just about every image-editing professional on the planet. It's that ubiquitous. Photoshop CS3 is the professional image-editing standard.

Photoshop CS3 has some strong ties to Adobe Premiere Pro CS3 and the entire DV production process:

* **Edit In Adobe Photoshop**—Right-click (Windows) or Control-click (Mac OS) any Photoshop CS3 graphic in Adobe Premiere Pro—in either the Timeline panel or the Project panel—and choose Edit In Adobe Photoshop (or Edit Original). This starts Photoshop CS3 and lets you immediately edit the graphic. Once saved within Photoshop CS3, the new version of the graphic appears in Adobe Premiere Pro.

* **Filmstrip export**—This feature is specifically designed to export a sequential collection of video frames for editing in Photoshop CS3. You open the filmstrip in Photoshop CS3 and paint directly on the clips—a process called rotoscoping.

* **Create mattes**—Export a video frame to Photoshop CS3 to create a matte that will mask or highlight certain areas of that clip or other clips.

* **Cut objects out of a scene**—Photoshop CS3 has several tools that work like a cookie cutter. You can remove an object and use it as an icon, make it into a button in a DVD menu, or animate it over a clip.

In the reverse direction, images created in Photoshop CS3 in multiple layers can be imported into Adobe Premiere Pro with the layers intact. We looked at importing Photoshop CS3 files as footage in Lesson 4. In this mini-lesson, we will import a layered Photoshop CS3 file into Adobe Premiere Pro as a sequence.

1 Open Lesson 17-1.prproj. Notice there is a bin in the Project panel named finished. Expand the finished bin and open the finished sequence, if it's not already open.

2 Play the finished sequence, and notice the title at the bottom of the screen is animated in layers. Titles appearing at the bottom of the frame like this are often referred to as *lower thirds*. The lower third graphic is a nested sequence called finished lower third. We are going to open that sequence to see how it was made, and then recreate it.

3 Inside the finished bin is another bin named finished lower third. From there, open the sequence named finished lower third.

This sequence is built from a Photoshop CS3 image that has three layers.

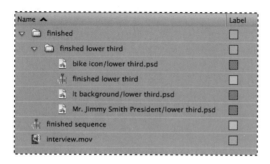

4 Move the CTI to about two seconds into the sequence. Toggle the track output off for each track (click the eyeball), and then toggle them back on to see the contents of each track. Examine the motion settings of each clip, and notice that the Motion effect was used to animate each clip to achieve an interesting appearance. We will now recreate this lower third by importing the Photoshop CS3 graphic into a new sequence.

5 Collapse the finished bin in the Project panel so you are back at the root level of the bins.

6 Import lower third.psd from the Lesson 17 folder. When prompted, choose to import as a Sequence rather than as Footage, and click OK.

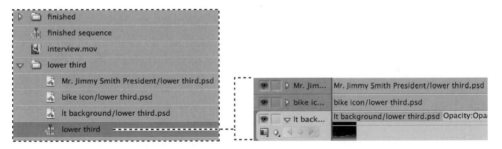

7 Expand the new bin called lower third that has been added to the Project panel. This bin contains three clips that constitute the three-layered Photoshop CS3 file. It also contains a sequence called lower third that has the three layers assembled in the same layered order as they were in Photoshop CS3.

8 Open the lower third sequence by double-clicking it in the Project panel and press the backslash (\) key to expand the view in the Timeline.

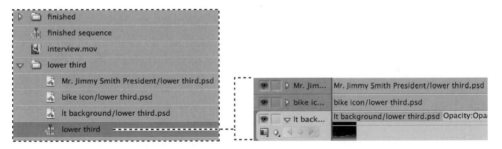

Re-create the lower third animation

1 Select the lt background clip, and open the Effect Controls panel.

2 Expand the Motion fixed effect, and then position the CTI at about one second into the clip.

3   Enable keyframes for the Position parameter by clicking the stopwatch. This will place a keyframe at the position of the CTI. Move the CTI to the beginning of the clip, and adjust the Position value to 360, 400. This will add a keyframe at this position and move the lower third background below the bottom of the frame.

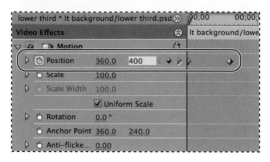

4   Play the sequence to verify that the lower third background rises from the bottom of the screen over the first second of the clip. Right-click (Windows) or Control-click (Mas OS) the second keyframe, and set Temporal Interpolation to Ease In. Play the sequence again, and notice what a nice touch the Ease In setting has on the animation.

5   Select the bike icon clip, and expand the Motion fixed effect in the Effect Controls panel. Set a Position keyframe just after one second, at about 00;00;01;15. Set another keyframe at the one-second point. Set the value of this position keyframe to -350, 240. This will position the bike icon off the left side of the frame at the beginning of the clip.

6   Play the sequence. You can adjust the speed the bike travels by moving the second keyframe farther from or closer to the first keyframe. Experiment with this until you have the speed you desire. Also set the Ease in option on the second keyframe as we did on the background clip motion.

7   The text of the lower third should follow the bike, so we can copy the bike's animation and paste it in the text clip. Select the bike icon clip, and choose Edit > Copy.

8   Select the Mr. Jimmy Smith President clip, and choose Edit > Paste Attributes.
The animation of the sequence is complete. The only thing left to do is to superimpose this lower third over the interview clip.

9   Create a new sequence by choosing File > New Sequence. Name it *Practice*.

10   Drag the interview.mov clip to the Video 1 track of the Timeline and press the backslash (\) key to expand the view in the Timeline.

11 Drag the lower third sequence we just animated to the Video 2 track above the interview clip. Adjust the position of the lower third so that it starts about one second after the interview clip starts.

12 To polish it all off, drop a Cross Dissolve transition on the end of the lower third sequence clip.

The lower third animation sequence references the original Photoshop CS3 file. So, if you change the original Photoshop file, the changes will ripple through any instances where it was used in Adobe Premiere Pro. For example, you might open the lower third. psd file in Photoshop and change the background or text color. When you save the Photoshop file, the changes will immediately be reflected wherever that file was used in Adobe Premiere Pro.

Editing Encore menus in Photoshop CS3

We will export video to Adobe Encore CS3 in Lesson 18 by using built-in menu templates in Encore. All the menu templates in Encore are actually Photoshop CS3 PSD files. You can learn to edit the existing templates in Photoshop or create your own new menus. The Photoshop CS3 engine is built into Encore, so when you choose Edit Menu In Photoshop while you're in Encore CS3, any changes you then save in Photoshop CS3 show up immediately in Encore.

To create Encore menus in Photoshop CS3, you need to follow Encore menu layer naming conventions. Assign certain prefixes to layer names to ensure those elements perform the functions you intend, such as whether video can appear in a button or if you want some text to be a link to the main menu.

We won't go through all the layer naming conventions. If you intend to build Encore menus from scratch, open Adobe Encore CS3 Help, and then choose Menus > Creating Menus.

Editing an existing Encore menu in Photoshop CS3

Note: This section requires the use of Photoshop CS3 to make changes to the menu template.

The easiest way to learn how Encore menus are designed is to customize an existing menu. Once you become familiar with them, you can try creating menus from scratch. In this mini-lesson, we will open an existing menu template in Encore and customize it by editing it in Photoshop CS3.

1 Start Encore CS3. Click New Project. Give your project a name and click OK.

Note: If this is the first time you've started Encore CS3, you might be asked to specify a Default Television Standard. For this lesson, we'll use the NTSC standard. You may change this option later in Encore Preferences.

2   Select the Library panel, and choose Corporate as the set.

Note: If this is the first time this library set has been opened, Encore will take a few minutes to initialize it.

3   Open the Blue Grid Menu by double-clicking it in the Library panel. It opens in the Menu panel.

We want to do a simple customization of this menu by changing the hue of the menu from blue to brown. The background is not a simple solid color that we can change in Encore. It is a complex graphic, but it is no problem to change in Adobe Photoshop CS3.

4   Right-click (Windows) or Control-click (Mac OS) the menu name in the Menu panel, and choose Edit Menu In Photoshop. This starts Photoshop CS3 and opens this menu as a layered Photoshop file.

5   In Photoshop, notice this menu has six layers. The layers with the plus sign (+) are Encore buttons. We will customize the Background graphic layer. Select the Background layer in the Photoshop CS3 Layers palette.

6   To change the hue of the background to brown, choose Image > Adjustments > Hue/Saturation. Move the Hue slider all the way to the left. This changes the hue of the background from blue to brown. Click OK.

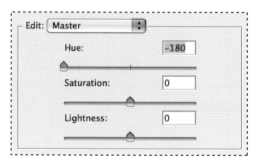

7   Save the menu in Photoshop CS3 by choosing File > Save.

8   Switch back to Encore CS3, and you'll see that the menu has been updated there.

This is just one sample of the many ways you can customize existing Encore templates by using Photoshop CS3.

Dynamic Link with After Effects CS3

Note: *The Adobe Dynamic Link feature requires the purchase of Adobe® Creative Suite® 3 Production Premium. Purchasing Adobe Premiere Pro CS3 and After Effects CS3 separately will not allow Dynamic Link to work. Dynamic Link is a suite-based feature.*

After Effects CS3 is the tool of choice for editors who want to produce exciting and innovative motion graphics, visual effects, and animated text for film, video, DVD, and the web.

After Effects users tend to fall into two distinct camps: motion graphics artists and animated text artists. Some production houses specialize in one or the other. There is so much that After Effects can do, it's hard to wrap your brain around all of it. You are likely to use only a subset of its creative prospects.

After Effects features

After Effects has numerous options:

• **Text creation and animation tools**—Create animated text with unprecedented ease. After Effects offers dozens of groundbreaking text animation presets. Simply drag them to your text to see them in action.

- **Leading-edge visual effects**—More than 150 effects and compositing features enhance your images well beyond the capabilities of Adobe Premiere Pro.

- **Vector paint tools**—Use built-in vector paint tools based on Photoshop CS3 technology to perform touch-up and rotoscoping tasks.

- **Comprehensive masking tools**—Easily design, edit, and work with masks using flexible auto-tracing options.

- **Tight Adobe integration**—Copy and paste assets, compositions, or sequences between Adobe Premiere Pro and After Effects. Preserve layers and other attributes when you import Adobe Photoshop CS3 and Adobe Illustrator CS3 files. The Dynamic Link feature (remember, available only in Adobe Creative Suite 3 Production Premium) means you no longer need to render an After Effects composition before moving it between After Effects and Adobe Premiere Pro or Encore.

- **Motion Tracker**—This option accurately, quickly, and automatically maps the motion of an element and lets you add an effect to follow that action.

A brief look at the After Effects workspace

In this mini-lesson, we will animate the same lower third graphic that we did at the beginning of this lesson. We will import the same Photoshop CS3 file into After Affects, use After Effects tools to animate the three layers of the graphic, and then use Adobe Dynamic Link to link the After Effects animation into the Adobe Premiere Pro Timeline.

1   In Adobe Premiere Pro, open the Lesson 17-2 project.

2   Start Adobe After Effects CS3.

3   In After Effects, open the ae finished.aep file by choosing File > Open Project and selecting ae finished.aep from the Lesson 17 folder.

Notice many similarities to the Adobe Premiere Pro user interface.

Composition

As with Adobe Premiere Pro, After Effects has a Project panel, but the icons and terminology are a bit different. For instance, Adobe Premiere Pro sequences become compositions in After Effects.

Double-clicking a composition (highlighted in the previous figure) opens it in the Timeline panel. Instead of tracks, you work with layers in After Effects.

4 Scrub the After Effects Timeline to see the final animation we will create.

5 After Effects may not be able to play back the animation in real time, depending on your computer speed. However, After Effects can do a RAM preview when you press the 0 (zero) key on the numeric keypad. This will render the Timeline to RAM, and then play back smoothly in real time.

6 Close the ae finished project by choosing File > Close Project.

Animating the lower third

We will start a new project in After Effects, and create the animation you just saw in the finished example.

1   With After Effects still open, import the lower third.psd file by choosing File > Import > File and selecting lower third.psd from the Lesson 17 folder. Change the Import As parameter from Footage to Composition, and click Open.

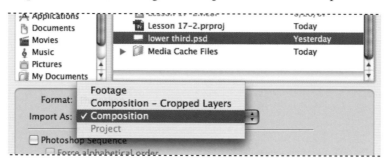

2   Double-click the lower third composition icon in the Project panel to open the composition in the Timeline panel.

3   Notice the Photoshop CS3 layers are intact and in the correct order in the Timeline. Scrub the Timeline, and you will see this is a static graphic. No animation has been applied yet. Return the CTI to the beginning of the clip.

4   Locate the Effects & Presets panel, and expand the * Animation Presets folder. Within that folder, expand the Transitions – Movement folder. Drag the Zoom – 3D tumble preset to the lt background layer of the Timeline.

Note: The preset will be applied at the CTI location on the layer where you dropped the preset, so make sure the CTI is at frame zero for step 4.

5   Do a RAM preview of this effect by pressing the 0 (zero) key on the numeric keypad.
Next we will animate the bike icon.

6   Position the CTI at the one-second mark, just as the lower third background
animation is finishing.

7   Drag the Slide – Straight preset (located in the Transitions – Movement folder) to the
bike icon layer. RAM preview the Timeline.

After Effects has some dazzling animation presets designed especially for text. These
animations are aware of individual characters, words, or lines of text. We'll use one of
these text effects on our text layer. However, because we didn't create the text in After
Effects, it doesn't know the layer is text. We need to tell After Effects that the top layer
(Mr. Jimmy Smith) is text.

8   Select layer 1 (the Jimmy Smith text layer) and choose Layer > Convert To Editable
Text. Now After Effects will treat this layer as text; the text can now be edited and
animated with special text effects or presets. After Effects indicates this is a text layer by
showing a T icon to the left of the layer name.

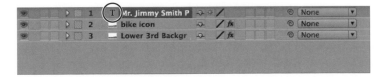

9   Position the CTI at the one-second mark on the Timeline.

10   In the Effects & Presets panel, expand the Text folder within the *Animation Presets folder. Within the Text folder, expand the Animate In folder and drag the Raining Characters In preset to the text layer in layer 1.

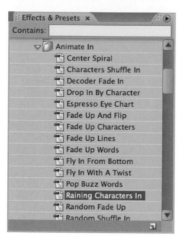

11   Do a RAM preview.

12   Save the project by choosing File > Save. Save the project in the Lesson 17 folder and name it *ae practice.aep.*

With the animation complete, it is time to use it in our Adobe Premiere Pro project, superimposed over the interview clip. In the past, this would involve rendering the animation out to a movie, importing the movie into Adobe Premiere Pro, and then placing it in the Timeline. If you ever wanted to change the animation, it would require editing in After Effects, re-rendering and re-exporting the movie, which was very time consuming. With Dynamic Link, the process is much simpler.

Importing a project from After Effects to Adobe Premiere Pro by using Dynamic Link

1   Leave After Effects open while you also open or switch back to Adobe Premiere Pro. It is not necessary to leave After Effects open for Dynamic Link to work, but we will be editing the animation again, so to save time we will leave it open.

2   In Adobe Premiere Pro, open the Lesson 17-2 project, and open the Practice sequence (it may still be open from the previous section).

3   Drag interview.mov from the bin to the Video 1 track.

4   Import the After Effects composition we just made via Dynamic Link by choosing File > Adobe Dynamic Link > Import After Effects Composition.

5   On the left side of the Import Composition dialog box, navigate to the Lesson 17 folder, click once on ae practice.aep, choose the lower third composition in the right window, and click OK.

6   The lower third/ae practice composition is added to the Adobe Premiere Pro Project panel. Drag it to the video track above the interview clip. Position it about one second after the start of the interview, and then trim the end to be the same length as the interview clip.

7   As a nice finish, add a Cross Dissolve transition to the end of the lower third dynamic link clip so it dissolves away with the interview clip.

8   Render and play the sequence in Adobe Premiere Pro.

We now have an After Effects animation playing inside Adobe Premiere Pro—and we didn't need to render or export the animation in After Effects. This is a real timesaving feature. The power of this feature becomes more obvious when you need to edit or tweak your animation.

Editing an existing dynamically linked animation

We will make an adjustment to the animation in After Effects to show the dynamic nature of this feature.

1　Leave the project open in Adobe Premiere Pro, and switch over to After Effects, which should still be open, with the lower third composition open.

2　Set the CTI position to the beginning of the After Effects Timeline.

3　In the Effects & Presets panel, expand the Image – Special Effects folder, which is inside the * Animation Presets folder.

4　Drag the Bad TV – Old preset to the lt background layer. Do a RAM preview to see this effect.

5　Without saving the After Effects project, switch back to Adobe Premiere Pro.

6　Play the sequence in Adobe Premiere Pro. Without saving the After Effects project, the changes we made in After Effects are already updated in Adobe Premier Pro. That's why they call it Dynamic Link!

Review

▶ ## Review questions

1   What is the difference between importing a Photoshop CS3 file into Adobe Premiere Pro as footage and importing it as a sequence?

2   Does Encore maintain all the layers of a menu created in Photoshop CS3?

3   What does the plus sign (+) indicate in front of a layer name in Photoshop CS3?

4   In some ways, Adobe Premiere Pro and After Effects have similar functionality. Only the terms are different. Give a couple of examples.

5   Once a dynamic link is established between an After Effects CS3 composition and an Adobe Premiere Pro project, must the After Effects composition be rendered after making changes?

▶ ## Review answers

1   Importing Photoshop CS3 files as footage brings them in as a single layered clip, with either all the layers collapsed, or a single layer selected. Importing as a sequence brings all the Photoshop CS3 layers into Adobe Premiere Pro in the same stacking order as in the Photoshop CS3 file. An Adobe Premiere Pro sequence is created to nest them all together.

2   Yes. Some of the layer properties are even editable in Encore. Those that are not can still be edited in Photoshop by choosing Edit Menu In Photoshop from the context menu.

3   The plus sign indicates that the layer is an Encore button.

4   Adobe Premiere Pro has sequences and tracks. After Effects has compositions and layers.

5   No. Once a dynamic link is established, changes made in After Effects are immediately available in Adobe Premiere Pro.

Export

MPEG

Media Encoder

EDL

Export to Tape

Device Control
- ☑ Activate Recording Device
  - ☐ Assemble at timecode: 00;00;10;00
  - ☐ Delay movie start by 0 frames
  - ☐ Preroll 0 frames

Options
- ☐ Abort after 1 dropped frames
- ☑ Report dropped frames
- ☐ Render audio before export

Export Status

Start Timecode: 00;00;00;00

End Timecode: 00;00;14;13

Current Timecode: 00;00;00;00

Dropped frames: 0

Status: Ready...

[Record] [Cancel]

Exporting your project is the final step in the video production process. You have many options. First, decide what you want to export: single frames, clips, or entire sequences. Then you choose the format: videotape, movie file, or DVD. The Adobe Media Encoder offers multiple high-level output formats: Windows Media, QuickTime, RealMedia, Adobe Flash, and MPEG. Within those formats you have dozens of options. You'll sort through them in this lesson.

18 Exporting Frames, Clips, and Sequences

Topics covered in this lesson:

- Export options
- Recording to videotape
- Making single frames
- Creating standard movie, image sequence, and audio files
- Using the Adobe Media Encoder
- Exporting to mobile devices
- Working with edit decision lists

Getting started

Adobe Premiere Pro offers a full array of export options—methods to record your projects to videotape, convert them into files, or burn them to DVDs.

Recording to videotape is straightforward, while file creation has many more options. You can record only the audio portion of your project, convert a video segment or entire project into one of several standard (but somewhat dated) file formats, or create still frames, sequences of still frames, or animation files.

Of greater relevance are the higher-level video encoding formats available in Adobe Media Encoder. You'll use that powerful tool to create projects to post to a website, for multimedia CD-ROMs, or for export to mobile devices using the new Adobe Device Central CS3 software. If you need to create Flash Video for websites, use the new tools to export Flash Video with web markers.

Export options

When you complete a project, you have a number of export choices:

• Select a single frame, a series of frames, a clip, or an entire sequence.

• Choose audio-only, video-only, or full audio/video output.

• Export directly to videotape, create a file for viewing on a computer or the Internet, or put your project on a DVD with or without a complete set of menus, buttons, and other DVD features.

Beyond the actual export formats, there are settings and parameters to be chosen as well:

• Any files you choose to create can be at the same visual quality and data rate as your original media, or they can be compressed.

• You need to specify frame size, frame rate, data rate, and audio and video compression techniques.

You can use exported project files for further editing, in presentations, as streaming media for Internet and other networks, or as sequences of images to create animations.

Checking out export options

1 Start Adobe Premiere Pro, and open the Lesson 18-1 project.

2 Click somewhere in the Timeline to select it and its single sequence (otherwise Adobe Premiere Pro will not present Export as an option in the File menu).

3 Choose File > Export.

Adobe Premiere Pro offers nine export options (some options might be unavailable due to the particulars of the files in your sequence):

• **Movie**—Create Windows AVI or Apple QuickTime desktop video files or sequences of still images.

• **Frame**—Convert a selected frame into a still image using one of four formats: BMP, GIF, Targa, or TIFF.

• **Audio**—Record an audio-only file in one of three formats: WAV, AVI, or QuickTime.

• **Title**—Since Adobe Premiere Pro stores Titler-created objects in the project file, the only way to use the same title in more than one project is to export it as a file. To use this option, you need to select a title in the Project panel.

- **Export To Tape**—Transfer your project to videotape.

- **Export To Encore**—Send your Adobe Premiere Pro project directly to Adobe Encore CS3.

- **Export To EDL**—Create an edit decision list to take your project to a production studio for further editing.

- **Adobe Clip Notes**—We reviewed this feature in Lesson 16.

- **Adobe Media Encoder**—Transcode your project or a segment into one of four high-end file formats: MPEG, Windows Media, RealMedia, or QuickTime. Use these for web streaming video or, in the case of MPEG, to play on DVDs.

Recording to videotape

Even with something as straightforward as dubbing your sequence to videotape, Adobe Premiere Pro gives you multiple options. All you need is a video recording device—most commonly, the same DV camcorder you used to import the original raw video.

You can use an analog videotape recorder without video control, but doing so takes some extra effort. That will be explained at the end of this mini-lesson.

1 Connect your DV camcorder to your computer, just as you did when you captured video.

2 Turn it on and set it to VCR or VTR (not Camera, as you might expect).

3 Cue the tape to where you want to start recording.

> 💡 **Bars And tone or Black Video**
>
> *If you're going to have a post-production studio duplicate your tapes, add 30 seconds of bars and tone to the beginning so the studio can set up its gear. Otherwise, give your project a little breathing room on your DV tape by adding black video to its beginning. To do either one, click the New Item button at the bottom of the Project panel and select Bars And Tone or Black Video. The default duration is five seconds. Right-click (Windows) or Control-click (Mac OS) the clip in the Project panel, choose Speed/ Duration, and change the time to suit your needs. Then drag that clip from the Project panel to the start of your project (hold down Ctrl (Windows) or Command (Mac OS) to insert it and slide all other clips to the right).*

4   Select the sequence you want to record.

Note: When using the standard DV device control videotape export method, you can only export an entire sequence, as opposed to a selected segment. To export a segment, follow the analog videotape recording instructions later in this mini-lesson.

5   Choose File > Export > Export To Tape.

That opens the dialog box shown in the next figure. Here's a rundown of its options:

• **Activate Recording Device**—When selected, Adobe Premiere Pro will control your DV device. Deselect it if you want to record to a device that you'll control manually.

• **Assemble At Timecode**—Use this to select an In point on the tape where you want recording to begin. When this option is note selected, recording will begin at the current tape location.

• **Delay Movie Start**—This is for the few DV recording devices that need a brief period of time between receiving the video signal and recording it. Check your device's manual to see what the manufacturer recommends.

• **Preroll**—Most decks need little or no time to get up to the proper tape recording speed. To be on the safe side, select 150 frames (five seconds) or add black video to the start of your project (see previous "Bars And Tone or Black Video" tip).

The remaining options are self-explanatory.

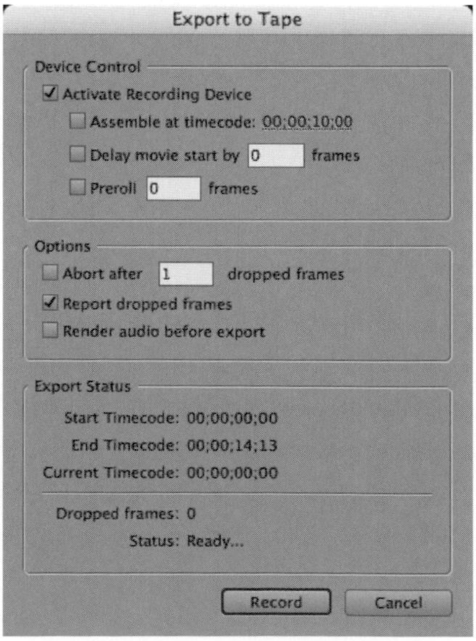

6 Click Record (or Cancel if you don't want to make a recording).

If you haven't rendered your project (by pressing Enter for playback instead of the Spacebar), Adobe Premiere Pro will do that now. When rendering is complete, Adobe Premiere Pro will start your camcorder and record your project to it.

Recording to an analog recorder without device control

To record to an analog machine without device control, set up your camcorder for recording.

1 Render the sequence or portion you want to record by pressing Enter.

2 Play the sequence to make sure that you see it displayed on your external recording device.

3 Cue your tape to where you want recording to begin, position the Timeline CTI to where you want playback from your sequence to begin, press the Record button on your device, and play the sequence.

4 When the sequence or segment finishes, click the Stop button in the Program Monitor, and then stop the tape on the device.

Making single frames

There are two basic export-to-file processes: standard files and Adobe Media Encoder files. Each uses its own interface. Single frames and frame sequences fall into the category of standard files.

1 Move the CTI to the frame you want to export.

2 Choose File > Export > Frame.

The Export Frame dialog box appears. You will see a window like this for all standard (not Adobe Media Encoder) files. The currently selected file type will appear in the Summary window.

3 Click Settings to change to a different file type.

Note: The format choices available for Mac users are TIFF and Targa.

4 Choose a format for File Type (only GIF has an additional Compile Settings option). You can deselect Add To Project When Finished if you choose.

5 Click OK to close the Export Frame Settings dialog box.

6 In the Export Frame dialog box, specify a location and filename, and then click Save (or Cancel if you don't want to make a file).

Creating standard movie, image sequence, and audio files

You can export a clip, an entire sequence, or a portion of a sequence as an audio/video, audio-only, or video-only file, or as a sequence of still image files. You can use those image sequences in animation programs or apply graphic elements to them (a process called *rotoscoping*) in programs such as Adobe Photoshop CS3 and Illustrator CS3.

Before looking at specific export options, you need to be aware of how to specify what you are exporting.

Export an entire sequence

1   Select the sequence in the Timeline or Program Monitor.

2   Choose File > Export. Details of each export option will be explored below.

Export a portion of a sequence

1   Place the ends of the work area bar at the beginning and end of the segment you wish to export.

2   Choose File > Export. For the Range to export, choose Work Area Bar rather than Entire Sequence. The Range field will appear in the settings of the movie or Adobe Media Encoder export settings.

Export a clip

Select the clip in the Source Monitor or Project panel, and click in the appropriate panel to make it active. To specify a range of frames within the clip to export, set an In point and Out point in the Source Monitor.

Movie and clip export options

1   Select the sequence or clip you want to export, and choose File > Export > Movie.

2   Click Settings. The Export Movie Settings dialog box appears, open to the General category of options.

For movies, you have a few additional options beyond those available when exporting a single frame:

• **File Type**—Examine the pop-up menu and note that there are six image file types for the image sequence option as well as QuickTime and AVI. Windows Waveform is for audio-only, and is one of the file types you'll find in the Export Audio option.

Note: QuickTime is the only export movie format available for Mac users.

• **Range**—If you selected a clip in the Source Monitor or Project Panel, you have the choice of exporting the Entire Clip or In To Out. If you selected a sequence, your choice is Entire Sequence or Work Area Bar.

• **Export Audio**—Deselecting this option means you'll create a video-only file.

• **Embedding Options**—Choose whether to include a project link in the exported file. That means you can open and edit the original project from within another Adobe Premiere Pro project or from another application that supports the Edit Original command.

• **Save and Load**—You can save and later quickly load export settings that you use frequently.

3   Click Video to open the Video category of options.

Here you can choose a compressor (if one is available for the file type you selected) as well as color depth, frame size, quality, and pixel aspect ratio.

Note: To see most of the compressors available for video files, choose QuickTime as the file type in the General category. QuickTime has more than 20 codecs (compression/ decompression algorithms) associated with it. Each video and audio compressor has attributes that work best under certain circumstances.

4 Click OK to close the Export Movie Settings dialog box.

5 Specify a location and filename in the Export Movie dialog box, and click OK (or Cancel).

Export audio only

You can use the Export Movie Settings dialog box to create audio-only files by deselecting Export Video in the General category, but it's more intuitive to use the Export Audio command.

1 Choose File > Export > Audio, and click Settings in the Export Audio dialog box. The Export Audio Settings dialog box appears, open to the General category of options. This gives you access to the four audio file types: AIF, WAV, AVI, and QuickTime. The latter two formats are primarily intended for audio/video files, but they also handle audio-only.

Note: The format choices available for Mac users are AIF and QuickTime.

2 Open the Audio category of options in the Export Audio Settings dialog box.

Here you can set audio quality. You can choose from different audio compressors.

3 Click OK to close the Export Audio Settings dialog box.

4 Specify a location and filename in the Export Audio dialog box, and click OK (or Cancel).

Using the Adobe Media Encoder

The Adobe Media Encoder offers several flavors of MPEG encoding, plus Adobe Flash Video, Windows Media, RealMedia, and QuickTime streaming media (as opposed to the QuickTime MOV files you encountered when exporting movies and audio).

Each of the five encoding engines has so many presets that few editors will need to do any parameter-tweaking. That said, there are customizable options aplenty.

Rather than attempt to explain each encoding engine's unique characteristics, we will review them and explain a couple of general concepts. For detailed explanations of all the options for each encoder, open Adobe Premiere Pro Help and go to Exporting > Adobe Media Encoder Basics.

Choose File > Export > Adobe Media Encoder.

The Adobe Media Encoder consists of a preview display on the left and tabbed panels containing export settings on the right. In the preview display, you can choose to view either your source or output video. The Source tab displays your sequence before any export settings have been applied. The Output tab shows how your video will look after it's exported.

A time ruler lets you scrub through your video. You can crop the source video using the Source display, or switch to the Output display and deinterlace.

Note: Use the Deinterlace option if the video in the sequence is interlaced (all standard DV is interlaced) and you are exporting to a non-interlaced medium, such as progressive scan video. Interlaced video displays images in fields of odd-numbered, then even-numbered, horizontal lines. NTSC displays in 29.97 frames (or 59.94 fields) per second.

Export settings

When setting export options, you can choose from a number of presets or create your own custom settings. Custom settings can be saved as presets for future use. As you make changes to your export settings, the Output tab in the preview display updates to reflect your changes.

Adobe Flash Video

Adobe Flash Video is based on Adobe Flash Player technology, so it's ready to play on any computer with a Flash-enabled browser. You don't have to worry about the platform or the format. With Adobe Flash Video, when the page loads, the video plays.

1   Choose Adobe Flash Video from the Format menu under Export Settings in the upper right section of Adobe Media Encoder.

2   Open the Preset menu under Export Settings, and choose a preset. For this example, choose NTSC Source To 512kbps.

This is all you have to set to export your project to Flash Video. However, there are five tabs on which you can optionally fine-tune the export settings:

• **Filters**—The filter available for encoded output is Video Noise Reduction. Enabling this filter reduces the video noise introduced by slightly blurring the video. Export the project without this filter to see if noise is a problem. If it is, increase Noise Reduction in small amounts. Increasing noise reduction too much will make the video blurry.

• **Video**—The Video tab allows you to adjust frame size, frame rate, and bit rate. The default values are based on the preset you choose.

• **Audio**—The Audio tab allows you to adjust the bit rate of the audio and, for some formats, the codec. The default values are based on the preset you choose.

• **Multiplexer**—This tab has no editable values for Flash Video. Other formats have different properties and settings on this tab.

• **Others**—This tab primarily allows you to specify an FTP server to upload the exported video to when it is finished encoding. Fill in the appropriate FTP values supplied by your FTP host if you want to enable this feature.

3   Leave all the values set to default for the Flash NTSC Source To 512kbps preset, and click OK.

4   Specify a filename, and then click Save. Adobe Media Encoder encodes and saves your file.

Note: A unique feature of exporting to Flash is exporting cue points to be used in a Flash application. Flash will read Adobe Premiere Pro CS3 sequence markers as cue points that you can use to trigger events in the Flash composition.

QuickTime

QuickTime offers the most options, but has a limited number of presets—eight each for NTSC and PAL.

1 Choose File > Export > Adobe Media Encoder, and then choose QuickTime from the Format menu in the upper right section of Adobe Media Encoder.

2 Choose NTSC Source To Streaming 512kbps from the Preset menu.

3 Click the Video tab, open the Video Codec pop-up menu, and note that as with QuickTime's Export Movie option, you can select from a list of more than 20 codecs. Several have additional options.

4 Click the Alternates tab, and note that there are options unique to the QuickTime format.

RealMedia

RealMedia takes a more consumer-friendly approach to its codec options. Its collection of presets is similar to those in QuickTime.

1 Choose RealMedia from the Format menu.

2 Select the NTSC Source To Download 512kbps preset from the Preset menu.

3 Click the Audiences tab.

This is where you can customize the bit rate from the selected preset and choose one- or two-pass encoding. Both RealMedia and Windows Media offer this option. If two-pass encoding is selected, the encoder analyzes the original video project before transcoding it. Encoding will take almost twice as long, but the resulting video will look better than a single-pass version using all the same parameters.

Note: *RealMedia export is not available for Mac users.*

Windows Media

This is the most versatile video format for use in Windows PCs and for playback on the Internet. You can create single files with multiple bandwidth bit-stream rates (as a means to compensate for varying Internet user connection speeds), or you can create high-definition, wide-screen videos with 5.1 surround sound for playback in theaters or on HD TVs.

1 Choose Windows Media from the Format menu.

2 Open the Preset menu, and choose NTSC Source To Download 512kbps.

3 Click the Video tab. Notice the one- or two-pass encoding option for Windows Media encoding. Choose two-pass encoding for the best quality.

Note: Windows Media export is not available for Mac users.

MPEG encoding

MPEG (Moving Picture Experts Group) is a working committee of the ISO (International Standardization Organization) and the IEC (International Electrotechnical Commission).

MPEG is in charge of the development of standards for digital audio and video compression. Established in 1988, the group has produced several compression standards, including:

- **MPEG-1**—The standard on which Video CDs and MP3 audio are based. MPEG-1 video is VHS-quality video with CD-quality audio at up to a combined data rate of 1.5 Mbps (megabits per second). Its resolution is 352x240 (about 25% of full DV quality).

- **MPEG-2**—DVD and satellite digital video with a data rate for standard definition video from about 3 to 15 Mbps (7–9 Mbps is the generally accepted range for high-quality DVD video) and 15–30 Mbps for HD. MPEG-2 also supports multi-channel surround sound audio encoding.

- **MPEG-4**—Multimedia for the fixed and mobile web.

All MPEG standards use similar encoding techniques. They compress video by selecting keyframes or *Intra-frames* (I-frames), and then removing a few of the frames between I-frames and replacing them with B-frames (backward frames) and P-frames (predicted frames). The B- and P-frames store only the differences between I-frames.

💡 Standard DV can't match broadcast-quality or film

You probably shot your videos using standard DV, also known as DV25, so named because of its 25 Mbps video data rate. Combined with audio and error correction data, DV25's actual bitrate is 3.6 MBps (megabytes per second). Broadcast quality DV—DV50—has twice that data rate, due to extra color information. So when you view DVDs that started out as DV25 videos, do not expect them to have the visual quality of broadcast or satellite TV or Hollywood feature films.

1   Open the Format menu, and note that there are six MPEG file formats:

• **MPEG1**—1.7 Mbps with MPEG-1 audio.

• **MPEG1-VCD (Video CD)**—1.15 Mbps with MPEG-1 audio. This file format is specifically to view about an hour of less-than-VHS-quality video on a CD that will play on most consumer DVD video players and computer DVD and CD drives. You'll need to use standalone CD-writing software to create a VCD.

Note: MPEG1 export and MPEG1-VCD export are not available for Mac users.

• **MPEG2**—The presets are geared to high-definition and progressive scan videos. If your goal is to create standard DVD content, select MPEG2-DVD. If you want to tweak the MPEG-2 parameters, select MPEG-2.

• **MPEG2 Blu-ray**—The presets are geared to high-definition video for distribution on Blu-ray disc.

• **MPEG2-DVD**—Offers the most presets. Select a preset that gives you the best quality while not exceeding the 4.7 GB of space on a DVD. To help you find the right fit, Adobe Media Encoder has an Estimated File Size display that updates each time you change a preset or a customized setting. You'll take a look at that in a moment.

• **MPEG2-SVCD**—Super Video CD. Like a VCD, SVCDs can play on most consumer DVD players. They hold about 35 minutes of low bit rate (2 Mbps) MPEG-2 video.

Note: MPEG2-SVCD export is not available for Mac users.

2   Select MPEG1.

Look at the Estimated File Size display in the lower right corner of Adobe Media Encoder. It should read about 3.4MB.

Note: The sequence is 30 seconds long. If you were to export it as an AVI file (with its DV25 bit rate of 3.6 MBps) it would be about 53MB—16 times larger than the MPEG-1 file.

3   Select MPEG1-VCD.

Depending on the Preset you select, the Estimated File Size will be about 25% less than MPEG-1.

4   Select MPEG2.

5   Choose NTSC DV High Quality from the Preset menu.

Note that its Estimated File Size is more than twice the size of an MPEG-1 file, but still much smaller than the AVI file.

6   Click the Video tab.

7   Scroll through the many options available for fine-tuning the MPEG encoding settings. Many of these settings are beyond the scope of this book. Leave them at their default values unless you are confident in making changes and understand how the various settings interact. One of the most common settings you might want to adjust is the Bitrate Encoding setting:

• **CBR** (constant bit rate)—This works well for Internet applications, because the bit rate does not fluctuate.

• **VBR** (variable bit rate)—Generally gives you better picture quality than CBR at the same bit rate, because it increases the bit rate during action scenes. It offers a one- or two-pass option. Two passes take longer but create a higher quality image. Use VBR when creating a video for a DVD.

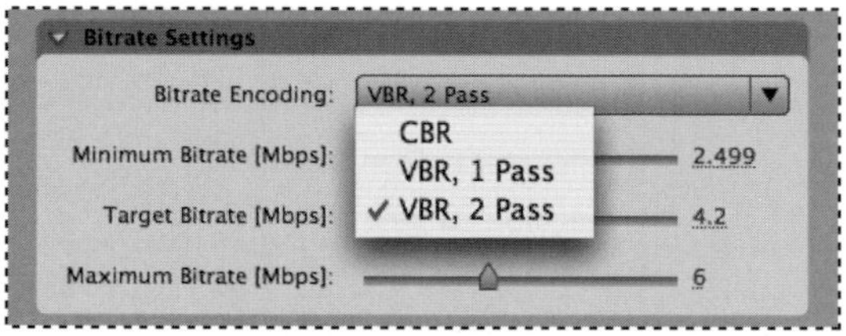

8   Click the Audio tab, and change the Audio Format to Dolby Digital.

That gives you a wide range of options including surround sound (in the Audio Coding Mode menu shown in the next figure).

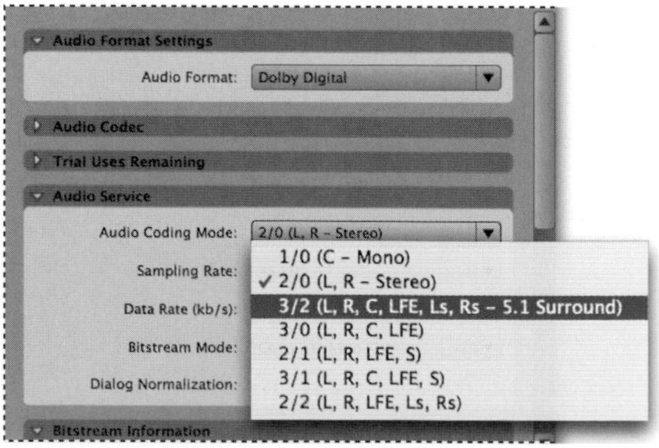

9   Click OK, give your file a name, click Save (or Cancel), and then rendering (transcoding) will begin. Depending on the quality level settings and the speed of your computer, this can take about two times the duration of your project.

Exporting to mobile devices

With the array of mobile devices that support video, it would be nice if there was a way to see what a video project would look like on various mobile devices. That is exactly what Adobe Device Central is designed to do. In this mini-lesson, we will export our project to Device Central and see how the video would look on various mobile devices.

Most mobile devices, such as iPods and 3GPP cell phones, support video encoded with the H.264 format. There are two flavors of H.264 available in the Adobe Media Encoder Format menu:

• **H.264**—An MPEG-4-based standard for encoding for a variety of devices, including high-definition displays, 3GPP cell phones, video iPods, and PlayStation Portable (PSP) devices.

• **H.264 Blu-ray**—An MPEG-4-based standard for encoding in high definition for Blu-ray Disc media.

We will be using H.264 for this mini-lesson.

1   Make sure your timeline sequence is selected in the Lesson 18-1 project, and then choose File > Export > Adobe Media Encoder.

2   Select H.264 as the encoding format.

3   Open the Preset menu.

Notice the variety of mobile devices set up for easy export. For example, it's easy to create video that will play on the Apple iPod by choosing the iPod preset. Many popular mobile device presets are already listed, and you can create or fine-tune your own presets. We'll work with a generic preset for now.

4   Choose the 3GPP 320 x 240 15fps preset, which we can test on multiple devices.

5   Make sure the Open In Device Central option is selected, and click OK.

6   Name the file, and click Save. Adobe Media Encoder encodes your project, saves the encoded file, and opens your encoded file in Adobe Device Central.

The available devices are listed in the left panel of Adobe Device Central by category or manufacturer.

7   Open the Nokia category, and choose Nokia 5300 cell phone by double-clicking it. This will load your encoded video into an emulation of the Nokia 5300 phone.

8   In the right panel under Scaling, select Fullscreen Mode, and click the Play button under the phone emulation to see how the video will appear when it is played horizontally in the phone.

9   Choose different options from the Reflections menu under Display to see how the video might look under different lighting conditions.

10   Double-click Nokia 5200 to see how the video will look on this phone with a smaller screen.

11   Double-click Nokia 6151. Notice the video will not play on this phone. This phone does not support the video file format that was exported. You can click the Device Profiles tab to get more information on the mobile device you are viewing.

12   Quit Adobe Device Central. Remember your exported encoded file is in the file location you chose in the export options.

Working with edit decision lists

An edit decision list (EDL) harks back to the days when small hard drives limited the size of your video files, and slower processors meant you could not play full resolution video. To remedy this, editors used low-resolution files in an NLE like Adobe Premiere Pro, edited their project, exported that to an EDL, and then took that text file and their original videotapes down to a production studio. They'd use expensive switching hardware to create the finished, full-resolution product.

These days, there isn't much call for that kind of off-line work, but filmmakers still use EDLs because of the size of the files and other complexities associated with going from film to video and back to film.

The EDL format used in Adobe Premiere Pro is more than 30 years old. AAF (Advanced Authoring Format), discussed in Lesson 16, is a significant step up from EDL. AAF was created to be something along the lines of a "super-EDL." Its purpose is to foster more cross-platform interoperability. The AAF that comes with Adobe Premiere Pro is compatible with a competing product, the Avid Xpress product line.

CMX is gone but its EDL lives on

There is no standard EDL format. Adobe Premiere Pro uses a format compatible with the CMX 3600, a switcher created by CMX Systems, a pioneer of production studio and broadcast-TV computer-controlled video editors. Formed as a joint venture by CBS and Memorex in 1971, CMX owned 90% of the broadcast video editing market by the mid-1980s. It discontinued operations in 1998, but its EDL remains the de facto standard to communicate edit decisions.

If you plan to use an EDL, you need to keep your project within some narrow guidelines:

•   EDLs work best with projects that contain no more than one video track, two stereo (or four mono) audio tracks, and no nested sequences.

•   Most standard transitions, frame holds, and clip-speed changes work well in EDLs.

•   Adobe Premiere Pro CS3 supports a key track for titles or other content. That track has to be immediately above the video track selected for export.

•   You must capture and log all the source material with accurate timecodes.

•   The capture card must have a device control that uses timecode.

•   Videotapes must each have a unique reel number and be formatted with the timecode before you shoot the video to ensure there are no breaks in the timecode.

To view the EDL options, Choose File > Export > Export To EDL to open the EDL Export Settings dialog box:

•   **EDL Title**—Specifies a title to appear in the first line of the EDL file.

Note: The title can be different from the filename. After clicking OK in the EDL Export Settings dialog box, you will have the opportunity to enter a filename.

•   **Start Timecode**—Sets the starting timecode value for the first edit in the sequence.

•   **Include Video Levels**—Includes video opacity level comments in the EDL.

- **Include Audio Levels**—Includes audio level comments in the EDL.

- **Audio Processing**—Specifies when audio processing should occur. Options are Audio Follows Video, Audio Separately, and Audio At End.

- **Tracks To Export**—Specifies which tracks to export. The video track directly above the video track selected for export is designated as the key track.

Review

▶ **Review questions**

1 What's the basic difference between Export Movie and Export Adobe Media Encoder?

2 When you click Record in the Export To Tape dialog box, your camcorder remains paused. What's going on?

3 What are the three streaming media options in Adobe Media Encoder?

4 How are MPEG-1 and MPEG-2 different?

5 What is the encoding format used when exporting to most mobile devices?

6 Why use an EDL instead of exporting to an AAF?

▶ **Review answers**

1 Export Movie is geared solely to standard, PC-based files. Adobe Media Encoder offers newer, compression-oriented files. In general, use Export Movie and select AVI to retain the full original quality of your digital video. Use Adobe Media Encoder to create files for use on the Internet, CDs, or DVDs.

2 Before Adobe Premiere Pro can start recording a project to videotape, it has to render it. You can do that in advance by opening a sequence and pressing Enter. Otherwise, when you click the Record button, you'll have to wait a while for Adobe Premiere Pro to render the unrendered portions of your sequence.

3 Windows Media, QuickTime, and RealMedia. Windows Media offers the most options.

4 MPEG-1 is VHS quality and is intended for use on CDs or PCs. MPEG-2 is much higher quality, has a wider spectrum of quality control possibilities, and is the standard video format for videos and movies on DVDs and digital satellite TV.

5 H.264 is the encoding format used when exporting to most mobile devices.

6 EDLs are geared primarily for projects that will have additional work done on them in a production studio. AAF is oriented toward moving a project to other NLE editing software, typically either Avid Xpress or Adobe Premiere Pro.

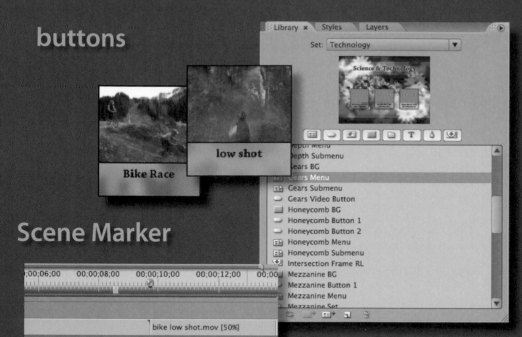

buttons

Scene Marker

DVD authoring

links

DVDs let you present your productions in their best light. They use high-quality MPEG-2 video compression, can include 5.1 surround sound, and are interactive. Adobe Premiere Pro CS3 can export timelines directly to Encore CS3, a full-featured DVD authoring and burning application. The new Encore CS3, included with Adobe Premiere Pro CS3, supports output to standard DVD, Blu-ray Disc, and Flash.

19 | Authoring DVDs with Adobe Premiere Pro CS3 and Encore CS3

Topics covered in this lesson:

- Overview of DVD authoring in Adobe Premiere Pro
- Adding Encore chapter markers to the timeline
- Creating an auto-play DVD
- Creating a menu DVD
- Creating a Blu-ray Disc
- Exporting DVD projects to Flash

Getting started

DVDs are a tremendous media delivery platform. Their images and videos are full-screen (including 16:9 widescreen), the audio quality is top drawer, and they are interactive. Simply click a menu button to jump immediately to a video, a scene, or behind-the-scenes stills.

Creating those interactive DVDs, with all their menus and buttons, used to take a Hollywood feature-film budget and expensive hardware. No longer. Now, with Adobe Premiere Pro CS3 and Adobe Encore CS3, you can create professional-looking DVDs on your PC in minutes.

Encore is now included with Adobe Premiere Pro and has a collection of customizable DVD menu templates with backgrounds and buttons—static or animated. If you like, you can use your own images or videos as backgrounds.

Encore CS3 takes DVD authoring much further. Use Encore to create DVDs, Blu-ray Discs, and even output your DVD project to Flash.

Overview of DVD authoring in Adobe Premiere Pro

DVD authoring is the process used to create menus, buttons, and links to assets and menus. It is also used to describe behaviors such as what the DVD player should do when it gets to the end of a video—does it return to the DVD's main menu, to some other menu, or to another video?

Each DVD authoring product takes a different approach to creating interactive DVDs. Adobe Premiere Pro simplifies the authoring process by allowing you to export to Encore CS3, which is a full-featured professional authoring tool.

You have two options when exporting from Adobe Premiere Pro directly to Encore:

• **Auto-play DVDs**—These have no menus. They work best for short movies that you want your viewers to watch from start to finish. Before you create an auto-play DVD, you can add Encore chapter markers to the timeline. Markers let viewers skip forward or back through the movie by using the Next and Previous buttons on their DVD player's remote control.

• **Menu-based DVDs**—These have one or more menus with buttons that link to separate videos, slideshows, or scene-selection submenus. (Scene-selection submenus, as you probably know, let viewers navigate to scenes within the videos.)

And then, Encore can output a project to any of three different file formats:

• **Standard Definition (SD) DVD**—The traditional DVD format widely in use today for set-top DVD players.

• **Blu-ray Disc**—A delivery medium for high-definition (HD) video.

• **Adobe Flash**—With one step, Encore can export your DVD project to Flash content for the web. Not only is the video converted to Flash Video, but the menuing system and actions are converted to Flash content as well. A web-ready HTML page with links to the Flash content is also produced, ready to be uploaded to your website for client review or demonstration.

Adding Encore chapter markers to the timeline

Once you have finished editing a video in Adobe Premiere Pro, you can add Encore chapter markers in the timeline to denote chapters for the final DVD. You can move, remove, and add markers at any time in the sequence.

Note: Encore chapter markers are not clip markers or timeline markers. Clip markers and timeline markers help you position and trim clips. Adobe Premiere Pro uses Encore chapter markers solely for DVD menu creation and button links.

1   Open the Lesson 19-1 project and open the Race sequence. We will be exporting this short video project to an auto-play DVD with no menus. But first, let's add a chapter marker so users can click ahead with the DVD remote.

2   Place an Encore chapter marker where the bike low shot clip begins (about 00;00;09;22 on the timeline).

3   To place an Encore chapter marker, position the CTI where you want the marker to be, and then click the Set Encore Chapter Marker button (located near the top left of the timeline). Give this chapter marker a name of *low shot*.

Note: Adobe Premiere Pro CS3 automatically places an Encore chapter marker on the first frame of every sequence. You cannot move or remove this marker. You can move, remove, or rename any other chapter markers that you add.

Creating an auto-play DVD

1   Choose File > Export > Export To Encore.

2   Name the disc Bike Race DVD.

3   Choose DVD Single Layer as the Disc Type. Notice there are options for dual-layer and Blu-ray Discs as well.

4   Select Direct Burn Without Menus. (We will create a DVD with menus in the next mini-lesson.)

5   Choose 1 copy, and select Entire Sequence for Export Range. In other projects, you might want to choose Work Area Only, to limit the export to a small work area of the timeline.

6   Select Loop Playback. This will cause the auto-play DVD to repeat forever. Of course, you might not want to use this feature for all projects.

7   Leave Encoding Settings at the default preset (NTSC Medium Quality). This is a good setting for the average project. You might want to experiment with other encoding presets for longer or shorter projects.

Note: To actually create a DVD, place a blank DVD in your DVD burner drive. If you do not have a DVD drive or do not wish to burn a physical DVD, you can proceed, but Encore will advise you it is searching for valid media.

8   Click OK. At this point, Adobe Premiere Pro prompts you for a folder and filename for the DVD project. Select a folder to store the DVD project, give the file a name, and then click Save. Adobe Premiere Pro renders the video, and then starts Encore to encode and burn the disc. You will see progress bars as the encoding is underway, and then the files are written to disc.

9　When the process is complete, your DVD is ready to watch, via a set-top DVD player or on your computer, if it is equipped with a DVD emulator (a simple DVD-playing application).

10　Quit Encore. You are prompted to save the Encore project. If you would like to make additional copies of an auto-play DVD, save the project. If you do not need to make additional copies, it is not necessary to save the Encore project.

Creating a menu DVD

Adobe Premiere Pro CS3 does not have tools to create DVD menus directly. However, the Encore chapter markers you place on the timeline are transferred to Encore and can be used to create buttons or chapters. Adobe Premiere Pro passes the video assets along with the chapter markers to Encore, and Encore is used to build the menus and burn to DVD.

You can continue where you left off, or open the Lesson 19-2 project to complete this mini-lesson. We will export the same timeline to Encore, except this time we'll make a DVD menu.

1　Make sure the Race sequence is selected by clicking anywhere in the sequence, and then choose File > Export > Export To Encore.

2　Name the disc *Bike Race DVD,* and choose DVD Single Layer as the Disc Type.

3　Select Author With Menus, 1 copy, and Entire Sequence for Export Range.

4　Accept the default Encoding Settings, and click OK. Adobe Premiere Pro prompts you for a DVD filename and location. Choose an appropriate folder to store the DVD files and an appropriate filename. For this example, name the file *bike race.*

5　Your video renders, and then Encore CS3 starts and automatically imports your Adobe Premiere Pro video sequence into an Encore timeline. (You may need to open the Project and Timelines panels to see these.)

Note: *There are three assets in the Encore Project panel. Don't let this confuse you. The Bike Race DVD timeline was created by Encore and is what Encore uses to play your encoded video. Bike Race DVD.m2v is the encoded video file in MPG format. Bike race DVD.wav is the audio file associated with the video. Encore will make sure the video and audio stay in sync.*

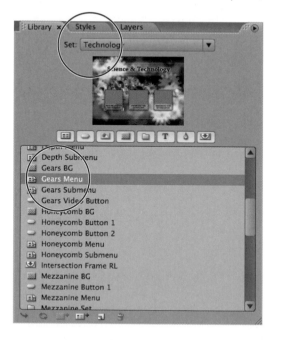

6 In Encore, select a menu template from the Library panel. Choose Technology from the Set menu. (If this is the first time you are opening a library set, Encore will take some time to initialize the new library set.)

7 Double-click Gears Menu to open that menu template in the Menu panel.

Note: *After you open the Gears Menu template, it is added as an asset in the Project panel. Also notice a new m2v file called NTSC Gears Menu.m2v has been added as well. This is a motion background that comes with the Gears Menu template.*

8   Drag the Bike Race DVD timeline from the Project panel to the Menu panel, and drop it on the leftmost square button. When you do this, Encore links the button to that timeline so that when a user chooses that button, the timeline will play. It also chooses a thumbnail image to display inside the button.

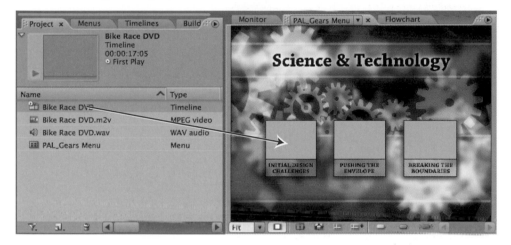

9   Select the Text tool (the T icon near the upper left corner of the screen) and change the button text label to *Bike Race.*

10   With the Text tool still selected, drag over the main title of the menu, and change it from Science & Technology to *Bike Race Menu.*

11   Switch back to the Selection tool, and drag the Bike Race DVD timeline from the Project panel to the center button in the Menu panel. This is the same video, but we want the second button to start playing the video from the chapter marker we set in Adobe Premiere Pro, rather than from the beginning.

12 Select the center button by clicking it.

13 On the Basic tab in the Properties panel, select the Sync Button Text And Name and Set Name From Link options. This will cause Encore CS3 to label the button using the chapter name you specified in Adobe Premiere Pro. The button label should change to read *Chapter 1*.

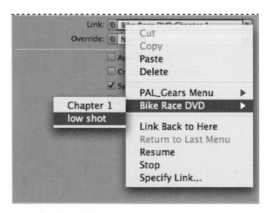

14 To cause this button to play the video from the second chapter marker, we need to adjust the link. From the Link menu on the Basic tab, choose Bike Race DVD > low shot as the new link. (Remember that in Adobe Premiere Pro we named the chapter marker "low shot.")

15 We won't be using the third menu button, so you can remove the button by selecting it and pressing the Delete key. Feel free to adjust the locations of the two remaining buttons on the screen, but don't let them overlap. Allow space between them.

Note: *If your buttons are too close together, causing an overlap, Encore will warn you by changing the button borders to red.*

The menu is almost done—just a couple more tweaks to finish it off. We have to tell Encore which asset to play first when the DVD is inserted into a DVD player. We want that to be the menu.

16 Notice in the Project panel that there is a small yellow circle on the Bike Race timeline asset. This icon indicates that this asset is currently set as the first-play item. To make the menu be the first-play asset, right-click (Windows) or Control-click (Mac OS) the NTSC_Gears Menu asset in the Project panel, and choose Set As First Play.

As a final step, we need to tell Encore what to do when the timeline finishes playing.

17 Select the Bike Race DVD timeline in the Project panel. In the Properties panel, click the End Action pop-up menu, and choose Return To Last Menu. This will cause the DVD to return to the menu when it is finished playing the video timeline.

That's it. We have made a complete DVD menu, in which the menu will appear when the DVD is inserted in a player, the first button will play the entire video, and the second button will play from Chapter 2 to the end.

Preview the DVD

You can preview the menu in Encore before burning to DVD to make sure it looks and works as you expect.

1 Since this menu has a motion background, it needs to render to preview properly in Encore. Choose File > Render > Project. Encore takes a couple of minutes to render the motion menu.

2 Preview the DVD by choosing File > Preview. Use the mouse as your DVD remote to choose the buttons. Click each button to ensure they all play as expected.

Burning the project to DVD

1 Close the Project Preview window, if it is still open. Then choose File > Build > Disc, or click in the Build Project panel. Adjust the size of the Build panel if necessary, so you can see the full width of the panel.

2   Although there are many options available on this tab, to build a DVD disc we need only to set Format to DVD and Output to DVD Disc, and then click Build. Make sure there is a blank DVD disc in your burner.

3   Encore prompts you for a project name. Select a folder and type an appropriate name for the project, and then click Save. Encore saves the project, builds the necessary DVD files, and then writes them to your DVD. The DVD ejects when the burn is complete.

Creating a Blu-ray Disc

Blu-ray is a format that supports high-definition (HD) video. HD video has a higher resolution, so it will not fit on a standard DVD. Blu-ray requires a Blu-ray-capable burner and Blu-ray disc media, and in order to play the Blu-ray disc you need a Blu-ray-capable player connected to an HD TV. Fortunately, Encore CS3 is ready to handle this new technology when you are. Burning a Blu-ray disc is as easy as burning a standard definition (SD) DVD.

Start where you left off the last mini-lesson, with the Bike Race Encore project still open.

1   Select the Build panel.

2   Change Format to Blu-ray.

3   Change Output to Blu-ray Disc.

4   Click Build.

Yes, it *is* that easy. As with standard DVD, you can also output to a folder or image file if you do not want to burn direct to a disc.

Exporting DVD projects to Flash

Creating Flash content from a DVD menu is a new feature in Encore CS3. Encore not only converts the video to Flash Video, but it converts the whole menu system to a SWF file that is viewable in a web browser. This allows you to demo DVD projects over the web with no knowledge of Flash, HTML, or scripting language—pretty amazing! The Flash controls even allow you to skip to chapter points via Flash web-friendly video controls. We will export the Bike Race DVD that we created in the "Creating a menu DVD" mini-lesson. Start where you left off in the Encore CS3 Bike Race project.

1   Select the Build panel.

2   Change Format to Flash.

3   Specify a location under Destination and a project name under Settings. Remember the folder and file name you use here, as you will need to navigate to it later with a browser.

4   Change the Quality to High, and click Build. Encore takes a few minutes to build the menu and convert the assets to Flash. You will see progress bars that provide details of the export process, and a complete message when it is done.

Encore CS3 converts your DVD project into an interactive Flash file that you can view in a web browser.

5   Open a web browser. (The browser needs to have the Adobe Flash plug-in to view Flash content.)

6   Navigate to the folder where you saved the Flash file.

7   Within the folder you specified, there will be an HTML file called index.html. Open this file in your browser to view your Flash application.

You will notice that the menu is fully functional, including the motion menu background, button highlights, and even semitransparent buttons. Clicking a button will play the Flash video and then return you to the menu, preserving the end actions you set up in Encore. All this is possible without your needing to know Flash or writing a single line of code.

Note: *If you upload this to a web server, be sure to upload a subfolder called Sources and all its content.*

As we've said before, Encore CS3 is a complete DVD authoring and burning tool (and more!). In this lesson you've seen a very brief example of building a fairly simple menu from an Adobe Premiere Pro exported timeline. It is beyond the scope of this book to explore all the menu-authoring capabilities of Encore, but hopefully this lesson has given you a taste of the amazing possibilities you have with Encore CS3.

Review

▶ **Review questions**

1   What are the two export-to-Encore options from Adobe Premiere Pro?

2   What is the purpose of Encore chapter markers in Adobe Premiere Pro?

3   What is the significance of the first-play object in Encore?

4   Is it possible to link an Encore button to a specific chapter within a timeline?

5   When you upload an Encore Flash project to a web server, which files must you upload?

▶ **Review answers**

1   Direct Burn Without Menus and Author With Menus.

2   Encore chapter markers in Adobe Premiere Pro will be passed to Encore when you export. These markers can be used in Encore to set chapter points and to name buttons.

3   The first-play object in Encore is the object executed when a user inserts a DVD into a player. Typically, the first-play object is the main menu, but it can be a video timeline that automatically plays.

4   Yes. A button can be linked to a menu or to a specific chapter within a timeline.

5   You must upload the contents of the folder you specified in the Build parameters, plus the Sources subfolder and its contents.

Index

Symbols

1-pass encoding 411, 414
2-pass encoding 411, 414
3-Way Color Corrector 343, 345
4 Color Gradient effect 342
4K film scans 11
5.1 Mix Down setting 288
5.1 surround sound.
    See surround sound
10-bit 4:4:4 HD format 374
12-bit recorded audio 264
16-bit recorded audio 264
24P and 24PA formats 375, 411
32-bit floating point data 264
32 kHz recorded audio 264
48kHz recorded audio 264

A

A/B editing 146–152
AAF (Advanced Authoring
    Format) 362, 366, 417
AAF Export Log information
    window 366
Absorption setting 285
accelerating clips 211–217
accelerator keys 353–359
Acrobat PDF files. See PDF files
action shots
    bitrate and 414
    chroma key effects and 327
    following action 30
    matching action in shots 32
Activate Recording Device
    option 402
active preview screens 128
Add/Remove Keyframes button
    209, 232
Add Marker command 357
Add Tracks dialog box 296

Adobe Acrobat PDF files.
    See PDF files
Adobe After Effects
    animation presets 394
    convert layer to text 393
    introduction to 389–397
    overview 390–391
    ram preview 391
Adobe Bridge CS3
    as part of Creative Suite 12
    defined 12
    labeling and rating files 94–98
    managing assets in 66, 90–91
    managing files and folders in
        92–94
    metadata functions 98–99
    navigating in 91
    opening 90
    slideshows 93
Adobe Creative Suite 3
        Production Premium
    benefits of 11–13
    workflow 13
Adobe Dynamic Link 12, 390
    editing 396
    importing 394
Adobe Encore CS3
    as part of Creative Suite 12
Adobe Flash 424
Adobe HD-SDI format. See HD-
    SDI format
Adobe Illustrator CS3
    as part of Creative Suite 12
    editing files 79
    importing files 78
Adobe Media Encoder 401,
    408–415
Adobe OnLocation CS3
    introduction 7
    analyzing audio 63–65
    field monitor 57
    live video 57–65
    overview 51
    scopes 59–65
    spectrum analyzer 63–65
    SureShot 54

Vectorscope 61–62
Waveform Monitor 60–62
Adobe Photoshop CS3
    as part of Creative Suite 11
    importing graphics 77
    rotoscoping techniques 381
    using with Premiere Pro 381
Adobe Soundbooth CS3 11,
    301–309
    audio effects 305
    Effects Rack 304
    fixing noise 302
    low frequency hum 302
    soundtrack creation 306
    spectral display 303
    Vocal Enhancer effect 306
Adobe Titler. See Titler
advanced 24PA format 375
Advanced Authoring Format
    (AAF) 362, 366, 417
After Effects. See Adobe After
    Effects
AJA hardware 374, 375
aligning
    clip markers 194
    text in titles 159
    transitions 148
Alignment list 148
Alpha Adjust effect 320–321
alphabetizing bins 89
alpha channels
    compositing techniques with
        transparencies 320–322
    filling holes with transparencies
        325
    in imported Illustrator files 79
Alpha Glow effect 321
amplifying audio 309
analog recording devices 403
analog video 39, 48
Anchor Point keyframe
    parameters 231, 235
anchor points
    for text 166